THE ANGLO-IRISH MURDERS

Foolishly, the British and Irish governments have chosen the tactless and impatient Baroness Troutbeck to chair a conference on Anglo-Irish cultural sensitivities. She instantly press-gangs her friend Robert Amiss into becoming conference organizer. Despite diverting encounters en route to Moycoole Castle in County Mayo, Amiss is in near-despair as the arrangements crumble around his ears. The interested parties seem intent on living up to their worst stereotypes. And driving rain and security problems make everything worse. When a delegate plummets off the battlements, no one can decide whether it was by accident or design. The next death poses the same problem and causes warring factions to accuse each other of murder even as the poiticians are busily trying to brush everything under the carpet in the name of peace. A wickedly funny crime novel taking an irreverent look at the Establishment.

THE ANGLO-IRISH MURDERS

Ruth Dudley Edwards

CHIVERS PRESS
BATH

First published 2000
by
Collins Crime
This Large Print edition published by
Chivers Press
by arrangement with
HarperCollins Ltd
2001

ISBN 0 7540 1596 3

I am grateful to A.P. Watt Ltd on behalf of
The National Trust for Places of Historic
Interest of Natural Beauty for permission to
quote from Rudyard Kipling's 'The Puzzler'
and on behalf of Michael B. Yeats to quote
from W.B. Yeats' 'The Curse of Cromwell'.

British Library Cataloguing in Publication Data available

To Carol, who endures the Irish without complaint, and to John, who doesn't.

And with thanks to Sean O'Callaghan, who suggested the idea, to Liam Kennedy, who identified and named the 'MOPE' syndrome, to Colm and Alva de Barra, Máirín Carter, Nina Clarke, Eoghan Harris, Gordon and Ken Lee, Kathryn Kennison, Robin Little, James McGuire, John and Una O'Donoghue and Henry Reid, all of whom helped with information and advice, to Georgina Hawtrey-Woore, a sensitive and tolerant copy editor, and, of course, to her wee boss, the exquisite, brilliant and ruthless Julia Wisdom.

This is a farce, so while I have drawn inspiration from conferences and people on the Anglo-Irish circuit, if anyone thinks they recognize themselves among my characters, they are in a bad way.

PROLOGUE

Amiss put yet another question mark beside yet another name on his long list and groaned. He picked up the receiver and dialled a Dublin number. 'Robert Amiss here. May I speak to Mr McCorley?'

' 'Fraid not, Robert. You're after missing Roddy. He's just this minute stepped out to church.'

'Will he be long?'

'You wouldn't know. It depends on if they're doing the works.'

'Sorry?'

'Loads of priests and communion and all.'

Amiss found it odd that a senior civil servant should absent himself from his desk in the middle of a weekday morning to pursue his religious duties. But then, he was finding much that was strange in his new-found incursion into Anglo-Irish relations. 'Ah, I see. He's gone to mass.'

'A funeral.'

'Oh, I'm so sorry.' Amiss retreated into shambling English embarrassment. 'How terrible. Was it someone very close?'

'Oh, not at all. 'Twas only the Minister's granny. But you know how it is.'

Though Amiss didn't, he said, 'I see. Could you put me through then to Mr McGarrity?'

1

'Sure isn't Joe after going to the same funeral?'

'Mr Devoy?'

'Johnny's gone an' all. There's no one in this division this morning only me, 'cause you see what with the Dublin Castle reception last night, they all had to miss the removal.'

'The removal?'

'The removal of the remains.'

'The remains?'

'The remains of the Minister's granny. Do ye not bury people in England?'

'We do. But clearly we don't take funerals as seriously as you do. Well then, in their absence, do you think you could help me, Miss . . .?'

'God, you're terrible formal. I'm Maureen. But I'd say I couldn't help you. Amn't I only the temp?'

Amiss's other phone rang. 'Just a moment please, Maureen, till I answer that.' He leaned over and pressed the speaker button. 'Hello. Robert Amiss.'

'We'll go a couple of days early,' boomed Baroness Troutbeck. 'I'll show you Ireland.'

'What are you talking about? I'm up to my eyes as it is. I can't possibly take any time off before the conference.'

'Balls. You're getting your knickers in a twist over nothing. You should have it all done by now.'

'Shut up a minute, Jack. I'm on the other

line. Call me back in a few minutes, will you?' He winced at the hopeless tone in which he made his plea. This would hardly impress Maureen.

'Can't. Going into a meeting. Anyway someone's already booking our tickets.'

'Jack, the arrangements are very complicated. Not to say sensitive. I can't abandon ship.'

She cut in. 'Never heard anyone make so much fuss about pulling a gaggle of Paddies together. Read them the riot act and tell them to get a grip. Like we should have done years ago.'

The phone went dead. Amiss returned to Maureen.

'I heard,' she said. 'Tactful, isn't he, whoever he is. Didn't think anyone called us Paddies any more. Who is he anyway?'

'She,' said Amiss grimly, 'is for the present moment my boss. Her name is Baroness Troutbeck. She is the key player in a conference intended to resolve some of the sensitive cultural issues in Anglo-Irish relations.'

There was a brief pause at the other end of the line. 'Well, shite and onions,' giggled Maureen. 'That should make for great gas.'

CHAPTER ONE

'Another fine mess she's gotten you into.'

Amiss glared across the table at his friend Detective Sergeant Pooley. 'You've got some crust saying that, considering how many fine messes you've gotten me into in your time. You're just jealous that these days she's wrecking my life with even greater regularity than you used to. Or maybe you're jealous for other—darker—reasons.'

Pooley flushed. 'That was a remark in very bad taste, Robert. On two fronts.'

'Two? Oh, sorry. I do apologize. I was intending to be offensive on one front only. I certainly wasn't intentionally making a stupid pun based on the fact that the girlfriend you inherited from Jack . . .'

'And from you,' said Pooley grimly.

'Doesn't count, Ellis. 'Twas but a fling, as you well know. Anyway I was not making a stupid pun about Mary-Lou being black. Unlike Jack, I do not spend my entire existence trying to stir people up. So let me try to answer your implicit question. The answer is the same as always. I was jobless, my defences were down and being the malleable creature I am, I was once again fair game for someone tempting me with what seemed an entertaining project.'

'Which is exactly?'

Amiss swallowed his last mouthful of steak too quickly, choked and then washed it down with the remains of his claret.

'You'd do better,' said Pooley kindly, as he leant across the table and refilled Amiss's glass, 'if you didn't try to talk and eat at the same time.'

Amiss cast an incredulous glance at him. 'Do you ever wonder, Ellis, how we manage to be friends? Very well, then. As you can see, I have cleared my plate, so I'm now free to tell you about my involvement in organizing and running this Anglo-Irish conference on cultural sensitivities.'

He paused. 'Well, to be accurate, it's Anglo-British really, I suppose, since someone decided to bring in a smattering of other Celts. The idea is that the peoples of these two islands—the Irish from both traditions as well as the English, Scots and Welsh—should learn better to appreciate each other's cultures.'

'What about our resident Asians and West Indians and Chinese and Africans and . . . ?'

'You're being a touch cosmopolitan, Ellis. Asian and Caribbean culture isn't big yet on the Celtic fringe. We're starting nice and easy with just four lots of peoples who've been at each other's throats for centuries.'

'Particularly the English and the Irish.'

'Well, yes and no. The Catholic Irish have hated the English and the Protestant Anglo-

Irish, certainly, though not necessarily vice-versa. But the English and the Welsh have always hated each other. The Protestants of Northern Ireland are mostly Scots and hate the English as well as the Irish and the Scots look down on everyone and since getting their own parliament to swank importantly in, have become as militant as the Micks. In the middle of this the poor old English are always wondering why people get so excited and why everybody else can't be sensible. You have no idea. But no idea! I never came across so many people with chips on their bloody shoulders. It's going to be murder.'

'That would be par for the course in any project in which you're involved.'

'Figure of speech, Ellis. Even Celts don't murder each other at conferences. Though, God knows, I might strike a blow on behalf of us Anglo-Saxons. The Irish are already driving me crazy by living up to several aspects of their national stereotype—particularly the "charming but unreliable". Nobody fills in forms or answers letters, they ring up when it suits them, usually to try to complicate things, and I've a nasty feeling there's an idea abroad that this is essentially a useful freebie to which to send their dumbos.'

He drummed his forehead in frustration. 'And then there's MOPE.'

'MOPE?'

'An acronym of the "Most Oppressed

People Ever"—a nickname for republicans which in this case applies to their cultural stormtroopers. I thought everyone knew it.'

'I pay as little attention to Irish politics as is humanly possible. If they're not bombing London, I forget about them.'

Amiss sighed. 'Great. It's exactly that attitude among our politicians that encourages MOPE's mates to bomb London if they're craving attention.' He leaned forward and poured himself some more wine.

'God, what a pain in the arse they are. It's bad enough that they're such a whingeing, aggressive bloody crew, but then on top of that you have to put up with their PC concerns about gender balance and parity of esteem with every other shagging delegation regardless of importance, size or consequence. I swear they'll probably measure the bedrooms to make sure no one's got a square foot more than them.'

'The whingeing seems to be contagious.'

'Stop being so unsympathetic. I haven't even told you about DUPE yet.'

'What?'

'It's what my new friend Simon Gibson—my Northern Ireland civil service go-between—calls MOPE's loyalist equivalents. You know, those fringe working-class Prods . . .'

'Prods?'

'Local argot for Protestants. DUPEs are the ones with paramilitary mates—stands for

"Downtrodden Unionists for Parity of Esteem". They're serious students of MOPE tactics and employ them to good effect in their own attention-seeking efforts.'

'It all sounds delightful.'

'I expect there will be consolations—like seeing how they all get on with Jack.'

'How did Jack of all people get involved in this anyway? I thought she was dead against conferences, do-goodery and diplomacy—not to speak of the Irish, Scots and Welsh.'

'Exactly. That's why it should be entertaining. Turns out it's ages since she's been to Ireland and she jumped at the opportunity on the grounds that it would be fun, especially since it offered the chance to knock a few heads together.'

'But why would anyone want her? Don't they realize what she's like?'

'All I know is that Jack had some late-night drinking session at the Lords with a visiting Irish delegation who were so taken by the general jollity and her enthusing about her girlhood excursions to the Emerald Isle that her name was fed into the official channels as an acceptable English co-chairman of the conference. Simon tells me they had had such problems in finding anyone the Irish would accept that they'd have agreed to exhume Dr Crippen if the Irish Department of Foreign Affairs had suggested him.'

'Who's the other chairman?'

'A superannuated Irish politician of an indolent disposition who will always take the line of least resistance.'

'You mean he'll let Jack push him around.'

'Even more than everyone else does.'

'Sounds grim. Rather you than me.'

'That's always the case, Ellis. Though you've been quick enough in the past to join in when things got interesting. I've become fatalistic. Even agreed to let Jack take me on a skite beforehand to show me Ireland.'

'I thought she hadn't been there for years.'

'She alleges she knows it well. Parts of it, anyway. There are relatives somewhere in the west. Anyway, after the hassle of the last few weeks, I suppose I need a break before I face Moycoole Castle.'

'Ah well,' said Pooley. 'If it all gets too bad, remember you can always lie back and think of England.'

*   *   *

'It may be a holiday for you. It certainly doesn't look like being one for me,' grumbled Amiss as he fell exhausted into an armchair in the airport lounge. 'I've had more crises in the last couple of days than you've had scandalous liaisons.'

'Rubbish,' said the baroness. 'You're making a big fuss about something very simple. Besides after a few days with me you'll be ready for anything.'

'That in itself is a sufficiently dubious proposition, without my having to, as you put it, "holiday" while lugging a laptop and mobile phone in a vain attempt to stop all or any of these Celtic loonies from wrecking this ludicrous conference.'

'"Holiday" is not a verb. Now stop going on and get me a snipe of champagne.'

'I'm not your batman, Jack,' said Amiss, nevertheless, from sheer habit, rising to obey.

'You're always complaining. Haven't I got you into first class? Most batmen would be touchingly grateful.'

He grinned. 'I grant you that was a fine performance at the check-in desk. Do you think she upgraded us because you're a baroness, because of your preposterous whispering about hush-hush peace-related secret negotiations or . . .'

'Neither. She fancied me. Didn't you notice the way she kept eyeing me?'

'It seemed like disbelief rather than lust from where I was standing. I think she found you sartorially overwhelming.'

'That's the idea,' she said, complacently smoothing the left sleeve of her emerald green tweed suit. Amiss surveyed her from the top down, taking in the trilby, its crowning pheasant feather, the vast Celtic brooch, the pale green chiffon blouse with an enormous cascading bow, the thick green stockings and

11

the stout brown brogues with an external tongue.

'Presumably you set out to create an understated effect?'

'You think I should have added a shillelagh for good measure? Quite a good idea now I come to think of it. I'd better pick one up on the way. Might come in handy.'

'I hate to be critical about your fashion statement, but isn't there a possibility the Irish might think you're taking the piss?'

'Me?!' She seemed outraged. 'All I'm doing is making obeisance to their dotty preoccupations with symbols and all that. Hence the jewellery and assorted greenery.'

'Do you have a similar treat in store for the Orange contingent?'

'No. When in Rome and all that. We're on Free State soil . . .'

'Jack, will you for God's sake get the terminology right. This has been the Republic of Ireland since 1949. It's only rabid republicans who think they should be running it and mad loyalists who want to insult it, who call it the Free State these days, and then only as a term of abuse.'

'God, you're so pedantic.'

'You'd be pedantic if you'd had all the crap about why nationalists are outraged if you say Ireland is in the British Isles, refer to Britain as the mainland or call the Republic Eire as unionists do, while unionists are outraged if

12

you call Northern Ireland the north as nationalists do or a statelet or the occupied six counties as republicans do.'

Her attention had wandered to a passing young brunette.

'Jack!'

She reluctantly returned to the conversation. 'As I was saying, the point is that the Orange brigade will swiftly be aware that I'm on their side rather than that of the Fenians [The Fenians were a nineteenth-century revolutionary organization: 'Fenian' is a term of abuse for republicans, which they wear as a badge of pride.] so there's no need for me to don sashes and bowler hats and start whistling "God Save the Queen".'

'Your subtlety does you credit, Jack.'

She beamed.

*   *   *

As he twisted the top off the second small bottle, Amiss's phone produced its tinny version of the Sailor's Hornpipe. 'Hello. Yes, Seoirse. What can I do for you? . . . No . . . no . . . I can't tell you that . . . Because the numbers keep changing . . . No. They're not the criteria we're using . . . No, we can't change them now . . . Everyone else has agreed . . . Fine, fine, fine. By all means. As it happens, she's right here.' He smiled grimly as he passed the phone over to the baroness. 'It's

13

Seoirse MacStiopháin of MOPE wishing to speak to higher authority. He's got a grievance.'

The baroness sank back in her chair, put her feet on the coffee table, took a large draught of champagne and jammed the phone to her ear. 'Troutbeck. What's the matter? What! Nonsense! Absolute balls! Your electoral mandate no more dictates the number of seats you get at this conference than how many seats you get to a Pavarotti concert . . . What? . . . Why? Because I'm in charge, that's why. I decide who gets invited. And if you don't like that you can bugger off and we'll do fine without you.' She handed the phone back to Amiss. 'Turn it off.'

Agitatedly, Amiss grabbed the phone. 'Seoirse, Seoirse. Are you there?' He switched off. 'He's gone. That's it then. We won't have MOPE. And after all the trouble I went to to persuade them to come.'

The baroness rolled her eyes upwards. 'God save me from half-witted, credulous liberals. Of course MOPE will come. They never want to stay out of anything. It's just that they seek every concession they can get by playing rough with appeasing simpletons like you. Smack of firm government, that's what these sods need. Pity we abolished national service. That would have sorted them out.'

'Is not the problem that the military wing of MOPEdom has gone in for a form of national

14

service which has involved them murdering people like you?'

She waved her hand dismissively. 'I'd like to see them try.'

'Don't tempt fate, Jack. They have friends who just might.'

CHAPTER TWO

'Step on it,' barked the baroness, as Amiss drove out of Dublin airport. 'I want to be in the west by mid-afternoon. Things to show you.'

'There isn't much I can do, Jack. The bloke in front isn't taking the hint.'

'Hint? Hint? You don't hint with wankers like that. Flash your lights, beep your horn and frighten him into the slow lane.'

'Bugger off, Jack.'

She stuck out her lower lip. 'I'll drive.'

'We've had that conversation,' said Amiss wearily. 'I think having you charged with drunk and reckless driving wouldn't be a good start to our Irish sojourn.'

She looked mutinous. 'The Irish have never bothered about that sort of stuff in my experience. But have it your own way. I'll go to sleep. Wake me at Athlone and we'll buy a picnic.' And before Amiss could say 'Picnic?' she had begun to snore heartily.

She woke instantly when he nudged her and sat bolt upright. 'Right. Let's get going. There's a lot to buy.'

'Like what? Can't this be simple?'

'It will be simple. I don't want a heavy lunch. Some soused herring, a knuckle of ham and good bread and cheese. And of course a decent claret.'

'I don't like soused herring.'

'Nonsense. Of course you do. Now, come on, we can't hang around all day.'

'Okay, Jack. Get what you like. Just find me a substitute for soused herring. I've got to listen to messages and make some phone calls.'

'Why didn't you make them in the car?'

'Because I'm a law-abiding Englishman and therefore switched off my mobile phone for the duration.'

'How quaint. All right, come along and you can hang around outside the shop gabbling away to your heart's content.'

By the time the baroness had stormed in and out of three shops—emerging each time to expostulate and shout 'ridiculous'—Amiss was leaning against a window gazing ahead of him in dull despair. He cried in pain when she dug him in the ribs. 'Why are you looking like a stuffed gannet?'

'Because no fewer than twelve people have left crisis messages, I've rung only three and everything's falling apart. Even your co-chairman's dropped out pleading illness and Dublin claims it can't replace him. I need to ring them all back and all I really want to do is throttle them. Except Simon Gibson, who sounds as furious as I do.'

'You'll have to wait till we've solved this much more serious crisis. This is utterly ludicrous. I don't know what these people live off but they don't appear to have the simplest everyday foodstuffs. No soused herrings, the cold meat is in plastic packages and the cheese is all factory-made. I pointed out that this country nowadays exports excellent cheese and was told they wouldn't know about that and what's wrong with processed cheese anyway? All this guff I've heard about Celtic Tigers and Ireland now being a haven for gourmets is obviously Hibernian codswollop. The only decent stuff they've got is brown bread.'

Amiss was beginning to feel peckish. 'Can't we settle for some sub-standard food of the kind that ordinary people survive on, Jack? I'd be happy with some ham and a piece of lettuce. Even some industrial cheese.'

'Certainly not. Can't have you ruining your digestive system by eating muck. I've got bread, some good radishes and a few tomatoes. That'll have to do. Let's go in here and get salt and butter.'

To Amiss's relief, she grumblingly accepted that in the absence of a salt-grinder, there was no point in demanding sea salt. Butter, however, proved an unexpected problem. They stood in front of the large dairy cabinet for perhaps three minutes before Amiss said finally, 'There just isn't any butter here. Only pseudo-butter.'

'That's impossible.' She charged over to the cashier. 'Where's the butter?'

'In the cabinet,' said the assistant, with the air and enunciation of one dealing with a foreign mental defective.

'No, it isn't.'

'Yes, it is.'

She stomped back to Amiss. Together they perused every label until she became incandescent with frustration, stormed back to the cash desk and bellowed in her most intimidating tone, 'Young woman, my companion and I have read the labels of a dozen packages claiming to contain nearly-butter or almost-butter or fat-free butter or other abominations. The one substance missing is straightforward butter. You know what I mean. The kind the United Kingdom buys tons of from you every year.'

The young woman transferred her chewing gum from one cheek to another and stared at her contemptuously. 'Is that so? Well, mam, the way it is is this. In Ireland, that's butter.'

Defeated and routed, the baroness stormed

from the shop. 'Christ,' she shouted at Amiss. 'That one lives up to the bloody Celtic stereotype all right. Get the rhetoric right and bugger reality. Take me to the river.'

'I don't want to take you to the river. May I remind you that it's October and cold. And what's more I have to deal with all these messages about cancellations and substitutions and demands for this that and the other and all the rest of the crap.'

'The sun's shining,' she interrupted, 'and I want to sit and ruminate by clear running water. *Carpe diem* and all that. Go on. You'll like it. Stop behaving like a grumbling old granny.'

'Twenty-four hours with you, and Job would turn into a moaning Minnie,' he said, as he switched on the engine.

*   *   *

The spot that eventually took the baroness's fancy was in a field with several dozen cattle. 'Is any of those a bull, do you think?' asked Amiss nervously.

'Very likely,' she said carelessly. 'Pass over the bag.'

'Are you good with bulls?'

'Yup. Important thing to do is to show no fear and bop them on the nose if they're troublesome.'

'Has anyone ever accused you of bravado?'

19

'Yes, oddly enough. Can't think why.'

She began to remove packages from the bag.

'I'm looking forward to the claret.'

'Wasn't any worth buying. Got bottled Guinness instead. Wish I'd some oysters to go with it.'

'I don't like Guinness,' wailed Amiss. 'It's too bitter.'

'It's that or nothing.'

'Shit. All right. Pass me a bottle.'

The baroness rummaged vigorously, disinterred two bottles and handed one over.

'Did you buy an opener?'

'No. I thought you'd be able to open them with your teeth. I would, except that one of my front ones is capped.'

'I don't open bottles with my teeth, Jack. Surely by now you've grasped that I'm too effete to do any of those manly deeds in which you specialise. Perhaps we should swap genders.'

'You're useless.' She heaved herself up with some difficulty and marched with her bottle to the wall that sheltered the field from the road. Amiss followed and looked on with interest as she sought first to lever and then, with increasingly impatience, to knock off the cap with the help of a sharp stone.

'Why don't you pretend you're in the real Wild West and just break it off?' he enquired genially.

She pretended not to hear and struggled on until a man appeared from behind a tree, leaned over the wall and observed, 'You'll do yourself harm if you don't take care.'

'Have you got an opener by any chance?' asked the baroness.

'Yerra, why would I be needing a yoke like that? Pass your bottle over here, missus.' Expertly, he tapped the top of the bottle against a stone and the cap flew off, followed by a substantial quantity of foaming stout. 'Grab that fast now and have a quick slug before you lose the whole works.' Amiss smiled triumphantly at the baroness and passed his bottle over for the attention of their new friend.

'I suppose ye'll be admiring them fine heifers,' he enquired, as he handed the opened bottle to Amiss.

'Oh, yes indeed.'

'Well, do you see that one kicking the sods over its back with its front feet?' Amiss and the baroness looked in the direction in which he was pointing. 'Now that lad happens to be a bull, and he's as big and mad as the Brown Bull of Cooley himself. I'd say if you don't get yeer bodies out of that field, ye'll be dead to the heel. Give us yer hand, missus, and I'll give ye a yank up.'

As several tons of bull detached himself from the herd, put his head down and began to run, the baroness and Amiss dropped their bottles and cleared the wall together.

*   *   *

After they had left the pub and the baroness had finished knocking out her pipe, with elaborate courtesy, their saviour assisted her into the car. 'God bless you, mam, and may you never see a poor day.'

'Long life to you, Mr Finnegan. May you never see your wife a widow.'

'And may you be the mother of a bishop.'

'That's pushing it, Mr Finnegan. But I'll look into it.'

'Well, that was enjoyable, anyway,' she said, exchanging enthusiastic waves with Finnegan as Amiss drove her away. 'At least the Irish understand about pubs.'

'I hadn't come across a pub-cum-undertakers before.'

· 'All the best Irish pubs are pubs-cum-something or other—grocers, hardware stores or whatever.'

'It was kind of him to fetch us that ham and brown bread.'

'I think after four pints and the whiskey chasers he probably feels he got the best of the bargain.'

'Blimey, did he have that much?'

'Indeed he did. While you were outside gabbling he was putting the black and the amber stuff away like billy-o. I think our modest sandwiches must have cost close on twenty quid in the end. But well worth it. He was most amusing on the subject of Irish politics, didn't you think?'

'Missed most of it. He doesn't seem keen on politicians.'

'No. Decidedly negative. I liked the bit where he said, "Celtic Tiger? Celtic Tiger my arse! Celtic Chancers the lot of them, that's what them hoors are."'

'Did you pick his brains on cultural sensitivities?'

'Well, as you might have noticed, I picked up a few cheery rural greetings from him. But on the wider issue of cultural sensitivities on this island, he takes a rather simple view. "Missus," he said, as he reached for his third pint, "God forgive me but them northerners are all gobshites of the first order." "Do I take it that you are less than keen on a United Ireland?" I asked. "I don't give a shite if we have a United Ireland," he confided. "As long as it has no effect whatsoever on the twenty-six counties."'

'I'm not sure that I follow that.'

'I think he means that he'll allow the island to be united on the understanding that this should have no deleterious effect on taxes, politics or jobs and that all the northern gobshites will stay confined to the six counties. I see his logic, though I foresee some technical difficulties.'

'Did you put any of them to him?'

'I made a small attempt. He responded by laughing uproariously, calling for another round and announcing "No one can tell what he's able to do till he tries, as the duck said when she swallowed a dead kitten".'

'How droll,' said Amiss. The Sailor's Hornpipe sounded. 'Oh, God.' He braked. 'Hello. Yes . . . I see . . . Nice to hear from you. Yes, got that. Spelled with a "y" . . . No . . . Yes . . . Yes . . . Indeed . . . Yes . . . How interesting . . . No, I don't think so, Wyn . . . Oh, really? . . . Yes, I do understand . . . Well, yes, but . . .'

'Hurry up or we'll never get there,' shouted the baroness.

'Yes, Wyn . . . Yes, yes . . . Look, I'm really sorry, and I'd love to talk, but I'm in a meeting . . . Yes . . . Quite . . . Give me your number and I'll ring you later . . . Yes . . . Yes . . . Got it . . . Yes, it is an unusual number . . . Yes, yes . . . Of course . . . So do I . . . Yes . . . Sorry, I've really got to go . . . Yes . . . Yes . . . Sorry, must dash. Speak to you soon . . . Bye.'

He slumped into his seat. 'Christ. I thought she'd never shut up.'

'Who?'

'Our Welsh representative.'

'What do you expect from Wales except windbags?'

They set off again and within a couple of hundred yards encountered a crossroads. 'Do I go right or left here, Jack? Where are we off to

24

anyway?'

She peered at the signpost. 'Left. We're going on a trip down memory lane to stay with my mother's cousins. The Micks pretty well rubbed out the Anglo-Irish so I'd thought I'd take you to one of the last outposts.'

'Which is?'

'County Galway. Knocknasheen, where my cousins live.'

'Oh good. What's it like?'

'Don't be so inquisitive. You'll see in due course.' She paused. 'There's just one thing.' She paused irresolutely and drummed her fingers on the dashboard.

'What is it, Jack? If I didn't know you better I'd think you were embarrassed.'

'Am a bit.' She cleared her throat. 'There's the business of my name.'

'Yes?'

'Bit of an altercation with Cousin Lavinia. Won't stand for "Jack". Never would. What was good enough for my parents was good enough for her, she's always said.'

'You're afraid of your cousin Lavinia? My admiration for her knows no bounds.'

Coyly, the baroness scratched her left calf with her right foot. 'Lavinia was a bit of a ring-leader when we were gels and anyway she's several years older. Old habits require me to do a bit of kowtowing. I won't be smoking either.'

Amiss beamed. 'How wonderful! At last I

25

get to call you "Ida".'

'You most certainly do not. If you think Lavinia would approve of a whippersnapper like you calling me by my Christian name you've another think coming. If you want to call me anything you call me "Lady Troutbeck". Be grateful I didn't stipulate "ma'am".'

'Fine, fine. And what do I call them?'

'You call Lavinia "Miss FitzHugh" and her younger sister "Miss Grace". Now get going or we'll be late for what passes for dinner. And tell me about your latest crises.'

The Sailor's Hornpipe rang out. Amiss dithered for a moment and then said 'The hell with the law' and picked up the phone. 'Hello . . . Oh, hello, Saoirse. Is Seoirse's problem sorted out? . . . What? . . . You're not serious . . . No, I'm not showing disrespect. I just can't see the point . . . Oh, he did, did he? . . . Well if you say so . . . I'll do my best . . . Yes, yes. My very best . . . I understand . . . Goodbye.' He switched off the phone and put his foot on the accelerator. 'That was MOPE again—Saoirse MacGabhain.'

'What sort of a name is that?'

'Simon tells me it means Freedom Smith.'

'These Micks call themselves by impossible names on purpose just to be annoying.'

'That may be, but what's bothering me is what Saoirse has just demanded.'

'What?'

'Simultaneous interpretation from Irish.'

'Tell him to fuck off.'

'It's a her. And I can't. Apparently the Irish government have been on to our lot and it's been agreed that this should be done as a mark of cultural sensitivity.'

'But there isn't anyone left in Ireland who doesn't understand English, is there?'

'Of course not, but unless Saoirse is lying to me, officialdom has caved in and I've got to find an interpreter.'

'Get me whatever pusillanimous dickhead in the Northern Ireland Office is responsible for this,' bellowed the baroness.

Amiss stopped the car and made a call. 'Damn. Simon isn't there. Are you sure you want me to find the perpetrator? What about Knocknasheen?'

'Knocknasheen can wait.'

Five phone calls later Amiss passed the phone across to her: 'It's Crispin Egglington. He confirms Saoirse's account of their agreement.'

'What sort of a pillock are you?' was her opening gambit, followed a moment or two later by, 'Has the elementary truth not sunk in that every time you give in to a lunatic MOPE demand they return to their Grievance Sub-committee to think up a few more . . . Certainly not . . . Damn sure it isn't coming off my budget.' Her voice rose. 'You can bloody well provide the interpreter. If you want to waste money on half-witted cosmetic gestures which set precedents that will haunt our grandchildren, do so. But don't expect me to help . . . No, I don't care. If you want a bloody interpreter find a bloody interpreter.'

She handed the phone back to Amiss. 'That should have sorted out the craven little cretin.'

Amiss winced. 'Crispin? You still there . . . Yes, I know . . . Yes, she is. Very. But then she was your choice . . . No, sorry . . . I'd never hear the end of it. I'm sure you'll be able to sort it with Dublin. Borrow one of theirs, perhaps? . . . Really? Well, well, life's full of these little ironies isn't it. Sorry, must rush. Bye.'

He grinned. 'Crispin says he doubts if the Irish can provide an interpreter easily. Seeing they all speak English all the time they have hardly any on the payroll.'

He switched on the engine and put his foot on the accelerator. The baroness was quivering with rage. 'Fine,' she said. 'So what we're actually doing is providing an interpreter to translate speeches into Irish for the benefit of a collection of people, most of whom can speak no Irish, at the behest of a gaggle of citizens of the United Kingdom who wish to join a state which never uses Irish anyway. Fine. Sets the tone for the whole weekend if you ask me.'

The Sailor's Hornpipe sounded once more and Amiss slowed down. 'Hello . . . Yes, Mr

Kapur. Can I help you? . . . Sorry . . . No, I didn't know she had asked you to attend this conference . . . You know it concerns cultural sensitivities in the British Isles? . . . I see . . . No, she didn't tell me. It must have slipped her mind. But then she's been so busy I've seen virtually nothing of her,' he added, glaring balefully at the baroness. 'Of course you'll be most welcome. As you say, I'm sure that the view of an objective outsider will be of considerable help. Right. Now this is how you get there . . .'

'Jack,' he asked with deceptive calm as he ended the call. 'I should be grateful for an explanation.'

'Don't get pompous on me. I didn't bother telling you since I wasn't sure he'd come. Anyway you might have objected. You're always objecting. Only thing to do was go for the *fait accompli*.'

'Why do you want him?'

'All packs need a joker.'

'Or more likely a loose cannon.'

'That too,' she said cheerily. 'There's always a chance it'll let off a ball straight into the enemy's flanks.'

'Or, of course, into one's own ranks.'

'Life is for taking risks. Anyway, Chandra will undoubtedly provide some fun and will definitely be on my side.'

'The problem, all too often, Jack, is knowing which side you're on.'

29

'Well it sure as hell isn't MOPE's. Now put your foot down.'

CHAPTER THREE

'It's just a few hundred yards on. Past the snipe bog.'

'I've never seen a snipe bog.'

'Not a lot to see.' She stared out the window. 'We're nearly there. Left. Now.'

Amiss turned abruptly through the enormous rusty iron gates. He had read enough novels about the slow death of the Anglo-Irish gentry to be unsurprised by the state of the structure that awaited them at the end of the overgrown drive.

'We'll stop here for a minute,' said the baroness. 'Get out.'

They had been standing in the twilight for a moment or two when she asked, 'Recognize the architecture?'

'I'm hopeless at that. Normanish?'

She snorted with derision. 'Sixteenth-century tower house. Replaced a castle that had a bad run-in with some rebels during the Elizabethan wars. Georgian wings.'

'Looks in pretty bad shape.'

There was a loud sniff from his left, followed by a mighty blowing of the nose.

'Jack, are you crying?'

'Nothing wrong with crying. I loved Knocknasheen as a kid. Hate to see it like this. Remember those lines of Yeats?

I came on a great house in the middle of the
    night,
Its open lighted doorway and its windows all
    alight,
And all my friends were there and made me
    welcome too;
But I woke in an old ruin that the winds
    howled through.

That's what it feels like.'
    'What happened?'
    'That ruin on the left is the wing that had been partially burned down by rebels in 1920 and now seems to have collapsed. The rest is decay. Costs went up, money ran out and the family died off or left the country until the only ones left were Lavinia and Grace.' She snuffled for a few seconds and then headed back towards the car. 'That's enough of that.'
    The handbell was rung several times before the peeling front door was opened a crack. 'I'm sorry to have taken so long, Ida,' said a commanding voice, whose owner was virtually invisible in the gloom. 'We normally use the back. Come in.'
    The door being too stiff to open properly, they had some difficulty pushing their way through to the hall. 'You are welcome, both of

31

you,' said the elderly woman, who though almost as tall as the baroness was fragile to the point of emaciation. She leaned forward and gave her cousin a chaste kiss on the right cheek. 'I am pleased to see you after so long, Ida.' She turned to Amiss and offered a cold, thin hand which he shook gingerly. 'I am Lavinia FitzHugh. You are Mr Amiss, I believe?'

As his eyes became accustomed to the dim light of the solitary bulb, he could see that the walls had the cracks and damp marks that along with the strong musty spell spoke of terminal decay. The only decorations were rows of riding boots hanging at eye-level.

'I brought you a small present, Lavinia,' said the baroness, handing over the large Fortnum & Mason bag she had rescued from the boot.

'That is kind of you, Ida.' Miss FitzHugh looked inside and smiled. 'You always were generous. To a fault, indeed, as I remember. Now, follow me upstairs.'

The bedrooms to which Miss FitzHugh showed them were at the top of the house and both austere and mouldering. 'Reduced to servants' bedrooms, now, Ida. Alas, the roof of the bedroom wing fell in last year. You will find a bathroom of sorts at the end of that corridor. I shall see you both downstairs in fifteen minutes for a glass of the madeira you have so thoughtfully provided.'

＊   ＊   ＊

'Thank you, Miss Grace.' Amiss took the delicate crystal goblet from Miss FitzHugh's smaller and even more fragile sister. When polite conversation about the journey and their route came to an end, he asked curiously: 'Forgive me, Miss FitzHugh, but do I gather from the dozens of pairs of riding boots that you or your sister used to give riding lessons?'

'Certainly not. We wouldn't have wanted snivelling adolescents with social pretensions near our horses. They're family boots.'

'Ah,' he said and took another sip.

The baroness took pity on him. 'It's a family tradition. When a member of the family dies, their boots are hung on the wall.'

'Servants too,' added Miss FitzHugh.

'When we had any,' added Miss Grace.

'And if they rode.'

'When did the last boots go up, Lavinia?' asked the baroness. 'I'm afraid I'm sadly out of touch.'

'Our nephew Jock. Remember him, Ida? Constance's son. Killed ten years ago taking a six-foot hedge unwisely.'

'I didn't know. Tell us about the others. It'll bring me up to date.'

'Grace'll do it. She's the family historian.'

Miss Grace led them back to the hall and began at the far end. 'These are Cousin Jock's. And these Mama's. O'Brien's are next to hers.

You remember O'Brien, Ida?'

'Indeed I do. He taught me to ride.'

'Our last butler. With us for more than fifty years.'

'These were Phineas's. And those his boys'. You'll remember them, Ida. Both killed in the RAF during the war.'

'Only just. I was a toddler when I met them.'

'And Cousin Gavin, poor boy. Such a romantic. Nothing would do him but to fight in the Spanish Civil War.'

'On which side?' asked Amiss.

Miss Grace looked at him askance. 'Republican, of course. Only Catholics fought for Franco.' She went back to the boots. 'Jim Flur, our gamekeeper. O'Sullivan, the head-groom. And father and Walter.' Her voice seemed to quaver.

'When did they die?' His voice was gentle.

Miss FitzHugh's voice cut in icily. 'They were shot by the IRA in 1920 for being Protestant interlopers.'

'How long has your family been here?'

'About eight hundred years. Give or take a few decades. Come on. Leave the boots and come into dinner.'

*   *   *

'Part of our problem is that money for the peace-and-reconciliation industry is virtually unlimited,' explained the baroness, as she

34

coped valiantly with a badly-charred trout by washing each mouthful down with copious amounts of the Brouilly she had provided. 'Ergo it's impossible to turn down any of MOPE's crazy demands simply on grounds of finance.'

'Are you telling me, Ida, that these dreadful people are subsidised by the crown?'

'I fear so, Lavinia. But so is your government, so we can't just blame the dreadful Blair.'

'The dreadful who?'

'Oh, for heaven's sake, Grace,' said Miss FitzHugh, 'you know who Anthony Blair is. He's the prime minister, that fearful fellow who's expelled Uncle Ralph from the House of Lords.'

'Oh,' squeaked Miss Grace. 'Yes, of course, I've heard of him.' She gazed worriedly across at the baroness. 'Is he as ruthless as Cousin Gertrude said when she wrote to tell us the news? You're not in any danger are you, Ida?'

'No, Grace, frightful, grinning little squirt though he may be, Blair will stop short of the tumbrils.' She paused. 'At least I think he will. Besides, I'm not an aristocrat.'

'At least, Ida,' said Miss FitzHugh, 'you still have the Queen as head of state instead of those hectoring lady lawyers we keep having forced upon us.'

Miss Grace was looking puzzled. 'Ida, do I understand that this Blair person has given you

35

huge sums of money to hold a gathering of terrorists?'

'No, Grace,' said the baroness with commendable patience. 'This is not a gathering of terrorists, although there will be the occasional erstwhile Seamus O'Semtex . . .'

'And,' put in Amiss, 'Davy McPipe-bomb . . .'

The baroness looked at Miss Grace's baffled face and threw in the towel. 'You explain it, Robert.'

'This conference,' began Amiss, 'is intended to help people in these two islands to appreciate each other's cultures.'

'Do you mean,' asked Miss Grace, clearly trying hard, 'you want the Reverend Ian Paisley to learn Erse [Gaelic] and that horrid IRA man with the beard to become a Protestant?'

'Well, Miss Grace, I suppose in an ideal world one should have such aspirations, but we seek only to encourage some further understanding and respect.'

'It's all balls obviously,' added the baroness and then, hastily, seeing Miss FitzHugh's nostrils flaring, '. . . I do beg your pardon, Lavinia. The expletive escaped me inadvertently.'

Miss Grace was not letting go. 'I am still perplexed, Mr Amiss. Why should the British government waste enormous amounts of money on something that Ida has no faith in?'

'The British and Irish governments think

that if you invite terrorists to conferences and cocktail parties, they'll give up murder. It is the presence of such people at this conference that has attracted vast amounts of money.'

'Should one write a letter to someone about this?' asked Miss Grace anxiously. 'Perhaps Gertrude might be able to do something.'

'Frankly, Grace, I think the best thing we can do is change the subject and have a snifter of that brandy I brought.'

'That would be agreeable, Ida,' said Miss FitzHugh. 'We can pretend we are living in more gracious times.'

*   *   *

'I don't know about you,' said Amiss, as they drove down the drive, 'but I'm chilled to the bone.' He looked through the windscreen at the driving rain and shivered.

'I'm forced to admit that Grace and Lavinia are a lot tougher even than me,' said the baroness, turning the heater to maximum. 'Mind you it's central heating that's made wimps of us all. Twenty years ago I wouldn't have noticed the cold. I'm really a bit ashamed of having chickened out of staying the second night. But very relieved I did.'

'It was the damp more than the cold. I swear those sheets were wet despite the stone hot-water bottle.'

'In my case it was because of. The bottle

37

leaked.'

'I'm not surprised you decided to cut and run.'

'Still, it came as little surprise. If you visit what the Irish allude to as the "ould dacency", these hardships are to be expected. At least the sheets were linen. Apart from the bits that were holes, that is.'

'As you know, Jack, I have no standards. I'd prefer dry polyester to wet satin, any day.'

'With luck we'll find a hotel that has dry linen. I have one in mind.'

'Do you think the ladies believed our excuse?'

'They absolutely accepted that you needed a phone socket that took a modem. Didn't know what you were talking about, but believed you.'

'Well, it's true anyway. God knows what messages I've missed. Especially since the mobile wasn't working at Knocknasheen either.'

She turned right and put her foot down hard on the accelerator. 'So what did you think of them? Good old girls, aren't they?'

'I won't forget them easily.'

She blew the horn at a wobbling cyclist, causing him to panic and almost tumble into the ditch. Passing him at high speed, almost too late, she spotted a signpost for Mayo and turned the steering wheel so violently that the car missed by only an inch crashing into a stone wall. She affected not to notice Amiss's intake of breath. 'Hardly anyone realises the Prods were all but eradicated in the south, since the Catholics are so good at the rhetoric of tolerance and have largely pretended discrimination and violence was a curiously northern phenomenon. The northern Catholics never shut up whingeing and the stiff-necked old Ulster Prods, of course, told their side of the story with all the charm and subtlety of an aardvark.'

'I know what you mean. Gardiner Steeples has caused me less trouble than almost anyone else involved in this conference, yet he comes across as truculent and churlish.'

'Who's Gardiner Steeples?'

'One of the very few unionists who look like turning up. Most of them think it's a complete waste of time and will be MOPE-driven.'

As they rounded the next corner, she jammed on the brake just in time to prevent them crashing into a tractor which was ambling gently down the middle of the road. 'Bloody fool. Why doesn't he pull in? Doesn't he realize it's me?'

Amiss ignored the increasingly petulant denunciations that accompanied the gesticulating and horn-blowing—all of which made no visible impact on the course of the tractor. They proceeded in a stately procession at eight miles an hour until suddenly and without warning the machine turned left into a hidden opening. As they shot by, the baroness shook her fist and the driver responded with a smile and a happy wave. 'Moron,' she yelled at his image in the mirror.

'I suspect he's deaf, Jack.'

'And blind. Shouldn't be on the road.'

'What does it matter? We're not in a hurry. We're supposed to be on holiday. You shouldn't be bringing to country roads in County Sligo that pace of life which everyone deplores back home. Especially in the middle of a deluge.'

'I'm in a hurry to get to lunch. I want to put the memory of that breakfast well behind me.'

'You've always trumpeted the wonders of porridge.'

'That wasn't porridge. That was gruel. Porridge is as thick as that tractor driver and you take it with lots of brown sugar, cream and whiskey. That watery stuff was inedible.'

'We're not doing too well on the gastronomic front, are we?'

'That's why I'm in a hurry. The centre of holidays is food. You can't properly appreciate the scenery unless you've got a happy stomach.'

Amiss reacted nervously to the sound of the Sailor's Hornpipe. 'Hello . . . Roddy . . . What! . . . Why? . . . What's she like? . . . Must we? . . . What can I say except that I'm not pleased? . . . This has come very late in the day . . . Bye.'

'What is it?'

'We've been lumbered with an observer.'

'What do you mean an observer? What is there to observe other than a lot of impossible malcontents complaining about each other?'

'This is not the view of MOPE. As a result of your beating-up of Seoirse MacStiopháin, they've lodged a formal protest about your bias and have tried to have you fired. Dublin claims to have worked night and day to achieve this compromise, viz, an observer to ensure fair play.'

'What do you bet McCorley's accepted whoever they came up with?'

'My shirt.'

She groaned. 'I can see it all now. No doubt it will be some poncey, left-wing, English academic who believes we should do what MOPE wants in order to atone for Cromwell.'

Amiss shook his head. 'Nope. It's an American.'

She banged her left fist on the dashboard. 'A fucking American? What business is it of theirs?'

'Now, now, now, Jack. You know very well that Americans have been meddling in Irish politics since the famine. Besides, Roddy said Dublin and London were happy that she's not political. Just a representative of a cultural organization.'

She glanced at him in deep suspicion. 'What cultural organization?'

'Roddy didn't seem too clear. Something to do with Irish-American heritage.'

41

'You know bloody well what that'll mean, Robert. One of those cretins who likes to fight battles at a three-thousand-mile remove.'

Amiss shrugged. 'I'm beyond caring. We're stuck with her anyway. Besides it should be quite entertaining watching you trying to prove to her satisfaction that you're impartial.'

'Pah! I'd like to see any bloody little Yank trying to cross swords with me.'

Amiss noticed with alarm that the speedometer had crept up to eighty, but he knew better than to encourage the baroness to greater excesses by challenging her. He hoped she wasn't noticing him gripping his seat hard. He was almost relieved when the phone rang. 'Hello . . . Yes, Gardiner . . . Tea? I don't think so. You won't be arriving until about six thirty, after all . . . Goodbye.'

'What's that about?'

'Gardiner Steeples wanting to know if he'll be there in time for tea . . . Look out, Jack!' There was an almighty jolt, the car lurched violently and only their seat belts saved both of them from being hurled through the windscreen.

The baroness jammed on the brake and the car stalled. 'What was that?'

'We hit an obstacle. Shouldn't we stop and look?'

'Haven't got time. The oysters call.'

'I don't like oysters.'

'You should.' She started the car again and

within a minute the speedometer had passed sixty.

'Jack,' he said desperately, forgetting his earlier self-discipline. 'Remember what happened only two minutes ago. This is a country road.'

'That's not going to happen again. Just a brick or something.'

Twenty seconds later there was another bang. When they had come to a halt, he said, 'I don't care how you feel about it. I'm going back to see what that was.'

'Oh, all right.' They got out together and surveyed the road. 'Good grief,' she said, 'that's an impressive pothole.'

'It's enormous. A deathtrap. And must be the second one we've met in less than a mile.'

'Odd. It's been a very good road until now. Well, come on, come on. Get in.' She switched on the engine, put her foot gingerly on the accelerator and uttered words Amiss had never thought to hear from her. 'I think I'd better go slowly for a while.' Her caution was fully justified. By the time they reached their destination, they had encountered more than three dozen substantial potholes.

It was not until they had located the restaurant, ordered lunch and the baroness had finished delving into her oysters that she looked over at Amiss, contentedly finishing his fish soufflé. 'I still can't fathom the craters.'

'Nor can I.'

'Better consult a native.' She summoned a waiter. 'We're puzzled by the condition of the road we took here. Without warning it turned from a class A road suitable for a Formula One race to a bogtrotters' boreen that would challenge a Landrover. It's the same country. It's even the same county. What's going on?'

Unlike Amiss, the waiter had not winced at the word 'bogtrotter'. He looked at her indulgently. 'What you've left out of your calculations, mam, is that it's a different constituency. And they won't give us a minister.'

'What do you mean minister? What sort of minister? Cloth? Government?'

'It wouldn't be a priest I'm talking about here, but a fellow down there in Dublin with the power to get good roads for his constituents.'

'Do you mean a minister for transport?'

'Not necessarily, mam. Any minister would do. Any fellow with the clout.'

Seeing their puzzled faces, he pulled up a chair and sat down. 'I can see you're not political people,' he observed kindly. 'Or maybe they do things differently in England. But the way it is here, do you see, is that Mickey Pat O'Shaughnessy in the constituency next door was Minister for Fisheries and was able to do a good turn for the boyo in charge of forestry who then did another deal with the lad who does transport who's a pal of the EU

44

commissioner. So, with help from Brussels and a bit more from the lottery, all the roads in Mickey Pat's constituency were attended to in the last few years.'

He gazed at them sadly. 'The way it is is they've got it in for us up here for reasons I won't trouble you with now but go back to certain matters I could tell you about that have to do with the Taoiseach's' [Irish for prime minister] grandfather. This shower would do anything to keep us from having a minister. They'd rather make the thickest BIFFO a minister than one of our own.'

'BIFFO?' asked the baroness, who was frowning with concentration.

'Saving your presence, mam, a BIFFO is a Big Ignorant Fucker From Offaly.'

He sighed. 'So we have to live with the potholes. Mind you, I'd say at the next election we'll get our revenge. Isn't Bandy Corcoran intending to stand as a candidate on the holes issue and won't he trounce the rest of them?'

'I know my grasp of Irish politics is slimmish,' said the baroness, 'but is it really possible to win parliamentary elections over an issue like potholes?'

'Sure, missus,' said the waiter, 'isn't one of the democratic joys of this country and our PR [proportional representation] system that you can win an election on anything as long as you're not up against a widda?'

'A widda?'

'Or a son. Or a daughter. You know, someone entitled to inherit the seat.' He looked at her kindly. 'It's all a bit beyond you, isn't it? But it'd take a good while to explain and I've work to do. You'll pick it all up eventually with the help o' God.' He collected their plates, smiled and exited.

Amiss looked at the baroness, who was in a reverie. 'Do you get the feeling that we've a lot to learn?'

She shook her head. 'Not fundamentally, I think. Just the small print. The fact is that Paddies are always up to sharp practices.' She smacked her lips. 'Enough of that. If my sources are accurate we're about to have the best wild duck in these two islands.' She raised her glass of Sancerre. 'I've feeling that our Irish trip will continue to be memorable.'

CHAPTER FOUR

Cullally Hall was a Georgian gem.

'Satisfactory?' asked the baroness as the porter carried their bags up the staircase.

'Wonderful.'

'I felt I owed you something good after last night. Now, sort yourself out and we'll meet in the bar in an hour. You'll have time for a bath.'

The porter delivered Amiss to a room full of rugs and prints and comfortable chairs. 'You can plug your modem in there, sir.'

Amiss tipped him, disinterred his laptop, plugged it in, dialled up his e-mail connection and waited in trepidation.

*   *   *

'One hundred and twenty-nine bloody messages! One hundred and fucking twenty-nine!'

'I'm not surprised you're late. You should have just ignored them. Have a drink.' She summoned the bartender. 'He needs champagne.'

'Do I?'

'Judging by your face you do. What's up?'

'I won't weary you with all the cancellations and changes except to tell you that this conference seems doomed to complete pointlessness. The southern Irish are melting away like flies on the dimmest excuses, the English are sending ever fewer and more junior representatives and all the big political names are sending substitutes. I knew I should have stayed in London.'

'What could you have done?'

He shrugged. 'Nothing, I suppose. But I could have tried.'

'Here's the champagne. Drown your sorrows.'

Amiss took a grateful sip. 'But there's worse.'

'More MOPEery?'

47

'Yup.'

'What do they want this time?'

'It's not so much what they want. It's what they've got.'

'From your obliging friends Crispin and Roddy, no doubt?'

'From everyone, really. Judging by the correspondence I've been copied, at every stage there was a little token resistance and then the British and Irish officials took it in turns to cave in first.'

She drained her glass, grabbed the bottle from the icebucket and refilled both of their glasses. 'So what have they got?'

'A wheelchair.'

'Are they bringing a cripple? And if so, why doesn't he bring his own wheelchair?'

'They said one of their number might need one. Hence the ramps, which the hotel is hastily installing even as we speak.'

She shrugged. 'Is that it?'

'No. There's been a big problem in finding someone to do sign language.'

'They're bringing someone deaf?'

'They might. The problem arises because the signer has to be bilingual.'

The baroness emptied her glass in one draught. 'Fuck them. Let's get pissed.'

*   *   *

'Well, despite one spartan night, the abortive

48

picnic and all that rain yesterday, Ireland has done us proud,' said the baroness the next afternoon, as she drove towards a glorious sunset.

'Mmmmm,' said Amiss contentedly. 'That was a wonderful hotel. Breakfast was even better than dinner. And lunch surpassed the two. The deprivations chez Lavinia and Grace are but a sweet, sad memory. Thank you. You've made amends for some of your misdeeds. And it's a pleasure to be driven by you when you're constrained by potholes.'

She wasn't listening. 'I'm looking forward to Moycoole Castle, anyway. Haven't seen it for thirty years, but still remember it vividly as a . . .' She interrupted herself. 'Ha! We must have crossed another boundary into the constituency of a cabinet minister.' She put her foot down hard and the car tore along the winding road. The sickening lurch that brought Amiss to near panic was caused by her slamming on the brakes just in time to avoid careering into a procession of cows.

'Jack, will you for God's sake please come to terms with the fact that we are in the country.'

She was slightly abashed. 'Oh, all right, then. Perhaps I've been living too urban a life of late. Very well, I'll surrender to the rhythm of the Celtic twilight.'

They crawled along behind the cows at one mile an hour. A relapse by the baroness into exhortations and impatience brought her to

49

within a foot of the nearest cow, who repaid her by stopping suddenly, lifting her tail and depositing a messy substance on the bonnet. 'Serves you right, Jack. Now we're going to pong all the way to the castle.'

This episode had restored her to complete good humour. 'Good old girl. I'd have done the same in her place. Besides I like the smell of cow dung. It's natural.'

As the cows turned right, their guardian appeared and stood by the window, which she wound down. 'Good evening.'

'How are you, missus? And isn't it a grand evening entirely?'

'Indeed it is. And that's a fine herd you have there.'

'Ah they're not the worst. And I see one of them has given you a little welcoming present. Sure, she must have taken a fancy to you. And why wouldn't she?'

'I feel very honoured,' she said solemnly.

'And where might ye be off to? Ye're not from around here. Ye'll be from London, I expect.'

'More or less. We're off to Moycoole Castle.'

'Oh, is that right? Taking the son on holiday, are you? Or is he taking the mammy?'

'That's not my son, my good man. He's my lover.' The ancient gazed with interest at Amiss, who managed to keep his expression impassive as he stared straight ahead of him.

50

'Is that right now? Well, now sure, I shouldn't be surprised. Aren't you the fine figure of a woman and aren't they up to everything in London? Not that they aren't up to it here too mind you. I could tell you a tale or two. Still, I'd better be getting the cows milked. Now I'll be saying good evening to ye and God bless. I hope ye enjoy yeerselves at the castle.'

Out of the corner of his eye Amiss saw the baroness directing a broad wink at the cattle driver. 'We will indeed,' she said roguishly. 'It's not often we get away for a romantic weekend.'

'Ah now, sure, wasn't a lady like yourself made for romance. I'd say it'll be a weekend to remember.' And with an attempt at a bow, he set off after his cattle.

'You two should be off for the romantic weekend,' said Amiss. 'A match made in heaven if you ask me. A pair of ham actors delivering themselves of unparalleled bullshit.'

'When in Rome . . .' She cackled happily as she put the car into gear.

*   *   *

The wind had risen and heavy rain began to fall by the time they reached a signpost saying 'Moycoole Castle, 1 km'.

'Now, I know you're a complete philistine, but you're to pay attention to this. And it's

51

good that you'll be seeing it in proper Mayo weather. That sunshine was an aberration.

'What we're about to see is one of the finest examples of Norman castle-building in the two islands. Can't say that I approve of such places being made into hotels, but I've been assured the whole effect is dazzling. Ah, here we are.'

She turned into a broad driveway, which after a few hundred yards opened out into a wide paved area. She braked and they surveyed Moycoole Castle in all its spotlit glory.

'Jesus Christ,' she said. 'The barbarians have taken over.'

Amiss contemplated the pink monstrosity that confronted them.

'Charming, Jack. Utterly charming. Your taste is impeccable. I particularly like the wings. What an interesting mixture of styles.'

'Vandals! Vandals!'

'You feel it's a bit ersatz?'

'Ersatz? Ersatz? This isn't ersatz. This is pure fucking desecration. They've stuccoed the castle and built on what look like Texan ranches.'

'Thatched Texan ranches. Sort of Hiberno-Dallas. And my, my, aren't the hanging baskets on the drawbridge an attractive feature?'

'I'm tempted to turn the car round and go home to Cambridge as a mark of aesthetic protest,' she grumbled, as she drove over the drawbridge. 'Look at that. A rose garden in the moat, for God's sake.' She peered further into the gloom. 'However, it's still pissing down, so I fear the thought of a whiskey-and-soda militates against such principled action.'

*   *   *

'It's comfortable, anyhow,' said Amiss soothingly. 'The decor may be awful, but at least the plumbing works. Now, do you want to know the latest? What the DUPEs have done? Not to speak about Wyn's musings about alternative modes of transport?'

'No, no, no, no, no. I can't think of anything now except this. It's OK for you. You're a philistine.'

'Even a philistine gets a nasty shock when he finds his bedroom is called "Darby O'Gill's Hideaway". What's yours?'

'"The Fairy Fucking Glen."' She jabbed her finger towards the fire. 'Look at it. An original Norman fireplace and they add a fake Adam mantelpiece.'

'But don't you like that heart-warming picture of merry peasants dancing at a crossroads?'

She threw him a withering glance.

'You're perilously close to losing your sense of humour, Jack.'

The only response was a growl.

'Try to be positive. At least it's a turf fire.'

'It is not. It's gas. The turf is simulated.'

'Nonsense. That's a basket of turf there beside the grate.'

'That's there for effect. I'll tell you it's gas. Look for a gas-pipe.'

He walked over and inspected. 'You win.' He sat down again and took a sip of gin-and-tonic. 'You noted the plastic suits of armour?'

'And the stuffed wolfhounds.'

'And the round-tower motif on the curtains.'

'And the Celtic motifs on the carpets.'

'And the names on the lavatories.'

She growled again. 'I don't think I want to hear, but I'd hazard a guess: Leprechauns and leprechaunesses?'

'Knights and Ladies.'

'Order me another drink. And tell the barman to turn off that appalling music. Muzak is an abomination at the best of times, but when it's bogusly ethnic it's even worse.' Her face twisted in pain as the sound of a distant pipe and a lamenting female voice came closer. 'What is this? Sounds like a cross between a dirge and a pissed-off banshee.'

Amiss caught the barman's eye and beckoned. 'That's not a dirge. It's supposed to be haunting and spiritual and it's highly fashionable. You need to grasp, Jack, that Celts are in. Celts are even cool. What you're listening to there is a pop promoter's musical portrayal of Celtic mysticism.'

'It sounds like a dirge to me.'

'You need to see it in context. Try to

54

imagine . . .' He sighed. 'I don't suppose you've ever heard of *Riverdance*.'

'You imagine correctly.'

'Try to imagine a stage full of short-skirted Irish beauties, male and female, whose Irish jigs are alternated with eerie music and long-haired pale-faced sopranos singing of priestesses and lost loves in a romantic mythological past. That's what this music is supposed to conjure up.'

'Load of bollocks. I know about Irish dancing. Saw it in my youth. Properly done, it's as mystical as my bottom.' She snorted. 'In its true form, before they invented all this Celtic codology, what happened was that in a pub or at a céilí, an old man full of stout would leap to his feet when the sound of the fiddle began to drive him wild and dancing alone and spontaneously, he would jig on till he collapsed with exhaustion. Apart from set-dancing, which is a different matter, authentic Irish dancing is about sexlessness. That's why in its purest form it's solitary, grim-faced and no part of the body is moved other than the legs. It has nothing to do with pretty girls showing their knickers in public.'

She paused. 'Not that I'm opposed to pretty girls displaying their knickers anywhere, you understand. But not in the guise of culture. Now get that crap turned off.'

'Are ye not fond of music then?' asked the barman, who had materialized in time to overhear her final sentence.

'I'm extremely fond of music. That's the problem.'

'Oh real music, do y'mean? Like classical?'

'That's right.'

'Oh, fair enough so. I'd say this stuff could be torture if ye really liked music. Don't you worry. I'll have it off in a flash. And I'll get ye the same again, will I?'

They nodded.

'Anyway,' he added as he turned away, 'it's time for Imelda to play the harp.'

Amiss tried not to look as appalled as he felt. The baroness, on the other hand, let out a roar of pain.

'Oh, God. It needed only that. I think I'd prefer the muzak.'

'Have you anything in particular against harp music? Or is it just general prejudice?' asked Amiss. 'Not that I'm disagreeing with you.'

'It's boring and pretentious and the audience always feels it has to look soulful.'

Amiss looked towards the door. 'Imelda's coming in now. Young and pretty, from what I can see.'

'Hah. I bet she's wearing her hair soft and loose, it's red or black and she's sporting a flowing gown of satin or velvet in green or blue. If I'm wrong, Celtic central casting isn't what it used to be.'

'You're right. Red and green respectively.

But still, she is definitely pretty.'

The baroness turned around and looked the harpist up and down. 'I see what you mean.' Imelda ran her hands over the strings and then addressed the drinkers in a soft, mellifluous voice. 'Ladies and gentlemen, 'tis a wonderful privilege for me to be having the chance to play to you as the ancient harpists played to our kings and queens in the glorious days when Celtic civilization was the envy of all who knew of it, when ours was an island of saints and scholars and the world was young. Here's a song about a boy and a girl, separated by fate but brought together again through the power of love.'

'Cancel the drinks and let's go into the dining room,' said the baroness. 'If we don't get out of here soon I'm going to behave like a marauding Viking on a wet Monday.'

*   *   *

'I'm Philomena. I'll be looking after ye.'

'At least you didn't say "Faith and begorrah",' grunted the baroness.

Philomena folded her arms and looked at her crossly. 'What's that supposed to mean when it's at home?'

The baroness looked slightly sheepish. Amiss broke in. 'May I apologize for my friend, Philomena. I'm Robert Amiss and this is Jack Troutbeck. And she's not as grumpy as

57

she seems.'

'Just as well if she's the Lady Troutbeck that's in charge of this conference.'

'That's part of the reason I'm grumpy, Philomena.'

'What you need is a decent dinner. Now for the love of Jesus, cheer up and tell me what ye want. The steak's not bad, but if I was ye, I'd have the bacon and cabbage. Ye can't go wrong with that. The food's all right here except when they get too ambitious and pour muck all over it for the sake of style.'

The baroness looked at her with respect. 'And what do you think for the first course?'

'Ye can't beat the smoked salmon. It's local.'

The baroness closed the menu. 'Thank you, Philomena. Excellent advice. I think we'll be very happy together.'

*   *   *

The Sailor's Hornpipe sounded as Amiss began to eat—causing him to dart from the room. When the conversation had finished he jabbed the off button savagely and by summoning up all his self-control just stopped himself from kicking the plastic door-stop shaped like a Viking helmet.

'What's wrong now?' the baroness asked as he sat down heavily.

'A Japanese. A fucking Japanese.'

'A fucking Japanese what?'

'A fucking Japanese male, that's what. Coming to the conference.'

'Why?'

'Crispin hummed and hawed and indicated that because of some sensitive negotiations going on at present, the Foreign Office thinks it helpful that officials accede to every legitimate request from a Japanese—even from one as peripheral as an Irish studies specialist.'

'Well, well.' She was beginning to look positively merry. 'At the rate we're going we'll have more observers than participants. As the joker, my old mate Chandra may even end up surplus to requirements.'

'I am pissed off. I am really, really pissed off.'

'Oh come on now, Robert. Where's your sense of humour? This is all bollocks anyway so we might as well enjoy it.'

'It's all very well for you, Jack, but if this thing is a complete shambles I'll be the one who'll get the blame in government circles.'

'So bloody what? Who cares about government circles? Bugger government circles. Come on, let's have a bit of the old spirit. Get your snout in the trough and cheer up.'

CHAPTER FIVE

'Philomena certainly has your measure,' said Amiss next morning as they left the breakfast room. 'I've rarely seen you behave as well.'

'At least there's no crap about her,' snorted the baroness. 'Unlike the rest of this place.'

'Speaking of which, look what we have here. The hotel gift shop.'

'I'm not going near it. I might be sick. I'm going outside.'

'I enjoyed that,' said Amiss, when he caught up with her ten minutes later. 'Apart from the call from MOPE to complain they hadn't been sent an up-dated list of participants. I explained that I hadn't either, but of course they think I'm lying.

'If they hadn't interrupted I might have bought you a present but I didn't have time to decide between the "I'M AN IRISH COLLEEN" T-shirt or the Virgin Mary who cries real tears if you squeeze her rosary beads.'

'Look, look,' she shouted, gesticulating wildly at the battlements.

'Why shouldn't they fly the Irish flag? This is Ireland.'

'No, you idiot. I can put up with the tricolour. But they've got the EU flag as well. Everywhere you go in this bloody country they're waving those yellow stars at you. Why?'

'Probably a mark of gratitude for all the loot they've been getting. Haven't you noticed posters all over the place crediting the EU with helping this and that project? Can we go in now, Jack? I'm shivering and it's just about to start raining again.'

As they walked towards the entrance the Sailor's Hornpipe sounded. 'Right . . . fine . . . I'll be there.' He slipped the phone back in his pocket. 'I must leave you now, Jack. I've got to meet a member of the Garda.'

'You're going native already. Call them Civic Guards. That's what Lavinia would do.'

'I'd expect her to refer to them as the Royal Irish Constabulary.'

'And why not?' said the baroness peevishly. 'This mania for change for change's sake pisses me off.'

'Don't let our prime minister hear you talk like that. He'll have you targeted as a leader of the forces of conservatism.'

'I indignantly refute that accusation. I'm a leader of the forces of reaction and proud of it. Now, where are we meeting Constable O'Plod?'

'I'm seeing Garda Inspector McNulty in a caravan near the gate. I'll go alone.'

'Why?'

'Because I wish to build up a decent relationship with him and I don't want you insulting him in the first two minutes.'

She looked baffled. 'Why should you think I'd do that? I will be my most charming self. Diplomatic, nay suave to the point of oleaginousness—or should it be oleaginy? Whichever it should be, I'm ready to be it.'

To Amiss's mingled irritation and relief she lived up to her own prospectus. Within five minutes of their arrival in the dingy, chilly caravan, McNulty seemed utterly charmed by her eloquent extolling of the unrivalled scenery, superb hospitality and matchless charm of the people of Ireland, who had conquered the globe with their words and their music. She even threw in some Yeats lines about a land where even the old were fair and the wise were merry of tongue.

At that point, observing a trace of scepticism on the inspector's gnarled features, Amiss broke in on her eulogy. 'Inspector, I know you're busy. How can we help you?'

'Sure, it's more the other way about, Mr Amiss. I'm happy enough. I've all the lads in place. But if you're worried about anything let me know.'

'When you say "in place"?'

'Around the grounds and round the front and back.'

'How many?'

'Well now, between the army and the gardaí, I'd say we've maybe thirty.'

'But I was told that security advice was that this event was low-risk.'

62

'Well it was, but now it isn't. We've had information that the boyos seem a bit restive.'

'Which boyos are these?' asked the baroness. 'I thought seeing we've got representatives of all the nuisances here that meant everyone was safe.'

'You'd think that, mam. But you see, though the IRA is quite respectable these days owing to putting on the good suits during the day and though the same is true of the UDA and the UFF and the UVF . . .'

'Sorry, Inspector, you've lost me.'

'I wouldn't blame you, mam. I get a bit lost myself among all the factions and initials. But anyway there's even worse boyos than them that would be delighted to blow up the whole lot of ye. And they're a bit on the busy side these days.'

The baroness shook her head. 'They're like the dragons' teeth, these terrorists, aren't they?'

'Or the Hydra's heads, mam. Just when you think you've got rid of the lot of them there's a new wave ready for more divilment.'

'Well, I suppose it keeps you in a job.'

McNulty looked at her with less affection than hitherto. 'There's some kinds of work you could do without, mam. I'd rather be dealing with ordinary decent criminals any day. At least you know where you are with them. They don't shoot you in the back one day and demand the next that you pay them compensation because they strained their trigger finger.'

'Are you worried, Inspector?' asked Amiss.

'Not really.' McNulty pulled at his grey moustache. 'Anyway, you can take it that no one's going to get in here without wearing an invisible cloak. And we've had the sniffer dogs over the whole place so it's not going to blow up. I think you'll be able to sleep safe in your beds, the lot of you.'

'Unless, of course, one of us is a wolf in sheep's clothing.'

'We have wolf's-bane, mam, in the shape of our intelligence sources. Let's hope it's effective.' He paused for a moment and an expression of great grimness crossed his face. 'Mind you, sometimes I wonder. There's a lad in Special Branch there and you wouldn't know he was on our side.'

Amiss put on his most sympathetic voice. 'I have exactly the same problem, Inspector. There are people who are supposed to be my colleagues and . . .' He threw out his hands in an exaggerated gesture.

'They wouldn't give you the clippings of their toenails,' said the baroness, beaming at her command of the vernacular.

McNulty was still musing resentfully. 'Mind you, he's from Clare. And I'll tell you what, Clare people wouldn't give ye wood enough to burn ye, earth enough to bury ye or water enough to drown ye.'

64

'Well, let's hope the terrorists are from Clare too and will grudge us explosives enough to blow us up,' responded the baroness merrily.

'But they're not. They're mostly from up north. And these days they're more like Kilkenny cats than anything else.' As Amiss and the baroness pondered this elliptical statement, McNulty rose. 'Now if you'll excuse me, I'll need to go and talk to some of the lads. Here's an umbrella. It's bucketing down.'

'What about you?'

'I've the clothes for it, mam,' he said, pointing to a pile of waterproofs in the corner. 'This part of the world, we take no chances.'

*　　　*　　　*

'If I'm not mistaken, Dr Watson, I think the Yank has landed,' observed Amiss, as he glanced out the window.

'How do you know?' asked the baroness. 'Is she waving the stars and stripes?'

'See for yourself.'

She heaved herself out of her armchair and stomped over to the window. He looked on with pleasure as her eyes widened. 'My God, I see what you mean. They don't make them on this scale in Europe. I feel positively slender by comparison. And as for the paraphernalia!'

'Colourful, certainly.'

They left the window as the object of their

scrutiny disappeared from view.

'Are you coming out to welcome her?'

'Are you off your rocker?'

'Come, come, Jack. Faint heart never won fair lady. You're on the hunt this weekend, after all.'

She looked at him disdainfully. 'I may be catholic in my tastes, Robert, but if you think I'd settle for something that looks like . . .'

The door burst open.

'Which-a-you'z in charge?' demanded a voice which closely resembled a corncrake that had had a bad morning.

Amiss stepped forward. 'Kelly-Mae O'Hara, I presume? Welcome to Moycoole Castle. I'm Robert Amiss. And this is . . .'

'It'z a disgrace. I'll be talking to my lawyers.'

'Please, Miss O'Hara. Do sit down and tell us what is troubling you.'

He ushered her towards the sofa, took her white, green and orange umbrella and helped her to sit down. She pulled off her matching baseball cap and tossed it on the floor. 'Whadda godawful journey! I'll be suing the airline. How dare they charge for two seats on the plane!'

'You weren't paying,' said the baroness. 'So why worry?'

She sat bolt upright. ' 'Snot about the money. It'z an insult. It'z offensive. It'z their fault if their seats aren't big enough for people of size.'

66

Amiss tried to look sympathetic. 'They do cut corners these days. I can hardly stretch my legs in economy . . .'

'And then they had the noive to ask if I'd take a later flight so two people could travel instead of me.'

'Since you're so early, I presume you refused,' said the baroness.

Kelly-Mae glowered. 'Of course I refused. Fattism is an abuse of my human rights.'

'Did you at least have a comfortable flight?' asked Amiss nervously.

'Did I hell! We're talking dangerous food here. Couldn't meet my special needs. Even ran out of diet soda. And then there was no one to meet me at the airport.'

'I didn't know what flight you were taking.'

'Huh! You shuddadone.'

After a pause, Amiss gestured towards the baroness. 'You haven't been introduced to our chairman, Jack Troutbeck.'

'Chairman!!!'

'Sorry, chairwoman.'

'Sexism as well as fattism.'

'Good morning, Miss O'Hara,' said the baroness. 'You must make allowances for different customs in different countries, as I'm sure you'll know from your travels.'

Kelly-Mae glared. 'Never been to Eu'rp before. And from what I've seen of it, won't be doing it again. No one told me about the rain.'

'I fear the west of Ireland is famous for it.'

'Can I get anything for you, Kelly-Mae, if it's all right to call you by your first name. Coffee? Er . . . soda?'

'No. I'll check in an' go to my room. Godda shower. That's if there *is* a shower,' she added, in tones of deepest sarcasm. 'I mean we're talking a taxi with no air-conditioning here.' She began the process of getting up and, as Amiss gave her his hand, seemed to mellow slightly. 'You guys from round these parts?' she enquired, as soon as she was vertical.

'No. From London.'

'London, England?'

'Yes. And Jack lives in Cambridge.'

'You're English!'

'Yes.'

'And you're running this conference? In Ireland?'

'Well, yes. But you see . . .'

'I guess the Irish are too stupid to organize their own conferences so the English have to do it for them. That it?'

'Yes,' said the baroness.

Amiss broke in. 'Kelly-Mae, this is not an Irish conference. It just happens to be located here. It's mainly composed of people from the United Kingdom—from Northern Ireland, England, Scotland and Wales.'

'Heard about dat. Celts. All under the British yoke. It'z a disgrace.'

'I fear it's beyond my powers to do anything about that, Kelly-Mae. Now let me show you to reception.'

*   *   *

Amiss banged his fists together. 'Sweet suffering Jesus, as Philomena would say, she certainly exceeds all expectations.'

'No, she doesn't,' said the baroness. 'She's Irish-American, isn't she?'

The Sailor's Hornpipe sounded. 'Hello . . . Yes, Inspector . . . OK, I'll be right there.'

'Anything wrong?'

'He's back in the caravan and wants a word. Do you want to come?'

'In this rain? You must be joking.'

The Sailor's Hornpipe sounded again. 'Hello . . . Yes, Simon . . . How are things? OK . . . Yes, sure. I'll pick him up . . . Half-an-hour? . . . Fine . . . Bye.' He slipped the phone into his top pocket. 'When I've finished with McNulty I'm going to meet Mr Okinawa at the bus station. Will you look after things here?'

'I'll sit here and finish the newspaper and people can come to me in time of crisis, if that's what you mean. But don't expect me to be chatty to Miss Bonkers USA.'

*   *   *

The inspector pulled on his moustache. 'I wouldn't go so far as to say I'm worried, but I wouldn't say either that I'm not worried. I'm

69

getting information that suggests that some of them dissident IRA gobshites might be planning something. Can't give you any details but it's a good source. They're not all just sheep-shaggers in Roscommon, you know.'

Amiss tried to keep his mind on the main issue. 'What are we talking about here? Bombs? Assassinations?'

'I doubt the bomb. I don't see any chance they'd run the risk of knocking off any of the MOPE contingent. The flak would be too hot and heavy for them to handle back in the republican heartland.' He yanked vigorously at the moustache for a moment or two before looking at Amiss in some embarrassment. 'Word is they're thinking of making an example of a Brit.'

'That's comforting. There's only a handful of us.'

'Quite.'

McNulty tugged even more strenuously. 'We've three options. We could advise you to cancel the conference for security reasons.'

'Don't tempt me.'

'We could increase our presence in the hotel as well as outside. Or we could try to infiltrate someone to keep an eye on things without it being known that they were there.'

'What do you think should be done?'

'I don't think we have the first option. Although from all that I hear—saving your presence—the word is this conference is heading for disaster, Dublin doesn't want that admitted. And mark my words, if it is a disaster, they'll blame anyone but themselves. So watch out.'

He shook his head mournfully. 'Them fellas would live in your right ear and let the other one out in flats. And then they'd complain about the accommodation.'

'You were saying about option A not being a possibility?'

'That's right. And B isn't either, since Dublin doesn't want to admit that republicans are anything other than peace-loving these days in case it hurts their feelings and drives them to war.

'You know, I've been a garda for nearly thirty years and I've suffered all my life from the wishful thinking of feckin' governments. And if you ask me this shower are the worst yet. They seem to think them vultures turn into doves overnight. And if you argue you're supposed to be against peace.'

He pulled harder. 'Don't get me started.'

Amiss struggled to be helpful. 'You're telling me that in practical terms your only option is C.'

'That's right.'

'So you want to know if anyone can be infiltrated?'

'That's about it. Any ideas?'

'Do you have a garda who could pass for an expert on culture?'

'Not so's you'd notice. Even if we were let do it.'

'Don't quite see how to smuggle one in then. Give me a minute to think.'

After a couple of minutes Amiss looked up. 'I've only one idea that might possibly work and it's a long shot. And at best it's only one person and I don't see how he'd be able to stop an armed gang. But he is smart and he could fit in.'

'Go on.'

'I've a friend in the Met who could easily pass for a civil servant and whose boss is also a friend of mine who is flexible enough to lend him discreetly if it's at all feasible and he's not actually up to his neck in something vital.'

'When you say he could pass for a civil servant?'

'All we've got to say is that he's from the British Ministry of Culture and here to learn in a practical way about pan-Celtic multi-culturalism. Only thing is, could you guarantee that should he be unmasked, you'll stop it turning into a international scandal about sneaky Brits getting up to their old knavish tricks?'

'Well, it wouldn't be good for my career to admit I was in on it, but then there isn't much left of that. So I'll swear on the Sacred Heart that if it comes out I'll say I asked him to help us out and that all that we were looking for was better security for all the participants and that we've no apologies to make for doing that.'

'Done.'

'Right. Now how do you get hold of this lad?'

'Leave it to me. I'll do the best I can.'

*   *   *

Chief-Superintendent James Milton picked up his pen. 'All right, Robert. Give me the relevant details.'

He scribbled down an address, telephone number and travel details. 'OK. I'll do it if I can. But I'm not promising. You know that. It's completely irregular. I should go straight to Special Branch with this . . . Yes, of course . . . Yes, I know. And I agree with you it would take days. So since I'd rather you and Jack Troutbeck weren't assassinated, that's why I'm considering an alternative to the proper procedures. But I have to do this in such a way that if things go wrong Ellis is in the clear.'

He jabbed his pen into his pad. 'For me, I don't care. I'm so fed up I'd probably be grateful to be sacked . . . Yes, I expect Ellis would love an escapade like this. He's as bored as I am, stuck on a fraud case that's going nowhere and involving tons of paper . . . No, I wouldn't worry about that. Whatever he's said about finding Irish politics bore him senseless will not stop him being instantly thrilled by the idea of hidden assassins.

'OK, leave this with me. I'll be back to you soon. How's Jack, by the way . . .?' He laughed. 'Par for the course. I wish I was there to enjoy the clash. Give her my love and tell her to keep her back to the wall.'

CHAPTER SIX

Amiss was already at the bus station when Okinawa arrived bearing suitcase and camcorder. He put the case down as Amiss went up to him. 'Mr Okinawa? I'm Robert Amiss.'

Okinawa bowed slightly, shook hands and said, 'Please be so kind as to do this again so I can film you.'

As Amiss obediently froze, Okinawa took a few steps backward and pointed the camcorder at him. Feeling like a total idiot, Amiss walked towards him again and repeated his welcome. Satisfied, Okinawa lowered the camera, beamed and said, 'Herro, I am pleased to meet you. Thank you. Now I am leady.'

The journey back to the hotel was mostly silent, since Okinawa was preoccupied with capturing the sodden scenery for posterity. When they arrived, Amiss ran for the entrance hall carrying the suitcase and waited there for five minutes as Okinawa stood in the pouring rain filming every last hideous part of the facade thoroughly. The baroness came downstairs as Okinawa came inside dripping and took off his raincoat. 'Please let me film you,' he begged, as Amiss introduced them. 'I am, you see, constructing an historical lecord for my students to help them see the Ilish as they truly are.'

She raised an eyebrow. 'I hardly come into that category.'

'Ah, but we must look more deeply and broadly to the lerationship between the sister islands. Is this not what the conference is all about? How ancient animosities must give way to new thinking as "peace comes dlopping srow", as the poet Yeats put it.'

'The way things are shaping up here,' responded the baroness, 'it'll be war that'll come dlopping fast. There look to be plenty of new animosities about to be created to bolster up the ancient ones.'

Okinawa put down his camera and looked confused. 'Solly, solly? Is something wrong?'

'Never mind. It'll all become clear in due course. Now hadn't you better register and get yourself dry?'

Making as gallant a bow as was possible for a small man so encumbered, Okinawa placed his camera back on his shoulder and walked over to reception.

'I don't think I'm going to be able to stand this,' said the baroness.

'Ssshhh,' said Amiss. 'He'll hear you.'

'Who cares? If he goes on like this it won't be safe to go to the bog without checking if he's there. I feel like swatting him. Tell him to stop.'

'Crispin was very anxious that we give him all the help and full facilities to do whatever he wants. Apparently he's somebody important's cousin.'

'Umph. Well, I suppose it'll be better when there are more people here to occupy him.'

As if on cue, there was the sound of an engine and the sight of headlights.

'That'll be the coach, I expect,' said Amiss.

His eyes bright with excitement, Okinawa came rushing towards the door, settled his camera cosily back on his shoulder and took up a position diagonally opposite the entrance. 'You can do the welcoming and all the rest of the smarming, Robert,' said the baroness. 'I'm going to observe from the sidelines.'

*   *   *

'Who are you?' asked the first arrival—a large man with a weatherbeaten face shaped like a slab of granite. 'I'm Gardiner Steeples.'

'Robert Amiss, Gardiner. We've spoken on the phone a few times.'

Presumably seeing no point in responding to such an obvious statement of fact, Steeples shook hands silently. Conscious that a queue

76

was forming, Amiss pointed. 'Reception's over there, Gardiner.'

Steeples caught sight of Okinawa. 'What's that wee scutter doing taking pictures of me?' he asked in tones of the deepest suspicion, turning his head away sharply from the camera. 'I thought there was to be no journalists.'

'Don't worry. There aren't. Mr Okinawa isn't a journalist, but an academic who's filming the conference for the historical record.'

'Waste of money, if you ask me,' said Steeples, and walked away.

Amiss thankfully turned to the beaming man next in line. 'Robert Amiss. You're very welcome.'

'Sean O'Farrell.'

'Sorry? Sean O'Farrell? I can't quite place you.'

'That's because you didn't know I was coming,' laughed O'Farrell. 'I'm here instead of Jimmy Mangan.'

'What's happened to Jimmy? I was talking to him only yesterday.'

O'Farrell twinkled with amusement. 'Ah sure, you know what Jimmy is like.'

'I don't,' said Amiss stiffly.

'Well, he's a great lad and all that, Jimmy, but you don't always know where you are with him. Anyway, he rang me last night and said something had come up so would I stand in for him. So here I am.'

'How kind of you,' said Amiss stiffly. 'Are the others with you?'

'Afraid not. Vincent couldn't make it either and Fintan had a heavy couple of nights so he's cried off.'

'Are you telling me you're the only person here from the southern Irish cultural committee?'

O'Farrell's merry laugh rang out again. 'Jaysus, we're awful and no mistake, aren't we?'

'You said it,' muttered Amiss under his breath.

'Have you met these two?' asked O'Farrell, throwing his arms around the pair behind him. 'Billy Pratt and Willie Hughes. Now they're great fellas entirely. If only all unionists were like them, sure we'd all be as happy as Larry.'

Pratt, who was thin with well-coiffed hair, and Hughes, who was bald and pot-bellied, laughed and shook hands with Amiss. 'And if all nationalists were like Sean,' said Pratt, 'all unionists would want to join a United Ireland.' The three of them went merrily off to reception together.

Amiss turned to the next trio, who had been posing for Okinawa. *'Is mise Laochraí de Búrca,'* said the buxom, henna-haired thirty-something woman, *'agus tá gearán agam.'*

Amiss put his hand out. 'I'm Robert Amiss, Laochraí, and I'm sorry but I don't understand

78

Irish.'

She shook his perfunctorily. 'Where's the interpreter?'

'Hasn't arrived yet.'

She glowered. 'I have a complaint. The bus driver couldn't speak Irish.'

'Sorry about that, Laochraí. But will you introduce me to your colleagues?'

She waved forward a tall, slim man of about her age, who looked at Amiss with some suspicion but put out his hand and nodded civilly. 'This is Liam MacPhrait,' she said, 'and this is *An tAthair* Cormac O'Flynn. They're standing in for Saoirse and Seoirse, who couldn't come.'

'Welcome, Liam. And you too, Antar.'

'Not Antar,' said the plump man in fatigues. '"*An tAthair*" means "Father". But I've no truck with titles or status, so you should just call me Cormac.'

It was a propitious moment for the baroness, who had clearly been getting bored, to heave herself to her feet and join them. 'This is Lady Troutbeck,' said Amiss. 'Jack, Laochraí de Búrca, Liam MacPhrait and Father Cormac O'Flynn, who prefers to be called Cormac.' He tried not to notice the expressions of contempt that greeted his mispronunciations.

'I know who you are,' said Laochraí. 'The conference chair.'

'The conference chairwoman,' said the

79

baroness, holding out a hand which, in turn, each of them took with some reluctance.

'I should warn you,' said Laochraí, 'that we reject the labels, titles and trappings of the British Empire.'

'Which are discriminatory,' added O'Flynn.

'I don't give a tinker's curse what you think about such matters,' said the baroness brightly, 'anymore than you should give a tinker's curse what I think. But if you're beefing about being expected to call me "Lady Troutbeck", that's one grievance you'll have to do without. Call me "Jack" as everyone else does, unless I'm in the chair, in which case you call me "Chairman", "Madam Chairman" or "Chairwoman". I do not answer to the preposterous politically correct alternatives.'

'The use of the word "tinker" is in itself . . .' began O'Flynn.

But Laochraí was already in full flight. 'We haven't resolved this matter of the bus driver not being able to speak Irish. He was almost dismissive when I complained.'

'Sorry about that,' said Amiss.

'I find it equally offensive that you, the sole organizer of this conference, are not bilingual. The very least you might have done was to have the interpreter here on time.'

Okinawa lowered his camcorder and came forward. 'May I be of help?'

'Only if you can speak Irish,' said Amiss wearily.

'Certainly I can speak Ilish.' He bowed in Laochraí's direction. 'Ah, so. You have here a native Irish speaker who knows no English. How unusual. I didn't think there were any reft.'

'No,' said Amiss grimly, 'that isn't what we have here. What we have here is a native English speaker who objects because I know no Irish.'

Okinawa bowed to Laochraí and spoke in what sounded to Amiss like fluent Irish. She looked perplexed and asked Okinawa a brief question, to which he responded volubly. Her puzzled response was again brief. Okinawa turned to Amiss. 'I think we need a diplomatic solution to this, Lobert. Raochrí cannot understand my Ilish.'

'Is that because it's a Japanese variant?' asked Amiss desperately.

'Maybe it is because I learned my Ilish in the south-west of Ireland, in Kelly, and she does not understand the dialect. Her diarect is difficult for me too.' He turned to Laochraí. 'Will it be easier if we speak in Engrish?'

She looked cross. 'It is my human right to have people speak my language.'

'But is it not their human light to have you speak theirs? However, if it helps you,' he bowed again, 'I will stay with you and do my best.'

Laochraí looked at Okinawa and then at Amiss. 'It's all right,' she said. 'It can wait until the official interpreter gets here.' And with her two friends, she headed towards reception.

Another set of headlights came into view. Okinawa picked up his camera and walked back towards his vantage-point, but not before giving Amiss a little grin.

The baroness watched him go. 'I've always been dead against foreign intervention in our affairs,' she said, 'but after watching the demolition of Lucrezia Borgia there, I'm beginning to change my mind. That is one useful Nip.'

*   *   *

After thirty minutes in which Amiss, with the help of the newly-arrived Simon Gibson, welcomed the baroness's Indian friend, one Scot, Welsh Wyn, one Englishman, a Dublin minister and his entourage, the interpreter and the signer and the main speaker, he was able to steal a moment alone with Gibson.

'What's going on with the DUPEs, Simon? They seem to be best pals with the Irish. Look at them. They're huggermuggering with the MOPEs now.'

'You'll see plenty more of that. MOPEs and DUPEs have plenty in common and specialize in the "let's-go-the-extra-mile-for-peace" lingo they've learned from the useful idiots who equate words with deeds.'

'Still, the DUPEs seemed a lot more

reasonable than the MOPEs.'

'I'm afraid these MOPEs are particularly grim,' said Gibson, 'but in some ways bloody O'Flynn aka Call-me-Cormac's the worst. He's been a nightmare addition to MOPEery.'

He shook his head. 'Not that there wasn't a kind of tragic inevitability about the kind of priest they would attract.'

'Quick drink before we go back on duty?'

'OK. I need it.'

When Amiss returned with their gins-and-tonic, Gibson had become contemplative. 'You know, you spend your life in that bloody place—Northern Ireland—trying to break down prejudices, and then people wilfully or ignorantly insist on reinforcing and indeed exaggerating the stereotypes you've been challenging.

'Thus the kind of Jesuit sent off to be a spiritual adviser to MOPEers isn't a perfectly sane chap with an interest in ethical philosophy and a desire to promote tolerance but a dimwit who thinks they don't sufficiently realise how thoroughly oppressed they are. So he sets out to make them develop a more bitter sense of victimhood than they already had.'

He took a large sip. 'You can't entirely blame Call-me-Cormac. He was no doubt doing useful things in South America and they took him away and posted him to Belfast. So naturally he runs around the place trying to

83

persuade the well-housed inhabitants on generous welfare benefits that they are trampled-upon peons who are entitled to rise up against their tormentors.'

'The British? The unionists? Who exactly?'

'Well you and I know that their main tormentors are their own so-called community leaders—MOPEs and DUPEs alike—who brain-wash the gullible and beat up anyone who challenges them. We also know the British government pours resources into the place that it would never devote to the quiescent needy closer to home.

'But these people are dangerous because of their great rage against people who have what they haven't got. It's like an underclass anywhere, but it's been given an ideology to justify envy and revenge. Anyway, in Call-me-Cormac's view all terrorism is a response to tyranny and therefore is usually justified. Unless it's the loyalist underclass killing Catholics, of course. Or even more so, any action by the state which smacks of heavy-handedness. IRA man shoots policeman dead—legitimate form of protest. Policeman accidentally kills terrorist in self-defence, call in Amnesty International and demand public enquiry.'

'Does the chap have saving graces?'

'Don't think so, unless a penchant for too much stout qualifies as a saving grace. Probably if he'd been a priest in Oxford rather than South America he'd have developed a taste for port. But since nowadays he's a friend of the poor and the Irish poor at that, stout it has to be. And it makes him sing even worse.'

'Sing what?'

'Protest and peace stuff, naturally. And accompanies himself badly on the guitar.'

'Oh, God. Does he . . . ?'

He was interrupted by the baroness, who plumped herself down beside them, waved her large Martini in a celebratory manner and said, 'Yum, yum. They certainly did all right on the interpreter.'

'Is that so, Jack? I haven't had time to notice. Unlike you, I've been too busy trying to grasp who is who to have time to study the carnal possibilities of anyone here.'

She smacked her lips. 'I could really take to Aisling. I've always liked blue-black hair and green eyes.'

'Well, well,' drawled Gibson. 'I hadn't expected romance to blossom so early in the proceedings. Gives us all hope.'

'Keep your filthy hands off our interpreter, Jack,' said Amiss. 'You shouldn't be mingling pleasure with business.'

'I long ago gave up thinking this had anything to do with business. As far as I'm concerned, I'm playing this one for laughs all the way.'

'Very wise,' said Gibson. 'Very wise.'

'Aisling's probably straight anyway,' said Amiss crossly.

'Only because she's never met *me* before.'

'Has anyone ever told you that you're quite repellent when you smirk?' She giggled with pleasure.

Amiss groaned. 'And that one of the most irritating things about you is that it's almost impossible to find any insult that you don't interpret as a compliment?'

She giggled again. 'Just as well, isn't it? Now tell me about this pretentious little jerk who is presumably about to bore the arse off all of us.'

'Why do you automatically assume he's a jerk?'

'Because of the title of his talk. "Silence and narrative: Heaney and the Peace." Bullshit personified.'

'I tend to agree with you,' said Gibson, 'but the Irish don't. McGuinness was pushed strongly by the Department of Foreign Affairs, who say he's intellectually red-hot.'

'That's because they're a bunch of spoiled writers and academics—like most of the Irish.'

'No one could accuse you of shirking the sweeping statement,' commented Amiss.

'So what's the alleged purpose of this session anyway?'

'He's to broaden our minds, we're told,' said Gibson, 'not to speak of extending our horizons, accessing our sensibilities, wringing our withers . . . all that sort of stuff. *Inter alia* he's looking at our cultural divisions from a

European perspective in the context of our universality, or something like that.'

'Can't wait. Anyway why isn't the little bastard here by now? We kick off in half an hour.'

'He is here,' said Amiss. 'Even as we speak I expect he is rehearsing in his room. He told me with immense solemnity that it had been hard to sandwich us in between his lecture to the Strasbourg Friends of the Peace Process and the Regional Hegemony Working Party in Stuttgart.'

'Oh God, he's one of these travelling academics. They're the worst. They talk multilingual balls.'

As the Sailor's Hornpipe began, Amiss retreated into a corner. 'Hello?'

'I'm on my way,' cried an excited Pooley.

'Great. Hang on a minute.' Amiss left the bar and found a quiet corner.

'Go on.'

'It's completely off the record as far as work's concerned. I'm supposed to be taking time off to visit a sick relative.'

'What's your cover? What I suggested to Jim?'

'No. Don't like the civil servant idea. Can I get away with being the employee of a mysterious American millionaire who wants to set up a similar conference which would involve flying all your participants to the US?'

'Ellis, you're a genius. Apart from anything

else, that should put the shits on their best behaviour. There's nothing they like better than trips to America where they can bewail their terrible lot in great luxury to tumultuous applause. Are you happy to keep your name?'

'Surname, yes. First name, maybe better not. I wouldn't like it on the record. Use my second name. Even though I hate it, it's one lie fewer.'

'What is it then? Stop being so coy.'

'Rollo.'

'Ellis, why did your parents do that to you?'

'It's to do with ancestors,' said Pooley stiffly. 'There are penalties attached to being born into the aristocracy, you know. Anyway, I can't hang about any longer. I've finished packing and am off to the airport. Should be at Knock at ten.'

'I won't be able to meet you, but I'll send a taxi.' Amiss paused and looked cautiously around him. 'Ellis—I mean Rollo—you do realise that this might be dangerous? Especially if somebody really wants to knock off Brits.'

'Of course I do,' said Pooley impatiently. 'That's half the attraction. If you spent as long as I've spent in the last few months trawling through financial records you'd offer yourself for active service in Afghanistan. See you.'

Amiss punched in some numbers. 'My friend Rollo Pooley is on his way. What do you think, Inspector? Who should know his true identity?'

'Not one single fecker except ourselves, if you ask me.'

'Lady Troutbeck has to know since she knows the bloke well.'

'Fair enough. But is there any reason to tell anyone else?'

'I'd be a bit unhappy not telling Simon Gibson. He's become a good friend and a very useful source of information since he knows everyone.'

'One thing I've learnt in a long career is that every person you tell anything to will pass it on to at least one more. As the fella said, "A secret shared is a secret blown". Mr Gibson may be decent and trustworthy as they come but you can't be certain that he's one hundred per cent discreet.'

Amiss shrugged. 'I suppose you're right. It's just that I feel I'm rather letting him down by hiding anything from him. But now that you mention it, discretion isn't what he's best known for.'

'Thanks for that. Anyone else you have to tell?'

'No one else. And incidentally, you needn't worry about Lady Troutbeck. She may be tactless and insensitive, but when she wants to be, she's as tight with information as an anal-retentive.'

CHAPTER SEVEN

Two minutes into Dr Gerry McGuinness's lecture Amiss thought things couldn't get worse. Three minutes later he realised that yes, indeed, they could. And what was more, they had. By now he had given up trying to extract any meaning and just let the words sweep over him. 'Syntactical hierarchy . . . resemblance and analogy . . . metonomy and the rhetorical treatise . . . temporalist discourse . . . audacity of the metaphor . . . elucidation of the enigma . . . seismatic patterns . . . utilitarian reality . . . referential poeticity . . . enigmatic signifiers . . . co-existentialism . . . revenge of rhyme on the reasoning paradigm . . . totalitising effect . . . intertextuality . . . condensing and contextualising the elliptical.'

He tried to allay his boredom by studying the audience. Gardiner Steeples and Sean O'Farrell were asleep, Okinawa was busy filming, Kapur seemed to be in another world and everyone else looked bored and shifted a lot in their seats. Although Aisling talked steadily into her microphone, the signer, a beefy chap with a hunted expression, had largely given up and seemed to be confining himself to translating the word 'one'—which, admittedly, occurred frequently.

Thirty minutes in, McGuinness looked

gravely at the audience. 'Now I will address myself to the association of cultures and civilizations with lexicogenetics and corpus linguistics. In Heaney's aspiration that "hope and history rhyme" one can see the semantic parallels, but . . .'

The baroness cut in. 'Dr McGuinness,' she announced benignly, 'you are probably too young to remember, but in vaudeville there was an excellent tradition that when the performer had outstayed his welcome, a long pole would emerge from the wings, its hook would be attached to his collar and he would be dragged off. My hook is only one of those metaphors of which you are so fond, but it will have to do. Your time is up.'

McGuinness looked at her incredulously and the suddenly revived audience gazed hopefully. 'But I have a great deal of ground still to cover.'

'I fear you won't be covering it. Not here anyway. Bugger off. We've had enough.'

McGuinness picked up his papers. 'I've never been so insulted in my life.'

'Pity.' She guffawed. 'At least I've got you to utter one comprehensible sentence.' She picked up her pipe. 'I need a drink,' she told the audience, 'and I bet all you do too. So let's go to the drawing room for the Irish government's reception.' The audience, studiously avoiding looking at McGuinness, followed with alacrity.

O'Farrell sidled up to Amiss. 'We'll probably have to register a formal complaint, but you know we won't really mean it. That little bollix had it coming. Sometimes I think half the EU budget is spent on sending arseholes all over the shop to talk shite at each other.'

Gibson joined them and smiled a jaded smile. 'I think Yeats might describe Baroness Troutbeck as "a terrible beauty", don't you? Do you know, for the first time, I am beginning to look forward to an entertaining weekend?'

*　　　*　　　*

The wine and spirits flowed lavishly. Since McGuinness had stormed off to the airport, there was no spectre to inhibit the light-hearted from character assassination. Amiss's consultation with the baroness about Father O'Flynn's request to sing grace was terminated with a quick 'Tell him to fuck off' as she reached over to the next group and pulled Aisling out of it. 'What did you think of that?' she asked.

Aisling shook her comely head. 'Worst yet professionally, and that's saying something. "Why am I here?" That's all I kept thinking. Why am I supposed to be translating an avalanche of pretentious and virtually incomprehensible words for which there are no known Irish equivalents?'

'How did you solve that problem?' asked Amiss. 'Sounds pretty insuperable.'

'Fortunately the two people I was translating for weren't actually listening to me since their English is considerably better than their Irish. So I knew that their earpieces were half-out and that I was going through this charade just so they could make a political point and nuisances of themselves.'

'Can't see the point of Irish myself,' said the baroness. 'If the only people who want to speak Irish are MOPEers trying to get back at the Brits, why do you collude with them?'

'Because I love Irish.'

'But it's dead.'

'So are Latin and Greek.'

'But they're different.'

'How?'

'Bases of the culture of western civilization.'

'So is Irish. It's a rich, wonderful language with a rich and wonderful literature and I for one believe it worth saving. Or are you one of those people who think that because it's not modern it should be discarded as uncool?'

Amiss sniggered. The baroness sucked her lower lip. 'I thought it was just political.'

'No, it isn't. Most people who love the language hate those who hijack it. It was nearly eradicated because for generations it was beaten into children as a political act. Now there's a chance it might survive among people like me if we can keep it out of the hands of those opportunistic bastards who anyway mostly speak dreadful Irish they half-learned in prison.'

The baroness beamed. 'Let's sit together at dinner, Aisling.'

'Jack,' hissed Amiss. 'You're supposed to be between the minister and Gardiner Steeples.'

'Bollocks to that. Aisling's sitting with *me*.'

Cursing under his breath, Amiss went out to break the bad news to Father O'Flynn and alter the seating plan.

*   *   *

Although Wyn Gruffudd, Liam MacPhrait and Kelly-Mae O'Hara proved to be teetotal, they were the exceptions. By seven thirty, when the participants moved to the dining room, most were in a genial mood. Amiss soon recovered his good humour, for he was beside the minister's private secretary, who was both attractive and indiscreet.

'You're spot on, Robert. Dublin thinks this has turned into a farce. The last straw is that the only nationalists from Northern Ireland are MOPEs and the only unionists are two loyalists and an Orangeman. Yer man was livid when he was told to stand in for the Minister for Foreign Affairs. Tried everything to get out of it.'

'He's putting a brave face on it,' observed

Amiss. 'In fact he seems to be having a high old time.'

'That's Packie for you.'

'Paki? I thought his name was Patrick?'

'It's short for Patrick.'

'How do you get "PAKI" from Patrick, Siobhán?'

She gurgled. 'Fortunately it's spelled "Packie" rather than what racists shout at Pakistanis. Still it sounds bad, but this is Ireland and we didn't know an Asian from a Roumanian until very recently. In fact it's only a few years since someone in the Department of Education caused deep offence by innocently sending to a Birmingham Irish language school boxes of books about the exploits of Packie and Máire.'

'It'll add greatly to the gaiety of nations if he becomes taoiseach. What's he like anyway?'

'Like all of them. You'll know yourself, having been in the civil service and all, that politicians will be slapping you on the back one minute and stabbing you in it the next.'

'Will he stay for the weekend?'

'He will in his arse stay for the weekend. There'll be an urgent summons from somewhere or other quite soon and in the morning he'll leave for Dublin in the Merc with the crocodile tears pouring down his face. Now tell me more about yourself. How did someone as clever as you get dragged into this shite?'

95

To Amiss's chagrin, it was at this moment that the baroness stood up and clapped her hands. Her first couple of words were both hesitant and apparently incoherent. She bent down and whispered to Aisling, who whispered back and then left the table to return to her translating duties.

Spotting Amiss's anxious look, Siobhán whispered, 'It's OK. I think she's trying to say "*A cháirde*". It's the Irish for "friends". Aisling must have been tutoring her.'

'A cardie,' boomed the baroness with a little more confidence. 'I'm sorry to do this to you, but it's time for the speeches.' Appearing to realise this was less than tactful, she offered a hasty amendment. 'That is to say, I can see you're all enjoying the sound of your own voices, but now it's time to listen. First, here is the Irish Minister for Culture, Mr Packie Barrett, who wants to welcome you on behalf of his government. I hope he'll also be apologizing for what developers have been allowed to do to this castle.'

She sat down and beamed triumphantly in the direction of Aisling, who was now sitting behind Laochraí and Liam MacPhrait talking into her microphone. The signer was gesticulating vigorously at the end of the room, watched intermittently by the idly curious.

Siobhán had warned Amiss he wouldn't understand the first few sentences. 'We have a quaint convention known as the "*cúpla focal*"

—the couple of words—which requires our politicians to gabble a few words of usually execrable Irish at the beginning of their speeches,' she had explained. 'This is to keep up the pretence that they can speak what is technically our first national language.'

Having lived up to her prediction, the minister produced in deeply sincere tones some rather incoherent flannel about his joy in being present at such a worthwhile coming together of hearts and minds from neighbouring cultures and his pride in being chosen to convey his government's deep commitment to the concepts of cultural diversity and parity of esteem for all. Even if everyone wasn't happy with the architectural innovations at Moycoole Castle, he said with some embarrassment, he knew they would be comfortable and well looked after with true Irish hospitality. And he ended by handing over 'without further ado to our gracious and distinguished hostess, the Baroness Troutbeck, whose inspired leadership will, I have no doubt, make this a conference to remember.'

'Thank you, Minister,' she said. 'Wasn't there a film about the *Titanic* called *A Night to Remember*?' She caught sight of his face. 'Sorry. Joke. Right, we have two speakers tonight, and though I've never heard of either of them, I'm told they're very entertaining in their way.' She pointed down the table. 'There's the first of them, Kevin Barry.'

The pairing of Kevin Barry and Paddy Reilly had been billed by the Irish as a lively look at Irish nationalism from two perspectives. Barry was a well-known controversial journalist of combatively nationalist views, while the historian Paddy Reilly was of a breed known in Ireland as 'revisionist'. Depending on your point of view, Gibson had explained to Amiss, revisionists were traitors selling out their glorious heritage or people who had the courage to challenge simple-minded nationalist ideology and seek instead objective truth. Irish ministers and officials mostly fence-sat on the issue.

Barry and Reilly had both been asked to speak for fifteen minutes on how they saw the history of Ireland since partition. Barry proved to be small, venomous and voluble. The Northern Ireland he described was one in which Catholics had ever feared to walk the streets lest they be beaten up by the constabulary or murdered by a passing loyalist. Their daily persecution had been orchestrated by the ruling unionist/Protestant class who hated them for their religion and who, having no culture of their own, were consumed with jealousy for the richness of the Irish tradition and so oppressed the Catholics viciously, until heroically, in the era of civil rights—goaded beyond endurance—they rose to claim what was rightfully theirs.

As for the other part of Ireland, while he

had some rude remarks to make about the Roman Catholic church, on the whole the story was of a plucky little nation emerging from under the long shadow of the British occupying forces to forge an identity as a creative and vigorous outward-looking democracy which was now the envy of the world.

After thirty minutes, with a final rhetorical flourish about the far-flung gallant Irish diaspora who, though driven from their native land by the tyranny of their foreign oppressors, had earned respect and love the world over, he looked at his watch, mumbled a vague apology and sat down to applause which varied from the minimum consonant with politeness to the prolonged and thunderous.

Neither Gardiner Steeples, who had stared stonily at the nearest wall throughout Barry's harangue, nor the baroness, who was scowling, clapped. When the noise died down, she stood up and said coldly, 'I had not realised your brief was to be so enthusiastically partisan. I hope your fellow countryman says something sensible.' Amiss put his head in his hands.

Paddy Reilly was large, scornful and equally voluble, the scorn being mainly directed at Irish historians who sought to perpetuate what he described as that 'ignorant, snivelling and self-pitying MOPE version of Irish history that collapses under any decent intellectual scrutiny.' All countries were colonized by

99

stronger neighbours. The truth was that as colonial occupiers went, the British had been benign.

'Brit-lover,' cried Kelly-Mae.

Reilly ignored her and moved on to Northern Ireland, which he saw as a place blighted by Catholics being bad losers who demanded separate schooling and tried to wreck the state. There had been discrimination, but nothing as bad as Protestants had suffered in the south, where through murder, intimidation and cultural and religious oppression they had been almost eradicated.

'Good,' shouted Kelly-Mae. 'Piddy they weren't all run out of the country.'

As the baroness rose threateningly, Laochraí intervened. 'That was out of order, Kelly-Mae. We have to be inclusive.'

The baroness looked at her in amazement. 'Blimey, I didn't expect you to talk sense. Now continue, Professor Reilly. And if that woman interrupts again she will be thrown out. Freedom of speech is not an inalienable right when I'm in charge.'

Reilly pressed on vigorously with an increasingly impassioned denunciation of the Anglophobia, rampant Romanism, hypocrisy, corruption, infantilism and necrophiliac aspects of the Irish state. 'We've reached adolescence,' he concluded, 'but the MOPE tendency remains in the kindergarten, playing with dangerous toys.'

The applause was even more uneven this time. The baroness clapped enthusiastically. She looked down at a piece of paper and read 'Gorrymeeleemahagat. For those of you who don't know,' she announced proudly, 'that means, "Thank you very much".' She turned to the minister. 'I'll master the coopla fuckill yet, Packie,' she added gaily. 'But you'd better learn to spout Kipling as a *quid pro quo*. You could start with "While the Celt is talking from Valencia to Kirkwall, The English—ah, the English!—don't say anything at all".'

'Hardly applies to you,' said the minister jovially.

'Exception that proves the rule, Packie.'

She looked down the table at Reilly. 'That was most illuminating, Professor Reilly.' Ignoring the hands that had shot up in the MOPE corner, she added, 'Now I know we were to have had some questions, but since both speakers talked twice as long as they were asked to, we'll adjourn immediately to the bar.'

As the crowd surged out, Amiss asked the minister's secretary to excuse him for a moment, caught up with the baroness and pulled her aside. 'Jack, you've to stop being partisan.'

'Why should I? I *am* partisan. I haven't been a bloody civil servant for a long time now. I feel gloriously, irresponsibly free.'

'But you complained about Barry being

101

partisan.'

'That's because he was partisan on the wrong side.'

'You're being very unfair. Barry, MOPE and the Irish have a perfectly legitimate complaint against you.'

'Nonsense, Robert. Absolute balls. I absolutely refuse to treat indecent people as well as the decent.' She grinned. 'So there. Now I'm going back to my raven-haired beauty.'

A great deal of wine had been consumed during dinner, and the bar buzzed with mostly merry chatter. While it was clear that people were tending to stick to their own kind, there was a certain amount of unexpected mingling. Amiss was surprised by the pairings of Kapur and Okinawa, Steeples and Wyn Gruffudd, and O'Farrell and the newly-arrived Pooley, as well as by the sight of Barry and Reilly, who were both drinking large whiskies, in deep and amicable conversation with the minister. Indeed Amiss heard them all laughing loudly at Barry's observation that of course revisionists believed that the victims of the Famine had all died of anorexia nervosa.

A sense of duty led Amiss to chat politely to several of the participants, particularly the signer, Joe, who announced his intention of getting drunk and trying to forget about everything. The baroness was afflicted by no inhibitions about indulging herself, so she stayed by Aisling's side throughout. By midnight, though, Amiss was in a corner gossiping happily with Siobhán, so it was therefore with intense irritation that he heard a violent altercation begin at the other side of the room. The source of the noise turned out to be Barry and Reilly, who were shouting abuse at each other. Insofar as Amiss could hear what they were saying, Barry's allegations appeared to be that it was well known that Reilly's grandfather had taken the King's shilling and that his father had been a turncoat and a traitor during the civil war. This Reilly countered by saying that Barry's father had been responsible for blowing up a whole convoy of Free State soldiers. 'Pity they didn't get more of those fucking Blueshirts [A 1930s Irish anti-IRA, pro-Mussolini and pro-Franco group],' cried Barry, which caused Reilly to denounce him as a thug and a life-long IRA groupie. 'And why not?' screamed Barry. 'It's better than being a sycophant and a lickspittle to the British establishment,' at which moment Reilly's fist connected with his head. Within seconds the two were slugging it out unsteadily.

'Bare-knuckle fighting,' said Siobhán. 'It's supposed to be all the rage in America these days.'

Their fight was short-lived. With the help of Steeples and Pooley, Amiss pulled the protagonists apart before they could do any

103

real damage, only for both of them to turn on their saviours. Amiss was denounced as 'a fucking Brit' by Barry and Steeples as 'a fucking unionist' by Reilly. Since neither of them knew anything about Pooley, he missed out on any insults.

'Why would a revisionist call anyone "a fucking unionist"?' asked Amiss of Siobhán, as they watched the pair being calmed by the minister. 'Don't they usually take their side?'

'Because when the Irish get pissed,' explained Siobhán, 'which we frequently do, we all turn into nationalists. It's in our blood.'

'It's tribalism,' said Steeples. 'It's bred into us, like bulls.'

The baroness came over with Aisling. She looked pleased. 'Things are livening up. That's certainly got things off to a good start. Pity you didn't let them go on longer.'

Amiss cast her a withering look and took Siobhán back to their corner.

*   *   *

'I want to apologize to you, Lady Troutbeck, for that appalling scene.'

The baroness, who was listening intently to Aisling, looked up crossly. 'Who are you?'

'I'm from the Irish Department of Culture. Theo Mathew is my name. And, as I say, I'm heartily sorry that this disgraceful scene has occurred. I wouldn't want you to run away with

104

the impression that Irish people normally behave like this.'

'Like what? You mean getting drunk and fighting? I thought they did it all the time.'

'I understand the purpose of this conference, Lady Troutbeck, is to show that these stereotypes are mistaken and outdated.'

She chortled loudly. 'Wishful thinking won't conceal the fact that there's always a lot of truth in stereotypes. And if that's what you're trying to do with this conference, your advisers have certainly gone about it in a funny way. Anyway I don't mind that the Irish drink and fight. I'm always in favour of people doing what they're good at. I'm a libertarian.'

Mathew looked shocked. 'I wouldn't know about that, Lady Troutbeck. Myself, I'm in favour of liberty, not license.'

'How pious.'

'I should tell you for the record, your ladyship, that the reputation the Irish have for drinking is most unfair. If you look at the statistics you'll find we drink less per head than the majority of the countries in the EU.'

'You're joking.'

'Indeed I am not. I'm only telling you the honest God's truth. We're a much maligned people and I would hope that this is a point that will be made and made forcibly during the next few days.'

'You'll have plenty of opportunity to do that, won't you?'

He looked at her shiftily. 'Alas, your ladyship, much to my regret, that will not be possible.'

'You're leaving already?'

'With great sadness, I assure you. But a crisis has arisen in the department. They need me and so I must go. Worse, I have just heard that the minister too has been called away. Still, every cloud has a silver lining and this does at least mean that I'll have a lift back to Dublin.' He smirked at her. 'We must count our blessings.'

The baroness stared at him. He made a slight bow. 'I'll make my farewells now, Lady Troutbeck. I'm very sorry to go, but I'm sure that in your capable hands the conference will be a tremendous contribution to harmonious relationships between our peoples. I wish you every success.'

'Listen,' she said, 'you can't just drop out like that. We're already short of several delegates.'

'I wouldn't dream of just dropping out. I've already made arrangements for a substitute. A most experienced man will take my place.'

The baroness stormed over to Amiss and brutally interrupted his tête-à-tête. 'That little creep Theo something-or-other's leaving.' She jerked her head towards Siobhán. 'And your creep's leaving as well.'

Siobhán's grin almost split her face in two. 'Really? That's surprising.'

The baroness looked grim. 'I hear the noise of scuttling rats abandoning ship.'

'Look on the bright side,' said Siobhán. 'You have to be better off without that craw-thumping little kill-joy with his pioneer pin and his rosary and his daily mass and his first Fridays and his scapulars and his novenas and his . . .'

'Calm yourself, girl. What's all this about?'

'Theo is a throwback to what we don't have many of any more but what used to be known as Holy Joes who lived lives of conspicuous virtue which they liked to ram down everyone's throat at all times under a cloak of supposed humility.'

'Uriah O'Heeps?'

'Saint Uriah O'Heeps.'

'What's all this baloney he was telling me about the Irish drinking less than any other European nation?'

Siobhán gurgled throatily in a way that Amiss found overwhelmingly attractive. 'That's one of our great Irish lies. It is of course true, yet it is not true.'

'Come again?'

'We drink less than other countries because half of us don't drink at all. The rest of us make up for it. So the drinkers drink more than anyone else in Europe but the semblance of moderation is there for statistic-massaging. Courtesy of Pioneers like yer man.'

'Pioneers?'

'Didn't you see that little badge in his lapel?'

'I thought it was something religious. Didn't it have a bleeding heart or something?'

'It's the symbol of the Pioneer total abstinence movement—which is indeed Catholic.'

'So that's what it is. I saw it the other day on a barman in Sligo.'

'You see it on a lot of barmen. Pretty rational, really.'

'Isn't it hypocritical to sell drink if you disapprove of it yourself?' asked Amiss. 'Rather like being a celibate brothel-keeper.'

'Why are you English so keen on consistency? We regard our inconsistency as part of our charm.'

She gurgled again. 'Anyway, you're much better off without Old Mother Mathew. He'd have driven you mad. And from what I've seen there's plenty to drive you mad as it is. Whoever you get in his place has to be an improvement. Forget about him. He's only an ould fossil.'

Amiss eyed the baroness. 'In that case, surely you should be cherishing him, Jack. He's part of Irish tradition. The kind of throwback you love so well.'

'I'll cherish what I like,' she said petulantly, and marched back to Aisling.

CHAPTER EIGHT

'Sweet suffering Jesus, Robert.' Philomena was quivering with rage.

'What's the matter, Philomena?'

'It's that fat whinge of an American. I've a litany of complaints from her that you wouldn't get from a reverend mother kidnapped into a hoorhouse.'

'Tell me.'

'Well, she comes down to breakfast and looks at the menu with a face on her like a wet Good Friday in Leitrim. "What would you like, madam?" says I. "Bagels, cream cheese and a Danish, with a strawberry milkshake on the side," says she. So as it happens, knowing the ways of Americans, we have some of that muck available. But when I brings it to her she says, "Is the bagel fat-free and the cream cheese lite?" And I says, "I don't think so." "And the milk for the milkshake," she says. "What about that?" "I can do you semi-skimmed, madam," says I. "That's useless," says she. "It's fattening."'

Philomena placed her hands on her ample hips. 'To tell you the truth, it was too much for me. I looks at the cow and says, "Tell you what, missus, if you're that worried about being fat you'd be better advised to start the day with a jog than a Danish." She got as mad as a wet hen.'

'I'll back you up if there's any trouble, Philomena.'

'I'll let you know. I'll tell you what though, I wouldn't be in your shoes if Jesus, Mary and the good Joseph went down on their knees and begged me to. I heard about the fighting last night. You've got a right shower there.'

*   *   *

'OK, let's do a tally, you two,' said the baroness. 'How many were we supposed to have and how many have we actually got?'

'Originally we were supposed to have thirty, of whom at least twenty were to be from the island of Ireland, representing every shade of nationalist and unionist culture. What was it we were promised, Simon? People of the highest quality, by-words for cultural achievement, rooted firmly in their tradition, yet cultivated and open and generous to other cultures.'

'I did warn you, Robert.'

'Indeed you did. But remember there was just you on the one hand, sounding cynical, while on the other were Crispin—and even more so, Roddy McCorley and co—telling me of a glittering line-up of prize-winning poets, artists and even—at one stage—the likelihood of an opening address from Seamus Heaney.' He clapped his hand to his brow. 'Crispin even told me the Poet Laureate wanted to become involved and make the conference a focus for a new poem on the changing face of these islands.'

The baroness was looking impatient. 'We know all this. Don't know why you're going over old ground again. They caved into the politicos. Surprise. Conference attendance got into the hands of the cultural committees. Surprise surprise. So we're left with cultural fundamentalists, freebie-lovers, the press-ganged and assorted other tossers. Now talk numbers. What are we down to?'

Amiss began to count on his fingers. 'Two from the south—Sean O'Farrell, who is here in a sort of half-hearted liaison role with Dublin and someone who has not yet arrived who will replace Theo Mathew. Billy Pratt and Willie Hughes, who represent the different cultural aspirations of two different loyalist paramilitary groups.'

'Isn't Hughes a Catholic name?' asked the baroness.

'They're all intermingled,' said Gibson. 'Gerry Adams's surname is English, John Hume's is Scottish and one of the most vicious loyalist murderers was called Murphy. Usually having a name from the wrong tribe makes them even more fanatical.'

'OK. That's four, assuming the Little-Nelly-of-Holy-God substitute turns up.'

'Mainstream Northern Ireland nationalists

111

aren't turning up at all,' said Amiss, 'and, I may say, only bothered to tell me they had so decided when pursued for an answer.'

'But that's because they had been beaten into submission on the cultural committee by MOPE, who in the end grabbed three places,' said Gibson.

'Not that that's an excuse for wimping out,' said the baroness. 'All right, that's Lucrezia, the fat and turbulent priest and the other fella, Liam Macwhateveritis.'

'Speaking of which, Jack,' said Gibson. 'Do you know what Liam MacPhrait is in English?'

'Not a clue.'

'William Pratt.'

'What!'

'Yep. He and Billy have the same name.'

'Well, well,' she said. 'I know my assumption has been that they use Irish names to upset people, but I can't say I blame him. I'd rather be called Liam MacPhrait than Billy Pratt any day of the week. Any more surprises?'

'Laochraí de Búrca is Lucy Burke. Laochraí is a completely bogus hibernicisation of something unhibernicisable.'

'Can we get on,' asked Amiss. 'We haven't much time. Eight, with Hamish Wallace from Scotland . . .'

'That funny-looking hairy creature who looks like a refugee from the Highland games?'

'Yes. And I still don't know who chose him.

112

Any more than I know who chose that garrulous Welshwoman, Wyn Gruffudd, who makes it up to nine.'

'And don't ask me anything about the English late substitute either,' said Gibson. 'All I know is that instead of three high-level delegates, we've got Charles Taylor, who is supposed to be some kind of cultural commentator, goes to the Wexford opera festival and . . .' He assumed an exaggeratedly upper-class accent, '. . . absolutely larvvves the Irish.'

'Ten,' said Amiss.

'Where are the Ulster Prods?' asked the baroness.

'We've Pratt and Hughes.'

'You know what I mean. I mean proper Prods. Decent unionists who support the state and don't kill people.'

'None of them would come except Gardiner Steeples, who is here as an Orangeman and wishes he'd stayed home.'

'Talk about the dreary steeples of Fermanagh and Tyrone,' snorted the baroness.

'Eleven,' said Amiss.

'Representatives of Anglo-Irish culture? Southern Prods?'

'Nope. Pulled out at the last minute pleading a sick headache or something equally convincing,' said Gibson. 'They're terrified of MOPE, so they must have got wind of what was happening.'

'Still, we've got various academics lined up,' said Amiss. 'They'll have opinions.'

'They're only coming to perform,' said Gibson. 'They'll all bugger off like Barry and Reilly did this morning and like McGuinness would have done if Jack hadn't sent him off in a rage last night. The only reason academics haven't pulled out completely is they don't want to get in the bad books of Dublin or London.'

'So they don't count,' said Amiss. 'But then of course we have Kelly-Mae O'Hara, Tomiichi Okinawa, your mate Chandra Kapur and Rollo Pooley.'

'Eleven participants, four observers and us.'

'I can tell you the hotel isn't too pleased,' said Gibson. 'It can sleep fifty and as a special concession had agreed to close to outsiders. And even though they'll be paid a flat rate regardless of how many cancel, they're going to lose out in bar receipts and so on.'

'Wouldn't count on it, from what I saw last night,' said the baroness. 'Right. I know where we stand now. Just one last question. Simon, what crime did you commit to be put in charge of this aspect of cultural relations?'

'I was insufficiently idealistic for the world of Anglo-Irish relations, where you will appreciate that to suggest that reality should intrude is to be recognized as a cynic, a nay-sayer, a person with an anti-peace agenda. Though God knows I can't imagine why any official with ambition should set out with an anti-peace agenda since the only way promotion is won in our world these days is to chant mindless peacenik mantras in response to every difficult question. Suggest that any of our feathered friends—loyalist or republican— are anything other than peace-loving democrats who need their confidence built up and a blank wall comes down.'

'So it was punishment . . .'

'. . . for innumerable heresies and tasteless jokes. Now, if you'll forgive me, I've a quick call to make before nine o'clock.'

*   *   *

'Tough luck,' said the baroness to Amiss, as they walked towards the seminar room. 'It was mean of the minister to take that piece of crumpet back to Dublin. You've missed your chance now.'

Amiss sighed. 'I certainly didn't expect him to be such a killjoy as to take off in the middle of the night. You're all right, though. Have you had your evil way with Aisling yet? Or is she remaining stoutly heterosexual?'

'Early days, Robert. Early days. She needs a little time to wake up to her bisexuality. I don't expect success for another day or two.' She snorted vulgarly. 'Night or two, I should have said.'

'Why don't you try a man for a change?

115

Simon seems keen on you.'

She sighed. 'I'll have a go if Aisling fails me. But it has to be faced that there aren't that many younger men who fancy someone of my age and weight . . .'

'Especially when you throw it around all the time.'

'They do seem to find me a bit frightening, though I'm buggered if I know why. No, apart from the faithful Myles, male lovers are a bit thin on the ground these days. Women, however, are still a happy hunting ground.' As Aisling came around the corner, the baroness smirked. 'And I'm still happily hunting.'

*   *   *

It was ten minutes past nine and several participants were still absent. 'I'm not going to wait any longer for the layabouts,' said the baroness. 'It's time we addressed ourselves to the rebarbatively titled issue of . . .' She looked down at her papers and wrinkled her nose. '. . . "Parity of Esteem: seeing others as they see themselves".'

She threw a lustful glance at Aisling, who was busily talking into a microphone. 'Now apparently every delegation is to show a film that'll make the rest of us . . .' She looked at her brief and snarled, '. . . culturally aware. There's seven of them to get through so we'd better get cracking. Who wants to go first?'

'*Ba mhaith linn bheith ag an . . .*' said Laochraí.

Steeples interrupted. 'Are you going to speak in Irish?'

'*Aisling, más é do thoil é,*' said Laochraí. Aisling looked up from her microphone. 'Laochraí wants me to translate from English into Irish as well. What Mr Steeples said was "*An bhfuil tú chun Gaeilge a labhairt?*"'

'*Tá mé.*'

'That means "yes",' said Aisling.

'Is anyone else intending to speak Irish?' asked the baroness.

'*An bhfuil aon . . .*'

'Hold it, Aisling, just for a minute.' The baroness narrowed her eyes to read their name cards. 'Father O'Flynn, do you want to speak in Irish?'

'Er, no.'

'Can't or don't want to?'

He cleared his throat. 'I entirely agree with Laochraí that proceedings should be conducted in what is Ireland's first national language, and if that requires translators, so be it.'

'But you don't speak it.'

'That is neither here nor there.'

'And Mr MacPhrait?'

'I agree with Cormac.'

'It would be an outrage to do anything else,' said Kelly-Mae.

'Do you know a word of Irish?'

'I know "Chuckee or law",' she said proudly.

'*Tiocfaidh ár lá*,' said Aisling. 'Our day will come.'

'The slogan of the IRA,' said Gibson.

The three MOPEs looked at the ceiling in embarrassment.

'So no one here understands Irish,' said Steeples, 'except Miss de Búrca and the interpreter.'

Okinawa pointed to his nose. 'I also,' he said. 'Though my English is better.'

'And of course,' said Charles Taylor, 'it may be that Mr O'Farrell and the other Irish representative might wish to speak it.'

The baroness shot him a look of such venom that he gazed at the table for the rest of the debate.

Steeples looked around the table. 'The only reason this woman wants to speak Irish is that people like me can't understand it.'

'*Tá teangeolaí anseo*,' said Laochraí.

'There's an interpreter here,' contributed Aisling.

'This is a shocking waste of time and money and it'll hold everything up,' said Steeples.

Aisling murmured into her microphone.

Hamish Wallace peered through the red foliage that enveloped most of his face. 'I'm wi' you, Gardiner,' he said.

Laochraí looked around her defiantly. '*Caithfidh sibh é a dhéanamh.*'

'You have to do it,' translated Aisling.

118

'I don't mind,' said Billy Pratt. 'We have to recognize each other's needs.'

Amiss observed with interest that Joe was manfully signing busily though no one ever looked at him.

'This is preposterous,' snapped the baroness.

'*Nae doot*,' said Steeples slowly. '*Nae nae doot. Thon scunners me. They're owre ocht thran gat.*'

There was complete silence for a moment, until Wallace peered through his hair again, smiled broadly, turned towards the MOPE contingent and said, 'Ay. Gie it a bye, will ye. Ye'r that constermacious.'

The baroness looked at Aisling, who shook her head. 'Sorry. I can't help. I don't do Ullans or Lallans, which is what we seem to have here.'

Steeples burst into fluent speech. '*An syne tha wickit winnae staun in tha big soartin oot tae cum, an wrangdaers wull no win ben tha maetin o tha guidleevin.*' ['Therefore the ungodly shall not stand in the judgment, nor sinners in the congregation of the righteous.' Psalms 1.5]

It was the sight of Wyn Gruffudd plucking up her courage and uttering what seemed to be a long string of disjointed vowels that galvanized the baroness into speech. 'This is most impressive,' she said. 'We can set ourselves to take this to its logical conclusion by throwing Hindi and Japanese into the

119

melting-pot, along, I expect, with some Latin, Greek and a few modern languages, thus ensuring that no one can understand anyone. Is this what you have in mind, Miss de Búrca?'

As Laochraí looked at her impassively and turned to Aisling for a translation, Kapur broke in. 'A suggestion I would like to make, Madam Chairman,' he said gently. 'Could we have your kindly agreement to a short adjournment? An idea I have to put to some of our friends.'

'By all means. We need the wisdom of the East brought to bear on this. Just say whom you want to talk to and the rest of us will go outside and await instructions.'

Kapur nodded at Okinawa, 'Please kindly to stay, Mr Okinawa. And Miss de Búrca and your two colleagues also be so good, please.'

Led by Gardiner Steeples, who marched purposefully out of the room, the others trailed out silently.

*   *   *

'My God, we could do with Plutarch,' said the baroness, as she and Amiss conferred in a corner. 'It'd be much better to have her here beating up MOPE than pining in those kennels into which you so callously thrust her.'

'You know I don't believe that you can deal with troublesome elements by bringing in one even more troublesome.'

'My career demonstrates that the truth lies the other way about. Most of my success can be attributed to my being more troublesome than the people I was brought in to sort out.'

'You are the exception that proves the rule, Jack,' said Amiss, with a certain froideur. 'In any case, you are not a cat.'

'If I were an animal I'd be a big cat. Bigger even than Plutarch. I'd be a king of the jungle.'

'Jack, may I once more display my pedestrian tendency and drag you from your egotistical fantasies to the more mundane level of timetable adjustments which may be necessary in the light of this delay.'

She snorted. 'The trouble with you is . . . Good grief! Here's Lucrezia already.'

Laochraí walked over to them and addressed them without a flicker of expression. 'We have decided as a confidence-building gesture and in the interests of reconciliation that we will for the moment cease to speak in Irish.'

'What do you mean "we"? It was only you.'

Laochraí glared. 'My colleagues and I have decided as a confidence-building gesture and in the interests of reconciliation that we . . . that is, I, will for the moment speak English if everyone else does.'

'Well that's hardly likely to be a problem,' said the baroness irritably. 'None of them ever wanted to speak anything else in the first place.'

Amiss scowled at her. 'Thank you, Laochraí. The gesture is much appreciated.' Pausing only to throw a dirty look at the baroness, Laochraí strode back towards the conference room.

'Jack,' said Amiss, 'for Christ's sake, do you have to alienate them needlessly?'

'Look, I alienate them just by existing. And vice-versa.'

'Yes, and I see both your points of view. But try not to let your antipathy show so obviously, will you?'

'I'll try,' she growled. 'But the world would be a better place if it was still possible to transport people like that to the colonies. Speaking of which, here's the miracle worker. How did you do it, Chandra? And why were you talking like a Delhi greengrocer?'

Kapur smiled. 'It seemed appropriate. They had to be nice to a poor native.

'What happened was that after a word with Okinawa, who can't stick MOPEs, we explained to them that they might not come out of it well if he released his film to the television news. They weren't sure at first, but when we said that sadly we would be obliged to express our disappointment that they had wrecked the conference, they caved in. It would not look good, they realized, to be criticized by a yellow and a brown man.'

'Cunning old oriental devils,' said the baroness delightedly. 'We should get you over to outwit them in Northern Ireland. Now we'd better get started again.'

As she was about to move, Aisling arrived. 'I've just heard,' she said. 'Well, that'll make your lives easier. However, it requires me to say goodbye.'

'What!' said the baroness.

'You don't need me now.'

'We certainly do.'

Aisling shook her head. 'Sorry, Jack, but rules are rules. Interpreters have no role other than interpreting.'

'We can soon change that.'

'We can't. The department wouldn't wear it. I'm really sorry, but I have to go. And the signer's going too. He's mutinied. Says his job is to help the deaf, not to make an idiot of himself at the behest of pillocks.'

The baroness jerked her head towards the door. 'Come with me, Aisling. Let's talk this over.' It was five minutes before she returned. 'What a disaster,' she moaned to Amiss. 'I feel like a cat who's seen the canary fly out the window.'

'Join the club,' said Amiss bitterly.

CHAPTER NINE

'All right, let's get this show on the road,' said the baroness. 'And no playing silly buggers this time. Who's going first?'

'I'm afraid the English are supposed to,' said Charles Taylor apologetically. 'Not that I mind. I'd be happy to make my presentation at any stage of the proceedings, but at Robert's instigation we had a sort of lot-drawing thingie earlier and I . . .'

'What the hell are you apologizing for now? Just get on with it, for Pete's sake. Give us your hooray for English culture.'

Taylor flushed, took a video tape from his briefcase and handed it to Amiss, who had appointed himself technical assistant for the morning. 'I'll let the video speak for itself, but I'm obviously happy to answer questions later.'

Amiss lowered the blinds and started the tape. Within a few minutes it became clear its contents had been determined by a committee bent on offending no one except perhaps white native English. The coverage of the joys of multi-culturalism included West Indians leaping about at the Notting Hill Carnival, Neasden Hindus celebrating Diwali, Birmingham Muslims at prayer, the opening of a Buddhist temple on the Thames, and shots of various Irish, Welsh and Scots in London hostelries respectively celebrating St Patrick's Day, St David's Day and Burns' Night. The only sightings of native English culture were a dozen elderly Morris dancers, a shot of Shakespeare superimposed on Stratford upon Avon, a Charles Dickens pub sign and an aerial shot of the Dome.

After it came to an end and Amiss had opened the blinds, there was a long silence.

'Taylor's contribution hasn't done much to liven us up, has it?' enquired the baroness. 'Has no one a comment or did you all fall asleep?'

'Ah now, Madam Chairwoman,' said Sean O'Farrell with a smile, 'you're very hard on us all and especially on poor Charles here. I thought that was grand.' He paused and added uncertainly, 'Oh and very inclusive. Yes. Most inclusive.'

'Huh,' said the baroness. 'I'd be more impressed with that judgement if I hadn't seen you sneaking in halfway through.'

Completely unabashed, O'Farrell grinned. 'There's no hiding anything from you, is there? You're a real divil.'

There was a half-hearted interjection from Laochraí to the effect that this was unduly cosmetic and failed to show the sad plight of the Irish in Britain but her heart wasn't in it. Silence fell once more.

The baroness glared down the table. 'Chandra. Any reactions?'

'Madam Chairwoman, I am a little surprised at the absence of the indigenous English,' said Kapur, who had clearly abandoned his poor-Indian routine. 'I admire the English for their great hospitality to foreigners and their kindness to strangers . . .'

An attempt by Laochraí to break in

125

indignantly was quashed by a 'shut up' from the baroness and Kapur continued smoothly '. . . but to the best of my knowledge the vast majority of that country is still occupied by white people who are English by birth and culture. Could we not have seen, for instance, something of the House of Commons? Surely the mother of all parliaments deserves acknowledgement?'

'Anyone else?'

'Yes,' said Steeples. 'I wonder what the grunts on the ground would say if they saw that. It was no more to do with English culture than my calves have to do with line-dancing. Typical government sell-out. And a waste of money at that, so it is.'

The baroness looked more cheerful. 'Any other comments? Robert?'

Amiss shook his head.

'Rollo?'

Pooley shook his even more vigorously. For about twenty seconds there was complete silence. 'Well then, Charles. What have you to say to Chandra and Gardiner?'

'Just that while I hadn't actually seen the film before now, I have to say I thought it got the balance right. We have to look to the future not to the past.'

The baroness looked at him with ill-concealed contempt. 'Is that it?'

He nodded.

'Right then.' She looked at her list. 'Let's

abandon this wasteland and see if the Taffies have done a better job.'

Wyn Gruffudd looked at her nervously. 'Now see, I know nothing about this,' she said. 'As I was telling Robert earlier, I am here at short notice, and I said, when they asked me, that I would not come if anyone thought . . .'

'Got you. We won't hold you responsible.'

The Welsh contribution was more entertaining and anything but inclusive. It took the company at a gallop through Welsh history, stopping here and there to contemplate anti-English avenging heroes like Owen Glyndower. Plenty of attention was given to the sufferings of coal-miners, but there were also clips from some great orators, a great deal of superb scenery, a fair amount of singing in pubs and at rugby matches and a nod to the new Welsh assembly. The presenter then plunged into Welsh (with subtitles), there were a few recitations, a bit more singing and then five minutes of an eisteddfod with people in white robes and hoods installing a new Druid. After a sentimental verse about forefathers from the valleys and another blast of song, it ended with another shot of declaiming Druids.

Kelly-Mae burst in. 'That's outrageous. You're showing the Ku Klux Klan like they were OK!'

Wyn flushed. 'Look you, Kelly-Mae, now you have to see that . . .'

127

'Miss O'Hara,' cut in the baroness icily, 'you are an observer. Observers observe. They do not speak if they are so ignorant that they confuse old Celtic ceremonies with southern white supremacist lynch mobs.'

Kelly-Mae looked towards MOPE for support, causing Laochraí to interject with some embarrassment, 'Kelly-Mae's reaction was very understandable. However, Kelly-Mae, this is a fine Celtic ceremony which deserves the respect of all of us, being neither imperialist nor anti-nationalist.'

Other than false praise from Sean O'Farrell and Charles Taylor, no one could summon up enough interest to say anything, so Amiss put on the Scots film. This was an altogether more lively affair, full of caber-tossing and bagpipes and Scottish reels and clips from films of martial Scots swarming over the Highlands in variously coloured kilts. There was no denying, however, the triumphalism and implicit anti-Englishness with which the 1999 establishment of the Scottish parliament was described. 'Scotland-the-Visionary faces the future looking towards Europe and away from the narrow Whitehall-driven agenda of the past,' was the last line.

When the strains of 'Scotland the Brave' had died away, there was a general murmur of approval, including a 'jolly good' from Charles Taylor that caused the baroness to snarl that clearly nationalism was OK for everyone except the English.

Laochraí, however, had a concern. 'That was a good film,' she said, 'but you avoided the issue of sectarianism and the discrimination under which the Catholic and particularly the Catholic Irish people in Scotland have lived and still live.'

Wallace peered through his foliage. 'Ach, we cannot always be harping on the past. These days we Scots are full of bounce.'

'We could have done with a wee parade in there,' said Steeples. 'There are 60,000 in the Scottish Orange, so there are.'

'Since you both feel that the issue of sectarianism should be addressed,' put in Taylor brightly, 'in a very real sense, Gardiner, you and Laochraí are in agreement.'

'We are not,' said Laochraí and Steeples in unison. And as they both broke into indignant and competing speech the baroness looked at her watch. 'This debate, I suspect, will be more appropriate to the next session. Now we stop for coffee.'

'That's it,' she said to Amiss as they left. 'Now I know the United Kingdom is finally finished. And I don't know that I'm sorry. We're better off without all the bloody Scots and Welsh. If we could only keep the modernisers and the wimps out of England and bring the decent Prods over from Ireland to join us, we could have quite a cosy time.'

No expense had been spared on the film from the Irish cultural group, which was essentially a highly professional marketing exercise. Awash with pop stars, fashion designers, models and internet whizzkids, it was full of lively music, vivid images of glorious scenery and merry people. Mellifluous voices declaimed the prose and poetry of winners of great literary prizes and the travelling Irish were seen skipping and laughing and singing their way around the world. 'Irish culture,' explained the presenter in conclusion, against a background of the inevitable mystical Celtic pipes, 'has enriched the world for centuries and nowadays is everywhere welcomed for its style, exuberance and cosmopolitanism.'

'Wonderful, wonderful,' said Charles Taylor. 'What it is for a vitiated culture like ours to see the magnificent vibrancy and spiritual openness of all that is great in the Irish. What I find so moving and yet energizing . . .'

As the baroness began to swell like a bullfrog, the Sailor's Hornpipe sounded. 'Hello,' whispered Amiss. 'Yes of course. I'll be right out.' He fled thankfully.

*   *   *

The florid man with a halo of white hair

chatting happily with the porter looked to be in his mid-fifties. Amiss approached him with his hand out. 'Hello. I'm Robert Amiss.'

The man took his hand and wrung it enthusiastically. 'Pascal O'Shea. Jaysus, I was just telling Pat here what a desperate journey I've had. What time is it now?' He looked at his watch. 'Christ's teeth, it's six feckin' hours since the car arrived for me. Six in the morning! What sort of time was that to expect a fella to leave home! And we've been crawling through the lashing rain ever since. God, I need a drink.'

'You wouldn't like to look in at the conference, would you? It's in its last hour for this morning. It'd give you a chance to say hello and get a sense of how things are going.'

'Robert Amiss, are you completely mad? You might drag me in this afternoon, though I'm making no promises. But Simon Legree himself wouldn't have expected a fella to spend six hours on the road and then go straight in to listen to a lot of tosspots banging on about cultural awareness.'

'I'm sorry, Pascal. I didn't mean to be unwelcoming. Of course I'm very grateful to you for standing in for Theo at such short notice . . .'

'For Theo? Are you telling me I'm standing in for Theo Mathew?' He roared with laughter. 'They didn't tell me that. That's a laugh and no mistake.' He clapped Amiss on the back. 'Well, you can accuse our side of lots of things, but you can't accuse them of lacking a sense of humour. The only thing that'd be funnier than replacing Theo by me would be replacing me by Theo.'

Amiss looked at him nervously. 'Would you mind awfully if I just pop back in to the conference? I'm afraid the bar won't be open yet, but let me organize a drink for you now.'

'Not at all. You get back in there and forget about me. I'll be grand. Pat here'll see me right. And I'll stand you a drink when you're free. How's it going anyway?'

'Bit early to say.'

'The minister left, I hear.'

'Called away.'

O'Shea clapped him on the back again. 'God love you,' he said. 'God love you. Now get back to them and I'll see you soon.'

Chuckling, he moved unerringly in the direction of the bar.

*   *   *

Laochraí was in full denunciatory mode when Amiss returned. 'A disgrace. The whole thing was a disgrace. Not a word about the national struggle or the suffering of our people.'

'Or inequalities and impoverishment created by the deliberate international capitalist policy of underdevelopment,' added Father O'Flynn.

132

'Which sought to weaken the poor by exacerbating sectarianism,' added Billy Pratt.

'Ah, now lads,' said O'Farrell, 'in the interests of peace and mutual understanding, would y'ever give us a break? Sure we don't want everything to be doom and gloom. Can't we cheer up a bit?'

'Anyway I'm sure you'll more than make up for the lack of whingeing with your film, Miss de Búrca,' interpolated the baroness acidly. 'Now, since no one seems to have anything else to say about that piece of ersatz Paddywhackery, I suppose we might as well get your contribution over with.'

*   *   *

The MOPE film was as ghastly as Amiss had feared: the difference between it and its predecessor being akin to that between a graveyard and a nightclub. It opened with a lengthy dirge which accompanied heart-rending Victorian sketches of Famine victims, then took the audience briefly back to earlier woes like the penal laws, Cromwell's sack of Drogheda and mass hangings after the 1798 rebellion. Then back again to the Famine (referred to as a holocaust and the worst act of genocide ever known to man), then a leap forward to the 1916 rebellion, complete with heroic pictures of Patrick Pearse and his comrades in the General Post Office being bombarded by British guns and culminating in the sound of rifle-fire over the pictures of those later executed. A quick leap through the war of independence followed, and then the focus went on to accounts of discrimination in Northern Ireland, sectarian oppression and what were euphemistically described as spontaneous outbursts of anger by the nationalist people. There were shots from a play showing brave women being battered by evil gloating policemen and the whole thing finished with one of them holding up a clenched fist and declaiming: 'We may be the most oppressed people ever, but we'll proudly gain our freedom in the end.'

Most of the participants gazed at the table after the film came to an end. The baroness looked enquiringly at Steeples, who shrugged. 'If that's culture, I'm the Pope, so I am.'

'Yet,' said Billy Pratt, 'it is a most constructive aid to the process by which we all come to feel each other's pain.'

Laochraí beamed at him. There was another silence.

'Do you feel, Rollo,' the baroness asked icily, 'that that was a fair account of Anglo-Irish history?'

'I couldn't possibly comment,' said Pooley. 'I'm too new to all this.'

'Charles?'

'All I can usefully do is apologize for the wrongs done to Ireland by my ancestors.'

'Not just your ancestors,' interjected Laochraí. 'You're still doing it.'

'Of course, for any continuing injustices also.'

The baroness surveyed him. 'Pusillanimous Albion,' she said. 'Why don't you admit to genocide and be done with it.'

Taylor looked at her nervously. 'Well . . .' He cleared his throat.

'Spit it out, man.'

'I think I should say . . .' his tone was hesitant, '. . . that is maybe for the record I should point out that the British didn't actually make the Famine happen on purpose.' He cleared his throat. 'Essentially, it was bad management.'

'Cock-up, Laochraí,' said the baroness. 'Not conspiracy. Can't you get that into your thick heads?'

Loud MOPE dissent dominated the next few minutes until the baroness restored order by asking for a comment from Kapur.

He smiled his gentle smile. 'Ah yes. That was most interesting. Though I think perhaps it is a pity to concentrate always on the negatives. There are things to be grateful for too. Where would you be without the English language, whose literature your countrymen have adorned with such distinction? And as Professor Reilly pointed out last night, would you really rather have been occupied by any other colonial power you can think of? For

135

occupied you would have been. And, you know, the history of the world shows that those places occupied by the British were peculiarly blessed.'

As the storm broke, his smile remained intact.

*   *   *

'Well, Jack, I have to admit that Chandra Kapur was an inspired recruit,' said Amiss after the session, as they clustered in a corner with Simon Gibson. 'I could almost feel sorry for the MOPEs. They're so used to presenting themselves as the friends of oppressed people everywhere that a brown imperialist is really hard going.'

'Yes,' said Gibson. 'I particularly liked the way in which he simultaneously pointed out to them that Indians have suffered infinitely more than the Irish while also explaining the virtues of the British regime. I thought Kelly-Mae was going to have a seizure.'

'It was also particularly nice,' added Amiss, 'when Okinawa put in that he had to admit that the Japanese record on the cruelty front was a lot worse than the Brits.'

'And when Wallace added that the Scots could have gone on about the devastation caused by the Highland clearances, but they didn't think wallowing in past miseries was the way forward.'

'Not to speak of Wyn Gruffud's lengthy contribution about how Welsh was doing much better under the British than the Irish language in the Republic.'

'Don't go overboard on the self-congratulation,' said the baroness. 'The shits are still in the ascendant. Now, who exactly is that unspeakable little jerk who talks like a mediator's handbook?'

'Billy Pratt? You know about him. He's one of the DUPE spokesmen—you know, the peace-loving loyalists.'

'It's a vague term. You mean those Prod proles whose idea of showing their loyalty to the state is to knock off the odd Catholic or blow up policemen.'

'That's about right. Though these days Billy would describe such activities as "unhelpful".'

'Why doesn't the other one speak?'

'It's his first conference, I think, and he doesn't know what to say.'

'There's nothing to choose between Pratt and the MOPE shower, as far as I can see,' said the baroness. 'In fact he's always jumping in obligingly to help them.'

'Apart from the little matter of the DUPEs wanting to stay in the United Kingdom and the MOPEs wanting a United Ireland, of course there's no difference between them,' said Gibson with a hint of impatience. 'For most purposes they're the best of buddies. Under all that rubbish about dialogue, moving forward and saying yes to peace, they both want Northern Ireland to be carved up into fiefdoms which their particular chums can rape and pillage to their hearts' content.'

'I'm close to the stage,' growled the baroness, 'that if anyone else mentions the word "peace", I'll reach for my gun.'

'I got there long ago, Jack. It's just that I don't have a gun.'

'Any chance that they might learn something from Chandra and Oki?' asked Amiss.

Gibson and the baroness looked at him pityingly. 'You're such an optimist, Robert,' she said. 'That shower would rather die than surrender their highly-honed sense of victimhood.' She rubbed her hands. 'All this is giving me an appetite. Let's see what Philomena advises for lunch.'

Steeples caught up with them. 'How's it goin'?'

'Fine,' said Amiss. 'And how are you?'

'I'm the best. But I'm looking me dinner. I'm starving.'

'Did you miss breakfast?'

Steeples looked at him as if he were mad. 'I did not. Why would I miss me breakfast? But I haven't had a bite since then. There were no biscuits with the coffee, so there weren't.'

'See that that deficiency is remedied in future, Robert,' said the baroness. 'We owe Gardiner a great debt of gratitude for stymieing Laochraí this morning.'

138

'What time is tea?' asked Steeples.

'Four o'clock,' said Amiss.

'That's a bit early, isn't it? We'll be famished by bedtime, so we will.'

'Sorry, Gardiner, I mean tea and biscuits will be served at four. Our next meal—what the hotel calls dinner—will be at eight.' Steeples looked at him aghast.

'I always have me tea at six.'

'But we had dinner at eight o'clock last night.'

'Yes, but I had me tea on the way here, so I did.'

'I'm really sorry,' said Amiss, 'but I can't help you with this one, except to suggest that you pocket some biscuits this afternoon.'

'If that's the way it's got to be, so be it,' said Steeples. He accelerated towards the dining room.

* * *

Apart from a warning against the chicken, Philomena was too enraged to be of much help. 'This is more than flesh and blood can stand. She wants to know the sodium content in the salad and then she says there's nothing she can eat on the lunch menu and to get her a take-away pizza, cos she needs American food. Glory be to God and his Holy Mother, I may be only an ignorant country waitress, but even I know pizzas come from Italy. And I don't know what sodium is but I bet there's plenty of it in a pizza. And then to follow she wants two chocolate puddings, but she says they have to be low-cal. Can't you turf her out of your conference and back on a plane home? She'll have me in the loony-bin.'

The baroness grunted sympathetically. 'You could just say no, Philomena.'

'No is against company policy. We had image consultants.'

'What?'

'People who tell you how to present yourself better, Jack,' said Amiss. 'You could do with them.'

'The country's full of them,' said Philomena. 'All image and no feckin' reality. Anyway they said we had to find the yesness in us—which turned out to mean that we have to put up with anything from the feckin' guests if there's any way of meeting their needs at all. Though if I had my way with this one, I'd have her doing press-ups on a diet of raw carrots.' She paused. 'Raw lite carrots, that is. Now what did you say you wanted, Jack?'

'A dry Martini first, Philomena, straight-up.'

'Shaken not stirred, I suppose?'

'And make it a large one. We've got a rough afternoon ahead.'

Pascal O'Shea materialized suddenly and introduced himself. 'I've a note for you, your ladyship. From Sean O'Farrell.'

'Jack,' she said. She scanned the letter,

140

laughed and tossed it across the table to Amiss. 'Dear Jack,' it read, 'I'm ever so sorry but I've been called away suddenly and didn't even have time to say goodbye. Still, you'll be in safe hands with Pascal and won't miss me.

'It's been a great conference so far and I'm really sorry to miss the rest of it. Keep up the good work.

'Be seeing you,

'All the best,

'Sean.'

Amiss didn't trust himself to speak.

'May I join ye?' asked O'Shea. 'God, I'm so hungry I could eat a nun's arse through the convent gates.'

'Pull up a chair by all means, Pascal,' said the baroness. 'But I have to hope that Philomena will have a more gastronomically attractive prospect to offer us for lunch.'

CHAPTER TEN

'We didn't know you could get money for doing this,' said Gardiner Steeples, 'so I got someone to do a wee compilation from existing tapes.'

Called 'For Bible and Crown,' the Steeples video mainly consisted of rather badly-shot parades and hymn-singing. There was much emphasis on banners showing William of

Orange and other Protestant heroes, but some of the band music was good and Amiss found himself absent-mindedly tapping his feet to the beat of the drums. It ended, predictably enough, with a rousing chorus of 'God Save the Queen'. The MOPE contingent sat stony-faced, but Kelly-Mae could not be contained. 'Racists,' she said.

'We're not.'

'Yes, you are.'

'I knew someone would say that,' said Steeples, 'so I brought this, so I did.' He handed Amiss another tape, which turned out to be a cheery procession of black Africans wearing Orange regalia and singing hymns.

Laochraí rallied. 'You're sectarian, which is just as bad.'

Kelly-Mae brightened. 'That's right. You're sectarian. You can't be a Catholic and join the Orange Order.'

Steeples looked across the table at Kelly-Mae. 'Do you parade on St Patrick's Day in America?'

'I most certainly do. I march proudly in New York.'

'And whose parade is it?'

'The Ancient Order of Hibernians.'

'And what do you have to be to join that besides being Irish?'

There was a pause.

'Catholic,' said Hamish Wallace.

'Dead on,' said Steeples smugly. 'So why's

142

that all right and the Orange isn't?'

There was a snore from Pascal O'Shea so loud that he woke himself up with a start. 'Whassat?'

'Nothing of consequence, Pascal,' said the baroness. 'Just a little tiff. Don't let us disturb you.'

He closed his eyes again.

There was another pause. 'Haven't I read that they don't let gays and lesbians walk in the New York parade?' enquired the baroness.

'Quite right too,' said Kelly-Mae.

The three MOPEs looked at her in horror. 'We dissociate ourselves from that comment,' said Laochraí. 'We are inclusive of all gender and sexual orientations.'

'The Pope isn't,' muttered Kelly-Mae.

'The Pope's a reactionary,' said Father O'Flynn.

'I agree with the Pope,' said Steeples.

'So do I,' said Wyn. 'Homosexuality is an abomination before God and man.'

'Anyway,' said MacPhrait hastily, 'Orangemen show they're sectarian by talking about the errors of the Church of Rome.'

'See now, why shouldn't they?' enquired Wyn. 'The Church of Rome is full of errors. That's why we had the Reformation . . .'

'Too right,' interrupted Hamish Wallace.

This caused uproar, with cries of 'bigots, bigots' from the MOPE corner.

'Shut up, all of you,' said the baroness. 'Yes,

143

Chandra?'

'I'm sorry to say that if our Protestant colleagues are bigots, so am I. I think Hinduism superior to any other religion. And as for Muslims . . .' He gesticulated gracefully.

'And Laochraí,' put in Okinawa, 'would you tolerate my country's main leligion?'

There was a puzzled silence.

'Shinto,' he said. 'Emperor-worship.'

Amiss had difficulty keeping his face straight. The baroness didn't try. 'Well?' she asked Laochraí with a big grin.

As the MOPEs looked at each other, Billy Pratt interjected, 'I have no time for the Orange Order myself. I am very annoyed that this film is supposed to represent my culture. The Orange Order has been a tool of exploiters who wanted to suppress the socialist instincts of the working class.'

The relief of the MOPEs was palpable. 'Absolutely,' said O'Flynn. 'Orangeism is one of those outmoded ideologies of the petit-bourgeoisie that we must rid ourselves of.'

'How about starting with nationalism?' enquired Kapur. 'Is the world not struggling to develop beyond this particular outmoded ideology that has brought with it only hatred and war?'

The baroness cut into the ensuing hullabaloo. 'It's four o'clock now so we haven't got time to slug this one out. Has anyone anything sensible to add about Gardiner's film?'

Kelly-Mae, who had been looking very confused, broke in. 'The difference is,' she shouted, 'that we have a culture and you Protestants don't. Some traditions are not worthy of respect.'

The baroness stood up. 'Well,' she said, 'we'll have tea now. I don't think we could better that as a conclusion to a session on tolerating each others' differences.'

*   *   *

Dr Romaine Fusco of Geneva was good to look at but produced no controversy. The baroness's perfunctory request for questions met a few brief and positive responses and then a dead silence to which she responded by terminating the proceedings abruptly.

'Can we have a ten-minute break?' asked Amiss. 'We have some housekeeping to do.'

Dr Fusco having shown little disposition to linger, Amiss walked her to the front door, uttered a few platitudinous expressions of gratitude, borrowed an umbrella from Pat, delivered her to her waiting taxi and ran back to the seminar room.

Gibson and the baroness were walking up and down outside. 'That was a crashing bore,' she said to Amiss. 'She was good-looking and more comprehensible than that ponderous idiot McGuinness, but blimey, was she tedious.'

'Can't disagree with you there.'

'I mean, for God's sake, the notion that the Swiss solution to having within its borders Italians, Germans and French could have anything to do with a mad place like Northern Ireland is completely . . .' She searched for the right word. '. . . Mad. If you scoured the entire world you'd be hard put to find people more different than the Swiss and the Irish. Look at them. The Swiss are peaceful, law-abiding and obsessed with being neat and tidy. And they're dull bastards as well. Say what you like about the Irish—they can be boring, they're self-obsessed and wrongly think they're endlessly fascinating, but they're rarely dull. Except when they get self-important like the McGuinness buffoon.'

She shook her head vigorously. 'What is it about academics?'

'They're trying to earn a crust like anyone else,' said Gibson wearily. 'She's just another typical member of the travelling circus of commentators on Northern Ireland.'

'That little shit got very enthusiastic about what she said anyway.'

'Billy Pratt?' asked Gibson. 'Well, he would, wouldn't he? So did Laochraí and Liam.'

The baroness snorted. 'Of course. That daft bint obligingly presented them with a theory of cantonization that helps them justify what their pals are doing in practice.'

'Precisely.'

She brooded. 'I hate DUPEs as much as MOPEs now. Who do you hate most among this mob, Robert?'

'Kelly-Mae, probably. But that creepy Jesuit is pretty grim too.'

'Good grief. Is he a Jesuit? Does Gardiner know? Don't Orangemen think Jesuits are Satan?'

'Of course they know,' said Gibson. 'They all know each other. But Gardiner will also know Call-me-Cormac was brought along to wind the Prods up and he's had more sense than to rise to the bait.'

'So far. The weekend is young. Now let's go back inside and deal with these practicalities with dispatch.'

*   *   *

'As for tomorrow morning . . .' said Amiss, when he had finished talking timetable alterations.

'I wanted to ask about that,' said Steeples. 'What are the arrangements for worship?'

Amiss looked at him hesitantly. 'Father O'Flynn and the local Church of Ireland vicar are conducting an ecumenical service here at nine.'

'Well that's no good to me.'

'There you are,' said Kelly-Mae. 'You won't go because Cormac is a priest.'

147

'I've no problem with priests doing whatever priests do, but I'll go to no ecumenical service. People should practise their own religion and not be looking the lowest common denominator. I've a friend down the road and he says there's a Presbyterian service in the local village at twelve and a mass in the chapel in Knock at the same time for those Roman Catholics who take the same view of ecumenism as I do.'

'I agree,' said Wyn Gruffudd in a low voice. 'That's why I'll be leaving early tomorrow and not coming back until Monday morning.'

'Elaborate, please,' said the baroness.

'I'm driving north to join a Baptist community for worship. As a strict Sabbatarian, I could not attend any secular events on a Sunday in any case, so I am no loss to you.'

'I don't want to be contentious,' interjected the baroness, barely concealing her wrath, 'but could you explain how a Sabbatarian comes to attend a weekend conference?'

'No one else would go,' said Wyn simply.

'Anyone else want a service other than the ecumenical one?' enquired Amiss.

'Yes,' said Gibson. 'I'm with Gardiner on this as it happens.'

'You're an anti-ecumenical Presbyterian?' asked the baroness in surprise.

'No. An anti-ecumenical Roman Catholic.'

'Well, bugger me, he's one of yours,' she

148

announced benignly to O'Flynn. 'All right, then. We'll swap the ecumenical service with our midday session and then everyone will be happy.'

'We'll order a taxi for about fifteen minutes beforehand to take Simon and Gardiner to their respective churches,' said Amiss.

Steeples shook his head.

'I won't need lifting. It's an Orange anniversary service, so I'll be joining the brethren on parade at the bottom of the drive around half past eleven.'

As one man, the other participants looked at him in astonishment.

'Deliberate provocation,' said Kelly-Mae. Steeples looked up and down the table. 'This is supposed to be about culture. Well, this is my culture. And I'm expressing it. As far as I'm concerned the rest of you can have a rosary procession or embalm Druids or do whatever you want to do. But that's what I'm doing the morrow, so it is.'

'It seems perfectly reasonable to me,' said the baroness. She looked towards the MOPEs. 'Does anyone want to make anything of it?'

Kelly-Mae looked hopefully at Laochraí, who stayed quiet.

'Good,' said the baroness. 'That's that settled. Sometimes I think we might be making progress.'

*   *   *

'I hadn't spotted you for a pape, Simon,' observed the baroness as they left the room.

'You're right in that I'm not a cradle Catholic. Came to it late.'

'What brought on the conversion?'

'Capriciousness? Boredom? Curiosity? A desire to give my mother a really good grievance?'

'What did you convert from?'

'I was born a Jew.'

'Wow. That's impressive. You've swapped a religion in which guilt is fed to you in your mother's milk for one which encourages you to put your conscience on the rack at every opportunity. Obviously you didn't convert to a namby-pamby Catholicism that has you holding hands with vicars.'

'Of course not, I'm unrepentantly a fan of the pre-Vatican II church.'

'Wonderful.' She put her head on one side and thought hard. 'Yes, you seem uniquely equipped to flagellate yourself with the sins of omission, commission . . .' She paused and chortled loudly, '. . . not to speak of emission.'

'What's the joke?' asked Amiss, as he caught up with them.

'Never you mind,' said Gibson.

*   *   *

Most of the evening went off without trouble.

The British junior minister sent to host the reception produced a speech of such blandness that even Kelly-Mae—dressed for the occasion in an enormous green-white-and-orange frock—could not object. In retrospect, Amiss was to blame Lord Galway's speech for the later trouble, for it went on so long that even more alcohol was consumed than on the previous night.

According to Gibson, the Irish had come up with Galway because they were trying to show that their inclusiveness extended to the old Anglo-Irish gentry. Having had a great deal of trouble finding someone who fitted the bill and who was prepared to travel such a long distance, they settled in the end, none too happily, for an octogenarian whose main claim to fame was that he was nice and had a large collection of Irish paintings.

Galway's brief had been to spend fifteen minutes or so thanking everyone who had to be thanked wittily and elegantly, to talk a little about art and to produce some liberal sentiments about mutual understanding and moving forward together in the new millennium. Instead, to everyone's bewilderment and, ultimately, horror, he embarked on a long account of childhood visits to Mayo, deeply tedious descriptions of hunts he had attended, the wonders of the local gamekeeper of his youth and mind-numbing tales of fly-fishing. He talked and he talked and he talked and when Pascal O'Shea opened a book on how long he would go on, even the optimists predicted an hour and demanded more wine.

Mindful of the baroness's summary dealing with Gerry McGuinness the previous evening, some of the gathering looked at her hopefully, but she just sat there drinking wine and staring into the middle distance. After about fifty minutes, Galway finished an incomprehensible anecdote about a point-to-point and thanked his audience for indulging an old man. 'You were surprisingly patient,' said Amiss to the baroness on the way out.

'What was I to do? Slug him?'

'It was one option.'

'Not him. He's a nice old buffer.'

She looked around her truculently. 'I've been thinking. And I've got very vexed. I can stand a lot. If we have to be exposed to the worst national stereotypes of everyone except—as it turns out—Indians and Japs, so be it. If necessary, I'll also put up with arrogant Frogs, humourless Krauts, suicidal Swedes and lachrymose Russians. But I have my limits. Even though I am English, there are limits to my tolerance.'

'And what is exceeding your limits?'

'The stereotypical bloody English we've been lumbered with. Or to be precise, the stereotypical New bloody English.'

'But why shouldn't we have stereotypical

representatives too? Isn't that fair?'

'Fair is only one bit of our stereotype. Why can't we have something robust? The roast-beef aspect of our national character? Why are you four such wimps?'

'Wimps are what the New English are supposed to be, surely? We're all Blair babes now. All in touch with the feminine side of our character. Except you, of course, who frequently gives the impression of being solely in touch with the masculine.'

'Someone has to in this emasculated world. Get them over here. I want to talk to them.'

'Who?'

'Our backsliding countrymen. Our pack of old women. Our Quislings. Taylor, Simon and Ellis.'

'Rollo,' said Amiss automatically.

'Rollo, Rollo, Rollo. Christ, you couldn't get a more effete name than that.'

'It's a thoroughly traditional name in the Pooley family. His ancestor Sir Rollo no doubt tilted a pretty lance during the Crusades.'

'Judging by his performance today, his descendant would probably respond to a Saracen onslaught by suggesting the issue be referred to arbitration.'

*   *   *

Taylor was the only one of the three to put up any defence against the baroness's assault, for

Amiss, Gibson and Pooley stoutly maintained that they were not participants, were required by their jobs to stay neutral and therefore had no case to answer. Having been denounced for being a placeman mouthing New Labour platitudes and a hopeless wimp with no pride in his country, Taylor replied smoothly that the new millennium called for new thinking and that while patriotism was acceptable, nay progressive, for those who had lived under colonialism, for the English it was regressive and must give way to a sense of being European. Her companions were profoundly grateful when an outbreak of singing elsewhere in the bar distracted the baroness from her ensuing apoplectic diatribe.

Pascal O'Shea, who turned out to be a strong tenor, provided a rousing version of 'Phil the Fluter's Ball'—a comic song whose speed and linguistic demands would have taxed even someone sober. Urged to reciprocate, Taylor—who explained he had once studied in Wyoming—burst into 'Home on the Range'.

When the clapping stopped, Laochraí stood up. 'That was inappropriate.'

'Sorry,' said Taylor. 'I'm not with you.'

'It's the same tune as a notorious sectarian song.'

'Not one that I've ever heard of,' said the hapless Taylor. 'I intended no offence.'

'That'll be "No Pope of Rome",' said

154

Steeples, who had been lowering Bushmills whiskey in company with Hamish Wallace and who was increasingly cheerful. 'Ach, Laochraí, it's only a wee joke. Why do you take everything so serious?'

'Quite right,' said the baroness, 'knock that off, Lucrezia. You can have a fight about it tomorrow. Tonight everyone sings whatever they like. Who's next?'

Willie Hughes, who was sitting with Billy Pratt and the MOPEs, and who up to now had not been heard to utter a word in public, suddenly put down his pint and burst into 'My Old Man's a Dustman', in which several others joined enthusiastically. He grinned bashfully after the applause and said, 'He was a dustman, you see, my old man was.'

Emboldened, Wyn Gruffudd, who had been drinking orange juice and exchanging information with Kelly-Mae about their respective cats, came in with a dreary and very long folksong in Welsh. Plucking ineffectually at his guitar-strings, Father O'Flynn delivered himself of an interminable lament from a South American peasant driven off the land by exploitative rubber-planters and then accompanied Laochraí equally dismally as she sang 'The Four Green Fields', an old woman's demand that her sons reunite Ireland by whatever means necessary.

In the ensuing depressed silence, the baroness turned to Gibson. 'One thing that

155

baffles me about MOPE is where they think the money would come from for a United Ireland once we've taken our billions away.'

Gibson smiled wearily. 'You've never heard MOPE on the subject of reparations?'

'What?'

'Reparations for all the wrongs we've done to the population of Ireland since the twelfth century. Their policy towards the British has been accurately summed up as "Fuck off, but leave your wallet on the mantelpiece". Now, if you'll excuse me, I'm off to bed.'

As he left, the baroness turned towards Steeples. 'Come on Gardiner. Give us an Ulster song.'

'Apart from the national anthem and hymns I only know one song,' he said.

'Save the hymns for tomorrow,' said the baroness cheerfully. 'Get on with the other one.'

Steeples promptly launched himself into the Orange anthem—'The Sash my Father Wore'—to expressions of thunderous disapproval from MOPE. The baroness and several others joined in the chorus with gusto.

'Well done, Gardiner,' she cried. 'An Orange a day keeps the papists away, what? Now have we any other volunteers? Simon? Chandra? Robert? What a collection of wimps you are. What about you, Oki?'

'I would do it and gradly,' said Okinawa, 'had you karaoke. I need an accompaniment.'

Seeing O'Flynn gesturing with his guitar, he added hastily, 'Only kalaoke. Please sing now, Jack.'

She drained her whiskey. 'If you insist. I'll give you my party piece. Flanders and Swann's "Song of Patriotic Prejudice".'

Amiss's face contorted. He looked at Pooley and said, 'Ooops.'

'Don't know it,' said Pooley.

Amiss shut his eyes as she burst into the opening stanza about the English being terrific and the rest of the inhabitants of the British Isles not being worth tuppence.

Wyn coped with the verse about the inadequacies of the Welsh, though she was seen to flinch at the lines about them being underground dwellers who resembled monkeys and sang much too loudly, often and flat. Wallace laughed at the lines about the Scotsman being tight-fisted, boney and covered with hair. Then came the last verse, which dwelt on the contemptible Irish, who slept in their boots, lied through their teeth, blew up policemen and blamed everything on Cromwell and William the Third.

As her deep baritone faded away, the baroness looked around triumphantly to see several of the audience applauding loudly and the entire MOPE contingent storming out. Billy Pratt came up to her. 'Although I consider myself British, I am devoting my life to trying to achieve peace and reconciliation. I share the hurt of Laochraí and the others and am therefore leaving.' He jerked his head at Willie Hughes who stood up, looked at Pratt, looked at the baroness and sat down again.

Pascal O'Shea pulled himself up reluctantly, staggered over to the baroness and whispered, 'I'm really sorry about this. And it's not that I mind myself. Not a bit in the world. But to tell you the truth if I don't back them up I'll never hear the end of it.' He lurched out.

'Well, bugger them,' said the baroness. 'Somehow it's all right for them to go on about how awful the English are but we're not allowed to say anything back.'

Kapur came up and put his arm around her. 'My dear Jack, you are a woman of great intelligence, but perhaps not the person I would expect easily to understand the sensitivities of those with a colonial inferiority complex.'

'They're not fucking colonials, damn it. Northern Ireland is part of the United Kingdom and the buggers in the south have been independent for eighty years.'

'You are in the business of applying logic, my dear Jack. They are in the business of emotion.'

'You've certainly given them a challenging trailer for tomorrow morning,' observed Pooley.

'What's that supposed to be about?'

'According to the agenda, it's called

"Confronting stereotypes: ourselves as others see us".'

'Doesn't augur that well considering the stupid fuss they've just kicked up. These people have no sense of humour. I was trying to make them laugh.'

'You're a sort of magnificent walking icon of cultural insensitivity, aren't you?' said Amiss.

She beamed. 'I've always wanted to be an icon.'

'Whoever suggested that Sunday morning session was pretty brave,' observed Pooley.

'Foolhardy is how I'd describe it,' said Amiss. 'It was Simon actually. He claims he was hoping that by this time they'd be at the stage when there might actually be some possibility of serious communication. But I think he was probably just being mischievous.'

'Do they have any idea what they're facing into?'

'No. All they have is the title. What do you think, Jack? Do you still have the bottle to go ahead with it as planned?'

'Don't ask stupid questions.'

Okinawa smiled. 'I think I will have a wonderful film, Rady Troutbeck. Thank you.'

She sat down and pulled him down beside her. 'Listen, Oki, you're a good scout. Tell me something that's always baffled me. This "l" and "r" business. What's wrong with you Nips that you muddle them up?'

'Solly, Lady Troutbeck.'

She put on her most patient expression and spoke slowly. 'All you Nips apparently say "l" when you should say "r" and vice-versa. Now surely you know that, so why don't you simply reverse it?'

His face cleared. 'Aa so. Now I understand. No, it is not that we reverse them.'

She was listening keenly. 'Hah. You said "r" there when it was supposed to be "r". Why didn't you say "l"?'

'As I am tlying to explain, it is random. It is just that you notice when we reverse them and don't when we get it light. We do not speak at the flont of our mouth and we simply can't diffelentiate between those two consonants. They come out as close as we can manage.'

'Excellent. I like having mysteries cleared up.' She called Amiss over. 'I've sorted out all this "l" and "r" business. Oki here tells me the problem is that all Japs suffer from a speech defect. Front of mouth doesn't work which is why it often comes out as flont of mouth. They've all got it.' Amiss looked nervously at Okinawa, who smiled. 'Cultulally we do not deal well with straight questions, but I am becoming more accustomed since I met Lady Tloutbeck. That is one of the prusses of this conference.'

'It's always good to have a Pollyanna around the place, Oki,' she said. 'Or do I mean Porryanna? Now does anyone want another drink or should we follow *les miserables* off to

160

bed?'

Hamish Wallace, who had been gazing into his whiskey, looked up. 'I'll have a double,' he said, 'and then I'll sing you "We're up to our knees in Fenian blood".' As one man, Pooley, Taylor and Hughes got up, muttered excuses and hurried out.

CHAPTER ELEVEN

'You're not looking too good this morning, Robert. Up half the night, were you?'

'Yes Philomena. And I didn't sleep too well when I got to bed.'

'They're all fighting again, are they?'

'Quite a few of them, I'm afraid.'

'Well, do you know now, maybe the best thing—the only fella that can help you at a time like this—would be St Jude, the patron saint of lost causes. I'll get him on the job.'

'It'd be a good one for him, Philomena. I'd say this is the lost cause to end all lost causes. And how are things with you?'

'Cookies, Robert. This is the new challenge to my yesness. "What kind of a hotel is this?" she asks me yesterday. "No cookies?" So I tell her I'll do my best for her and out of the goodness of my heart I go out and buy three kinds of chocolate bars and four kinds of biscuits and she creates merry hell because I

haven't provided any Hershey bars and anyway
. . .'

'Don't tell me. They're not fat-free and lite.'

'How did you guess? God forgive me, I'd
love to stab her, only I haven't got a long
enough knife and it'd be a mortal sin. She'd try
the patience of a saint.'

'I'll have a word with her, Philomena.'

'No, don't. She'd know I was complaining.
And I wouldn't give her the satisfaction. I'll
offer it up for the souls in purgatory.'

'Are you having trouble with anyone else?'

'No. That fellow Steeples has to be given
extra large portions, but I don't mind that.
And one of the others tried to get me to speak
Irish, but when I told her I'd forgotten every
bit I ever knew and wished I'd learned French
instead, she shut up.'

She picked up his empty plate. 'What are ye
up to this morning?'

'Being frank about what we think of each
other.'

'Jesus, Mary and Joseph. Ye go around
looking for trouble, don't ye?'

*   *   *

'Listen,' said the baroness, 'if any of you is
serious about this mutual-awareness claptrap
. . .' She paused and looked slightly abashed.
'That is to say, this mutual-awareness odyssey,
this is the session for you to make a

contribution.'

She turned her chair slightly sideways, pulled it back from the table and threw one leg over the other, revealing a flash of her familiar directoire knickers, which today were in a sombre black.

'Now, I expect some of you aren't going to like this—judging by the way you carried on last night. But that's tough. We're never going to get anywhere if we carry on with this mealy-mouthed-let's-all-love-one-another-and-cover-up-the-hatreds-of-centuries crap. The thing to do when you've got something wrong with you is not to pretend it doesn't exist but to get to the root cause and if possible chop it out.

'Why do we hate each other so much in these islands? Tribal reasons, of course. Historical reasons. Human nature. We all need other groups to hate for defining purposes. All that's a bonding business and not always a bad thing. It helps to bind the community together having a common focus for ire.

'The trouble in these islands is that some people have taken it to excess. Particularly some of the mates of some of you.

'What each of us is going to do this morning is to write down five things we most hate about each of the groups represented here. And you don't have to confine yourself only to the ones you are not a part of. I shall enjoy filling in the five things I hate most about the English quite as much as I will the section on Irish republicans.' She nodded towards the MOPEs. 'At least no one could accuse you buggers of being appeasers.

'OK then. You have the forms in front of you. Get cracking. You've got half an hour. And don't whinge at me that you should have had advance notice of this. We'd have ended up having hours of argument and anyway it's better that your prejudices come straight from the heart.'

The Sailor's Hornpipe sounded. As Amiss slipped out, the baroness called after him. 'And get that lazy sod O'Shea out of bed.'

*   *   *

'McNulty here. We've got a problem.'

'Big one?'

'Well it's not a threat to life or limb. But it could be a nuisance.'

'Tell me, please.'

'You didn't tell me one of your people was joining an Orange parade.'

'Sorry. I was surprised, because I didn't know you had them in the Republic, but he was so matter of fact about it I thought it was OK.'

'We only have the two. A big one in Donegal in the back of beyond every July and this little one here that escaped the republican purges.'

'What's bothering you?'

164

'Security.'

'But Gardiner's only going on a short walk to church.'

'And back.'

'Well, I suppose so.'

'If we'd known we could have cordoned off the disputed area.'

'Come again? What disputed area?'

'The hundred yards between the beginning of the village and the other side of the Catholic Church. The Slievenamná Residents' Group is protesting that they don't want a sectarian Orange march going that way.'

'Isn't there another route?'

'It takes another half mile and the local Orange master won't do it. Says he's been walking that route for two centuries, that they've never had any trouble before and this must be all a put-up job by northerners.'

'Is that true?'

'Certainly, it seems to be. As far as I can gather, the Slievenamná Residents' Group has never been heard of before this weekend and so far no one knows any residents of Slievenamná who are part of it.'

'Oh, shit. MOPE must have spilt the beans to some of their mates.'

'Probably.'

'Maybe you'd better have a word with one of them.'

'O.K. Put the de Búrca woman on. I'll see if I can persuade her to call off their hounds.'

*　　　*　　　*

'I resent that imputation,' said Laochraí haughtily. 'This has nothing to do with me.' She handed the phone back to Amiss and stalked out.

'Interesting,' said McNulty. 'You know, I believe her. But maybe one of her pals is responsible.'

'The good Father, perhaps?'

'Perhaps. I'll ask some more questions.'

'May I come and see what's going on?'

'Give me an hour to talk to people. I'll meet you outside at eleven fifteen.'

*　　　*　　　*

'How dare you!'

'It was only a joke,' said the baroness. 'Can't you Jesuits take a joke?'

Followed by Laochraí, Liam and Kelly-Mae, O'Flynn stormed out of the room. After a moment, Billy Pratt went after them. Hesitantly, Hughes followed.

'Who cares?' said the baroness. 'They'll be back. It's time for coffee anyway, followed by religion.'

She stood up. 'See you all here at two thirty. Robert, did you put a rocket up O'Shea's arse?'

'He was in the bar having a Bloody Mary.

166

Said he'd be straight in.'

'He's got the right idea. I'll join him.'

* * *

'What did she say?' asked Amiss wearily of Gibson as they left the room.

'Something about Father O'Flynn being prone to sophistry, but then what else would you expect from a Jesuit.'

'What beats me is why they put up with her. Look at them. They're all there—well, all except Kelly-Mae—queuing for coffee. They walk out of the room but they don't walk out of the hotel.'

'They don't want to leave the conference,' said Gibson. 'It's a five-star hotel, the food is free, the drink is free and it goes down on your CV. You don't know these guys the way I know them.

'Whatever ideals they had in the beginning are rapidly becoming eroded by the sheer joy of flitting from hotel to hotel and capital city to capital city being hailed as peacemakers by the sort of people who find them particularly attractive because they have about them the whiff of cordite.'

'But they're so touchy and she's so rude . . .'

'Yes, but she's also an object of fascination to them. They've never come across anything like her. Sometimes I think they've never met a single English person who didn't bow and scrape and apologize for existing—just like old Charlie Taylor.

'What's the worst our ministers have ever done to these people? Say "Tut tut, we have a slight problem about your being in government if you don't promise to get rid of your surface-to-air missiles and maybe ease up on shooting people".

'History would have been different if Jack Troutbeck had been in charge. She wouldn't have talked about the truth lying in the middle. She'd have talked about right and wrong.'

Amiss briefly tried to imagine the baroness in charge and—slightly dizzied—returned to the discussion. 'But they've had countless excuses to storm out of the room and they haven't taken most of them up.'

'Because they'd miss the fun. Never forget how boring a lot of these events are for them. They enjoy all the perks, they enjoy the status, they enjoy the way groupies and liberals fawn on them obsequiously and the further invitations generated, but even they have to get bored with each other. I mean can you imagine what it's like to be Liam, listening to Father O'Flynn drivelling on for the fortieth time about the imperialist struggle. And as for Kelly-Mae! Even they're embarrassed by her stupidity.'

'One gets the sense that Kelly-Mae has not—as they say in California—moved on with the mainstream of republicanism.'

'You can say that again. I can't make out if she's stupid or ignorant or has an entirely separate agenda.'

'Or all three, of course?'

'Of course. Or all three.'

'Anyway, just imagine, for instance, the three MOPEers and Kelly-Mae deciding to leave. What do they do? Call a press conference? They're relatively low level, so it would have to be pretty interesting to get the media worked up.

'They're going to have to explain that they have been insulted by a woman in late middle-age who is a mistress of a Cambridge college and a very articulate one to boot, who will defend herself by saying that she is a seeker after truth and wonders why they are opposed to free speech.

'It won't work. And they'll be seen by future organizers of conferences as potential nuisances. Nope. Jack's got their measure. Can I fetch you a cup of coffee?'

'No, thanks. I have to go out. See you later.'

*   *   *

'Someone phoned from the hotel public phone box last night to a number which the RUC tell me belongs to a republican who spends his entire life stopping Orangemen walking in his area and now clearly has colonial ambitions.'

'Who do you think?'

'Dunno. The priest? MacPhrait? The American?'

'I wouldn't have thought she'd have had the contacts to set up something like this.'

'Who knows.'

Coming up to the village, McNulty parked the car and they walked around the corner into the village. Their way was blocked by a line of people carrying a large banner saying 'RE-ROUTE SECTARIAN MARCHES'.

McNulty approached the group. 'Do you have a spokesman?'

'Over there,' said one of them, pointing to a man wearing a baseball cap backwards who was being interviewed in front of a television camera. As they came up behind him he was saying vehemently, 'All the residents of Slievenamná want is to have their lives free of sectarian harassment and violence. Is that too much to ask?'

'Excuse me,' said McNulty. 'I would like a word?'

'I hadn't finished. You're interfering with my freedom of expression.'

McNulty looked fixedly at the interviewer, who said, 'Don't worry, Mickey. This isn't live. We can wait.'

'Thank you,' said McNulty heavily. 'We all want to avoid any trouble, don't we? Talking to the press can come later. Now, do I understand you are the spokesman for this so-called residents' group?'

'I certainly am. I'm the democratically elected chairman of the SRG.'

'Your name is?'

'Micheál Ó Murchú.'

'Aka Mickey Murphy,' said McNulty. 'I've heard of you. You're not from here, are you?'

'What is the relevance of that question?'

'It would seem to be logical that the spokesman for a residents' group should be a resident.'

'This is not about logic. It's about democracy. It is for the democratically chosen group to decide whom they democratically choose to be a spokesperson.'

'In other words, you're not a resident.'

'So what?'

'Can you please point me to a member of your group who is a resident of this area?'

'No. I am the democratically elected spokesperson. You have to deal with me.'

McNulty glowered at him. 'I'd be very careful, Mickey Murphy, before I used words like "have to" when you deal with me. Where are you from?'

'I don't have to answer that question.'

'If you don't want to be arrested,' roared McNulty, 'you'll answer my questions. And civilly.'

'This is police harassment.' Murphy swung round to look for the interviewer. 'You've seen that.'

The interviewer shook his head. 'Look,

Mickey, it's no business of mine but if I were you I'd answer the garda's question. They can get a bit rough down here you know.'

Murphy looked back at McNulty. 'Am I being threatened?'

'Take it whatever way you want. Where are you from? Or do you want to come to the station now?'

'Derry,' he said grudgingly.

'So what are you doing here?'

'I was asked.'

'Who asked you?'

'The residents.'

'What residents?'

'The residents' group.'

'Which takes us back to my earlier question. Are there any residents present?'

'I can't answer that. You'll have to ask them.'

McNulty looked at him narrowly. 'I'll be back to you shortly.' He walked over to the dozen or so protestors. 'Which of you lives here?' There was silence. 'I asked which of you lives here.' Still silence.

After about fifteen minutes, individual questioning elicited the information that all of them came from across the border.

McNulty stormed back to Murphy. 'This is completely preposterous. You've no right to set yourself up as a residents' group when there are no residents in it.'

'Who says? We're here to represent their

interests and their legitimate right to freedom, justice and equality. We cannot stand idly by and see fellow nationalists insulted by triumphalist sectarian parades.'

A garda came running up the main street still fastening his tunic. 'Sorry, sir. I wasn't there when your message arrived.'

'McNamara, have you ever had trouble in this village with Orange parades?'

'No, sir. There's only this little one every year and no one takes a blind bit of notice. Sure, they're all neighbours anyway.'

'It is our democratic right to protest,' said Murphy. 'Civil rights campaigners came from all over the US to stand by their black sisters and brothers in the fight for their human rights. We have to do the same.'

'But there isn't a problem here.'

'You may say that. But we know there are residents here who are offended by this parade.'

'Where are they? Who are they?'

'I can't tell you who they are. They fear for their lives.'

'You are full of shite,' said McNulty. 'Now I'd like you to get out of town, quietly and quickly.'

'We will not. We have a democratic right to protest for the human rights of our fellow citizens.'

'They aren't even your fucking fellow citizens,' said McNulty. 'They're the citizens of the Republic of Ireland and you come from another state.'

'I shall be reporting that comment to the Department of Foreign Affairs. I carry an Irish passport. I'm as good an Irishman as you are. I'm not going. We're staying to make a peaceful protest.'

'It had better be peaceful or you'll be sorry. McNamara, keep an eye on them. I'll be back.' He and Amiss walked round the corner where McNulty exploded. 'Of all the brass neck. Those guys could start trouble in a Trappist monastery.'

'And then claim they were doing it for the sake of the Trappists.'

'Exactly. Mind you, what do you expect when you know he comes from Derry. Now there's a Fenian hole. Those bastards'd steal your eye and come back later for your eyebrow. And then they'd claim they brought the yellow maize to Ireland.'

'So what are you going to do?'

'Have a word with one of my opposite numbers in the RUC and find out what to expect. Come on, I'll give you a lift back. Nothing will be starting here for another hour or so.'

'But the parade will go ahead.'

'It certainly bloody will. I'm not going to be put up with their ould nonsense. Jaysus, I wouldn't give a fella like that the smell of an oul oil rag if he was out of petrol and late for

174

his mammy's funeral.'

*   *   *

Amiss stuck his head into the bar. 'Do you want to come and watch the parade, Jack? Apparently there might be trouble.'

'Excellent,' said the baroness. 'Wouldn't miss it for anything. Especially since it's stopped raining. Fancy a walk, Pascal?'

'Are you off your head?'

'Ah, you're anxious to attend the ecumenical service?'

O'Shea threw back the remainder of his drink. 'I wouldn't go next, nigh or near it if I had the choice, but it'd get back to Dublin if I didn't. God deserves better than to have that creeping Jesus wailing shite songs at him, but don't tell anyone I said so. Are you sure you won't have the other one?'

'Positive, Pascal. Have it for me. Come on, Robert. Let's go.'

*   *   *

They caught up with Steeples's parade a few minutes later, parked the car nearby and followed at a respectful distance. Ahead of them were a dozen or so mostly elderly men, each wearing an Orange collarette and a bowler hat, walking slowly to 'Abide with Me' played by a single accordion.

175

'They're not the most threatening bunch of people I've ever seen,' said the baroness. 'Mind you, I can't say that Gardiner's improved by a bowler hat.'

'I don't think anyone is. Isn't that why they died out?'

As they followed the parade around the corner, the 'REROUTE SECTARIAN MARCHES' banner suddenly appeared forty yards or so in front of them, and several of the protestors jumped from the pavement to form a human barrier to the parade. Prominent among them was Kelly-Mae. Another dozen protesters appeared from nowhere with posters of a faceless Orangeman with a line across his front and the legend 'SECTARIAN BIGOTS NOT WANTED'. Another was carrying a placard with very rough lettering: 'SLIEVENAMNÁ SAYS NO WALKING WITHOUT TALKING'.

The baroness and Amiss gained on the parade. As they passed it, she caught Steeples's eye, waved merrily and received a nod and a big grin in return. 'He improves with time,' she observed. 'Like a decent port.'

They reached the barricade and circumvented it. 'Ah, Kelly-Mae,' said the baroness. 'I see you are taking your observer responsibilities extremely seriously. We've come to join you.' She looked her up and down. 'My, combat boots. You do come well prepared, don't you? And a T-shirt saying

"OBSERVER"? What a good idea. You wouldn't have a couple of spares, I suppose, would you?'

'No,' said Kelly-Mae. She tossed her head. 'And I wouldn't give them to you if I had. The British can't be observers. They're occupiers.'

'Of what?'

'Of Ireland.'

'Really? Now I was definitely under the impression that we abandoned this part of Ireland a good eighty years ago, Kelly-Mae. Or do you know something we don't?'

'You're still occupying the six counties, so it's all the same.'

'I don't think I follow that, but I can't be bothered to talk it through.'

McNulty appeared suddenly leading four uniformed men and a small army detachment. 'Stand aside,' he said.

'I will not,' said Murphy and as one man all the demonstrators lay down on the street.

'By Jaysus, lads, if you think we'll tolerate that sort of stuff here, you're well mistaken,' said McNulty. 'This is the Republic of Ireland you're in, and we tolerate no shite from troublemakers. The bleeding hearts aren't in control the way they are up north. I'd advise ye to get off the road now or ye'll regret it.'

'This is a disgrace,' cried Kelly-Mae, and she rushed forward and lay down beside Murphy. 'And don't forget, I'm an American citizen and if you hurt me I'll call the

American embassy.'

McNulty looked at her appraisingly. 'Well, madam, I grant you we probably don't have the manpower to lift you and it's hard to get hold of a crane on a Sunday morning, but the parade can get round you when we've shifted the others.' He waved at his men. 'Clear a corridor on the left.'

The police formed two pairs and each picked up a demonstrator. One who kicked out wildly and caught a guard in the stomach received a blow on his shoulder from a baton that caused him to scream. Hearing it, the other one struggled less. Another guard was almost knocked flying by a young man who leaped on his back and began to pummel his head and kick his legs. The baroness grabbed a poster from one of the recumbent protesters and hit the assailant vigorously over the head. He emitted a loud cry and she stepped back beside Amiss looking triumphant. When the guards had consigned the bodies to the military, the man she had helped returned and said, 'Thank you, mam. I appreciated your intervention.'

'A pleasure, Constable.'

Her victim was rubbing his head. 'I'm going to sue you,' he said. 'I've suffered bruises and cuts.'

'Think yourself lucky that's all you've suffered,' said the guard.

'She has no right to attack me,' said the

178

youth. 'She's not an officer of the law.'

'There's guards and soldiers here who'll say she never touched you and if you try any funny business you'll find yourself charged with slander and assault. We don't put up with this sort of stuff down here.'

'Well,' said the baroness. 'I must say you have a more robust attitude to policing than we are used to these days in the United Kingdom.'

'More fools ye,' he said. 'I tell you we won't put up with that old shite. We'll take these lads off to the station now and give them a few good kicks and send them home. They won't be back in a hurry.'

'Blimey,' said Amiss, 'if that happened in Northern Ireland you'd all end up in the European Court of Human Rights.'

'Well thank God ye've these problems and not us,' he said. 'Yet, anyway. I wouldn't have that republican crowd for all the money in the lottery.'

'Well, well, well,' said the baroness. 'I think that's enough excitement for this morning. It's time we had a preprandial celebratory drink.'

The street was emptying quickly. Except for Kelly-Mae, the remaining protesters had chosen prudence over valour and were packing away their banners and posters in their cars under McNulty's vigilant eye.

'You're not waiting till they come out of church?' asked the baroness genially.

179

'They are not, mam,' said McNulty. He jerked his thumb towards Kelly-Mae. 'Except for her, anyone who is not away in ten minutes will be arrested. And down here they won't be martyrs.'

'Very impressive,' she said. 'See you again, no doubt.'

As they passed the recumbent Kelly-Mae, she called out, 'Can you help me get up?'

The baroness looked down at her. 'No,' she said. 'At my age one shouldn't lift weights.' Grinning delightedly at her own wit, she marched around the corner, leaving Amiss hovering indecisively behind.

CHAPTER TWELVE

'So how did Knock affect your romantic soul, Simon?' asked the baroness, as they sat down to lunch.

'I'm not cut out to be an Irish Catholic. Either old- or new-fangled.'

'That's what I expected. You're one of these cerebral Evelyn Waugh kind of converts, very happy in Catholicism as long as its practitioners have country houses with priests' holes, aristocratic confessors and not an Irish maidservant in sight.'

'That's a bit harsh, Jack. Simple faith is something I can respect, but I have to say that

180

the rosary procession and hymns to Saint Patrick were not quite what I joined up for. Vulgarity is all right when one is sneering at it in other people, but it hurts when associated with one's own side.'

'So when the Honourable Father Jeremy or whoever coaxed you out of the synagogue and into Brompton Oratory, he wasn't tempting you with Irish plebs?'

'My particular Father Jeremy was more a man for Gerard Manley Hopkins and exquisite theological debates about transubstantiation than for improbable apparitions and sanguinary hymns.'

'Perhaps the fact that you find yourself religiously in bed with MOPE will yet drive you back to the rabbi?'

'My dear Jack, MOPE aren't Catholic in any religious sense. They just use it as a weapon in their tribal struggle—like Billy Pratt uses Protestantism. The only person here—apart from Call-me-Cormac and I'm not sure about him—who I'm certain believes in God is Gardiner Steeples, with whom I couldn't possibly make common cause because his religion is too austere and logical. And I can't stand all that Old Testament. Didn't like it as a Jew. Don't like it as a Catholic. It's all so very . . . unsubtle.'

'Better keep your voice down,' said Amiss nervously. 'Here come the ecumenists.'

'How did your hands-across-the-religious-

181

divide service go, Pascal?' enquired the baroness cheerfully.

O'Shea looked nervously over his shoulder at a frowning young man in a clerical collar. 'Grand, grand, wasn't it, Canon?'

'I hope my few words did something to help Father Cormac deal with the hurt feelings of which he sang so movingly. It was inspiring to hear of his mission to root out injustice in every part of our island.'

'Unctuous toady,' said the baroness, as he passed almost out of earshot. 'Let's hear from Willie. Willie! Willie! Come and join us.'

Hughes looked surprised. 'I can't stop, but I'm looking for Billy.'

'What did you think of the ecumenical service?' she asked.

He looked at her suspiciously. 'Why weren't you there?'

'We had business elsewhere.'

'Well, I wish I'd been somewhere else, so I do.' He pointed at the Canon, who was sitting apparently very happily with Father O'Flynn, Laochraí and MacPhrait. 'It's the ones that are supposed to be on our side give me a headache. Everyone knows what the Free State did to the Prods so what's that weasel doing bowing and scraping to that mad priest?' And shaking his head, he walked away.

'That's a bit unexpected from him, isn't it?' said the baroness. 'I assumed he'd take his pal's pro-MOPE line.'

'You've got Willie wrong,' said Gibson. 'Maybe it's my fault, since I have a tendency to be rather sweeping in my judgements, but actually I've some time for Willie. He hasn't lost touch with his roots, I think, and he's never really swallowed all that PRB that is Billy's stock-in-trade.'

'PRB?'

'Peace-and-Reconciliation-Bullshit.' He looked around cautiously. 'Don't mention it because it's not yet widely known, but there's a bit of a territorial war going on between those two, in fact. They affect to be great friends but in fact they're deadly rivals for the next council seat. Willie has the upper hand at present owing to having form. He blew himself up in the early eighties trying to do for a republican and served five years. Whereas Billy's never done time.'

'I'll be glad to get back to dear old straightforward Blighty after this is over,' said the baroness. 'Philomena, Philomena, come here and tell me what to eat.'

*　　*　　*

The Sailor's Hornpipe sounded as people began to drift towards the seminar room. 'Hello . . . What! Yes, of course. At once.' He switched his phone off, chased after the baroness and pulled her aside. 'Come out and see Ellis. Billy Pratt's had an accident. And he's dead.'

Pooley and McNulty were waiting for them at the entrance. 'He fell off one of the battlements,' said McNulty.

'Definitely an accident?'

'Very likely, though I can't yet rule out murder or suicide. But why would anybody come all the way to a conference to commit suicide?'

'It might have been the conference brought it on,' said the baroness. 'I've been feeling pretty suicidal on occasion during the last day or two.'

McNulty looked at her disapprovingly. 'Hardly an occasion for humour, mam.'

'Nonsense, Inspector. Straightforward philosophy. As my granny always said, you should learn to laugh at nothing since most of the time there's nothing to laugh at.'

'Who found him?' asked Amiss.

'Routine patrol.'

'Where?'

'Round the back. Keep this quiet for the moment, but it looks as if the probability is that he fell when he was trying to put up a Union Jack.'

'Why the hell would Billy Pratt be doing that?' asked Amiss. 'He was a Grade A appeaser.'

Pooley shrugged. 'He was up to something. Why else the flag—and in this weather— wearing just shorts and a T-shirt?'

Amiss looked at them. 'What was on the T-shirt?'

McNulty looked at the baroness as if daring her to laugh. 'It said "PEACE".'

'I have to admit,' she said, 'that while every man's death diminishes us and all that stuff, Billy Pratt's passing is not going to leave me inconsolable. Now if you'll excuse me. I've been harping on about punctuality, so I'd better go in and tell them the afternoon session will start a bit late. Come on, Robert. We'll need to confer.'

McNulty eyed her as she went off in a flurry of plaid. 'Tough old bird, isn't she?' he said to Amiss.

'Bark worse than bite,' said Amiss, as he went off in pursuit.

*   *   *

'What the hell are we supposed to do now?' asked Amiss. 'This afternoon was earmarked for examining what the questionnaires revealed about our prejudices. Is it really possible to go through with it now?'

'Of course it is,' said the baroness. 'For one thing, it'll keep the little jerks under control and away from the telephone. If they're not corralled, MOPEs'll be roaming around looking for attention.

'This is what we're going to do. You call them together and we'll agree a pious

185

statement about what a loss to the universe and the human race was Billy and then we'll agree that he would have wished us to go on in the name of reconciling our differences, sharing our hurts and feeling each others' pain. Not to speak of reaching out to hearts and minds, building bridges and walking hand-in-hand in the new millennium.'

*   *   *

'A tragic accident about which we know nothing yet,' said the baroness firmly. 'Now, unless there are any sensible objections, I propose to issue this statement on behalf of all of us: "We sincerely regret the death of Mr Billy Pratt, whose contribution to our deliberations has been invaluable. Our sympathy goes out to his family and friends".'

'There should be an Irish version too,' said Laochraí.

Hamish Wallace groaned loudly and Steeples stared at the MOPEs. 'We'll not be starting all that again, will we?'

Laochraí looked at Okinawa, whose camera was pointing at her, and lapsed into silence.

'Fine,' said the baroness. She handed the piece of paper to Amiss. 'Do whatever needs to be done with that. Now, let's get back to what we laughingly call work.'

*   *   *

The hasty compilation of results Gibson had prepared at lunchtime made interesting reading. Of the twelve participants there had been quite a lot of agreement as to the deficiencies of the various communities. Taylor nodded in agreement with the description of the English as superior, patronising, snobbish, exploitative, uncaring, class-ridden, racist, appeasing (two votes) and blood-sucking (one). Wallace looked resigned at the news that Scots were mean, gloomy, quarrelsome, sectarian, bitter and unyielding. Wyn Gruffudd was not there to hear the Welsh dismissed as shifty, dishonest, boring, garrulous and self-pitying, but Pascal O'Shea laughed merrily at hearing his countrymen being described as sleeveens, gombeen men and *mé féiners*, ['Myself alone'—as opposed to Sinn Féin, 'Ourselves alone'.] who were priest-ridden and money-mad.

Accusations of Protestant bigotry, brutality, triumphalism, dreariness and land-grabbing seemed to depress Willie Hughes, but Steeples looked unmoved. MOPE bridled when they found themselves described as whingeing, hate-mongering, self-pitying murderers as well as hypocritical black propagandists with no conception of right and wrong.

Kelly-Mae in some ways had it worst, for the overwhelming view appeared to be that Irish-America was peopled with ignorant, narrow-

187

minded, cowardly armchair-generals. 'Some of the MOPEs must have broken ranks,' whispered the baroness to Amiss.

If anything could graphically prove how insular were most of those present, it was the shortage of pejorative adjectives for either Indians or Japanese. Indians were given a few votes for being violent, greedy and sectarian and the Japanese for being cruel and racist, but most people, reported Gibson, had awarded them no adjectives at all.

Kapur smiled. 'Oki and I did our best to denounce ourselves. I find it illuminating how little you know about us.' He looked over at Taylor. 'Or are prepared to say about us. Really, the tender consciences of the English are a constant source of wonder to me.'

The Sailor's Hornpipe sounded. 'Hello . . . yes . . . yes . . . Very well. I'll tell them.'

Amiss turned to the baroness. 'May I? That was Inspector McNulty, the garda in charge of our security. He's coming to speak to us now.'

Kelly-Mae glowered.

'That's a relief,' said the baroness.

No one seemed to disagree.

*   *   *

'Mr Pratt's death was either an accident or murder,' said McNulty. 'At least I can give you the consolation that suicide is almost certainly ruled out.

'You will understand that I am not prepared to go into details at present, but for reasons we do not yet understand, it seems that Mr Pratt intended to put an Ulster flag on the vacant flagpole. He seems to have placed a ladder against the pole, but unfortunately the bolt gave way, catapulting him over the edge of the battlements.'

'Bolt?' asked O'Shea. 'Why would a flagpole have a bolt?'

'So it could be brought down to the horizontal.'

'Why would you want to do that to it?'

'Flagpoles have to be painted sometimes, Mr O'Shea,' said McNulty patiently. 'Something 'twould be bit hard to do if it was vertical. So this one had a hinge at the bottom which would be secured by a bolt. And the bolt gave way.'

'How could the bolt give way?' asked the baroness.

'That's what we're investigating now, Lady Troutbeck.'

'What about the press?'

'We have issued a straightforward press release giving bare details of the accident along with your statement of condolence.'

She looked at her watch. 'So that presumably means that the reptiles will be staking the place out in a couple of hours.'

'I hope not, Lady Troutbeck. We're playing this down as much as possible. I'd be grateful if

189

you would all make yourselves available for interview by some of my men. We would like to have details of your movements earlier today.'

'Why?' asked MacPhrait.

'For the record,' said McNulty. 'Please, sir. Let's keep this simple. We're just doing our job.'

'So he is,' said the baroness. 'Let's not have anyone making a human-rights issue out of answering a few questions.' She looked at MacPhrait menacingly. 'You wouldn't want it thought that you didn't care about Billy's death, would you?'

There was no answer from MacPhrait.

'Right, Inspector. Now, tell us what you want to do and where you want us to do it.'

*   *   *

Irish television was short of news that night, so the death of Billy Pratt and the Slievenamná Orange parade made the first and second items respectively. The coverage was relatively low-key, for though Pratt was popular among Dublin's political chattering classes, he was little known to the average Irish viewer whose normal reaction to hearing the words 'Northern Ireland' was to change channels.

Over a picture of Pratt shaking hands with the Irish prime minister, the presenter spoke solemnly. 'Billy Pratt, who was admired and

190

liked in Ireland as a leading figure in the struggle for peace, died in a tragic fall at Moycoole Castle earlier today while participating in an Anglo-Celtic conference on reconciling cultural differences.' The Irish minister for foreign affairs, a DUPE spokesman and a British junior minister were pulled in to talk about Pratt's crucial contribution to bringing peace to Ireland.

By agreement between McNulty and the baroness, journalists were barred from the castle or its grounds allegedly for security reasons, but although conference participants had been asked not to speak to the media, Laochraí had broken ranks. Over a crackly mobile phone she spoke of her affection for Billy and how he had shown the way forward to a future when loyalists would recognize their Irishness.

'Great. That'll really get the Prods going,' said Gibson.

'Sshh,' said the baroness. 'This is us.'

'In an unrelated incident,' said the presenter, 'in nearby Slievenamná, the residents' group protested today at an Orange parade past a Catholic church.' He cut to an interview with Murphy. 'The Slievenamná residents have determined not to any longer put up with this flaunting of sectarian bigotry. Today we have made a stand in the name of peace and inclusiveness. We were appalled that as an act of deliberate provocation, an

191

Orangeman travelled from north of the border to take part in the parade.'

'When asked to respond to this allegation,' said the presenter, 'Mr Gardiner Steeples refused to comment.'

'You have to hand it to them,' said the baroness. 'Not only do they split infinitives, but they take hypocrisy to hitherto undreamed of levels and the media swallows it all.'

'I don't care about that,' said McNulty. 'It'll die a death. What's important is the Pratt investigation.'

'Have you learned anything from the interviews?'

'Nothing yet, but I want to keep an open mind. Dublin wants me to conclude it was an accident, but I won't till I'm ninety-nine per cent sure. I haven't yet been able to get hold of the maintenance lad who had charge of the flagpole.'

'Where's Billy's body?'

'In the local morgue awaiting the autopsy. Not that it's likely to tell us anything. Now, if you'll excuse me.'

*   *   *

The intention all along had been to leave people free to do what they liked on Sunday evening. As previously arranged, Steeples was picked up by his friends and taken to an evening service followed by a family get-together, while the MOPEs and Kelly-Mae were taken off to a local republican club. Kapur excused himself and disappeared to his room.

'So what are you going to do with yourselves?' asked Pascal O'Shea of the rest of the gathering as they clustered in the bar.

'Any ideas?' asked the baroness.

'I've heard there's a céilí on in the local,' said O'Shea. 'It's a good pub and it might be a bit of a laugh.'

Hamish Wallace and Okinawa brightened up, Gibson and Pooley looked alarmed and Taylor looked deeply worried. 'In view of the tragedy, would attending such an event not seem very hard-hearted?'

The baroness, who had been brightening up even more, shook her head. 'Nonsense, Charles. If you're embarrassed, you can say you wanted to stay here saying prayers for Billy's soul but that you felt professionally obliged to examine the local culture.'

'How would you feel about it, Willie?' asked Amiss.

'I'm that fed up at the minute,' he said, 'I wouldn't mind getting out of here.'

The baroness clapped him on the back. 'Good man, Willie. Right, all of you. I want no nay-sayers here. Let's get going. Though first I'm going to change. I have the very garment for the occasion.'

'It's striking, I grant you,' said Amiss, circling the baroness as she stood impatiently in the hall. 'But I thought you didn't approve of the ersatz?'

'Nothing ersatz about this.'

'I suppose you're right. *Outré* is a better word. I don't associate kaftans with County Mayo. And it's just such a very vivid green. Then there's the gold . . . what are they?'

'Harem pants.'

'I look forward to seeing what the locals make of it all.'

'They won't know what to make of it, but they'll be faintly flattered.'

'And I see from your footgear that you mean business.'

'Much as I deplore many aspects of modernity, I acknowledge that trainers have their place.'

'You're certainly an arresting mix of the old and the new.'

She looked at her watch. 'Come on. Where is everyone? Rout them out and let's get this show on the road.'

CHAPTER THIRTEEN

The pub, about whose unspoiled attractions O'Shea had eulogized in the car, was all he had promised and more. There wasn't a tourist in sight—just a few dozen young and middle-aged couples and a scattering of unattached youngsters and perhaps half-a-dozen solid citizens with red, lined faces who were, O'Shea explained, what were known as mountainy men. 'Some of these guys mightn't see a soul from one end of the year to the other. This lot would be the sociable element who come down for a feed of pints once a week and look in at the céilí maybe in the hope of finding a bride.'

He surveyed his companions, now arranged comfortably around a long wooden table. 'What'll you have, Jack?'

'A pint of stout, of course.'

'Robert?'

'Lager, please. Now don't start, Jack. I'll drink what I like.'

O'Shea took orders from everyone and disappeared for a while. He returned five minutes later with a tray, bearing a pint of lager for Amiss, pints of stout for himself, the baroness, O'Shea, Hughes, Taylor and Wallace and half-pints for Pooley and Simon Gibson. Okinawa had opted for a large whiskey, which O'Shea and Wallace were also having as chasers.

'*Sláinte mhait*—and thank God we're not fond of it,' said O'Shea, whose first swallow lowered the level of the black liquid by a third and whose second halved the amber.

Taylor made a face. 'You don't seem to be enoying that stout,' said Amiss.

'I don't really like it,' whispered Taylor.

'Why drink it then? *Noblesse oblige*?'

'Really, Robert, you make me sound patronizing. It's just that it seems offensive to refuse what is, after all, the national brew.'

As he spoke, a be-aproned woman emerged from the back of the bar and placed on it a vast platter. The baroness looked up and an expression of ecstasy crossed her face. 'Crubeens. Bliss!'

'Crubeens?' asked Amiss.

'Pigs' trotters. The greatest delicacy in Ireland. Greater even than their oysters, if you force me to a choice. Go on, Charles, you're nearest. Grab that plate.'

As clearly reluctant as he was obedient, Taylor departed and returned several minutes later with a tray containing a platter piled high with trotters, along with plates, cutlery and napkins. The baroness, who was almost slavering, grabbed the largest trotter. 'Get rid of those knives and forks and all the rest of that unnecessary paraphernalia. This is good peasant food. Let's behave like good peasants.'

Okinawa, Hughes and O'Shea followed suit.

196

Taylor caught Amiss's eye and then unhappily reached out for a trotter, put it on a plate and started work gingerly with a knife and fork.

'Cheer up, Charles,' said Amiss. 'Look on the bright side. It could have been pig's eyes.'

The evident enjoyment on the faces of their companions gave Amiss and Pooley the courage to investigate a trotter apiece. The baroness stopped eating long enough to berate Gibson, the only defaulter. 'Come on, Simon. Even yellow-bellies like Robert have passed this test. What's wrong with you?'

Gibson shook his head impenitently. 'Sorry, Jack. The ancestral stomach. Becoming a Catholic doesn't magically get rid of the old taboos. I could no more eat pig than Chandra could eat cow.'

'Hmm. That doesn't explain why you're doing so badly with your Guinness.'

'Alas, being a Jew is usually inhibitive of the enjoyment of vast amounts of alcohol.'

'I know that,' said Amiss. 'My ex-girlfriend was afflicted by hideous moderation. You lot are brought up with too civilized an approach to alcohol to understand why people get drunk.'

Gibson sighed. 'I can't imagine what it would be like to be an Irish Jew. Or do they get a special social dispensation from pig and drink?'

'Speaking of which,' said O'Shea. 'Will it be the same again?'

197

'Not for me,' said Gibson.

'Nor me,' said Pooley, who had made only a slightly greater impression on his Guinness. A few of the others, including Amiss, indicated more half-heartedly that they'd rather wait a while, but their protestations were brushed aside.

*   *   *

By ten o'clock, the pattern for the evening was clear. There seemed to be a common acceptance that Gibson and Pooley were allowed to skip several rounds, but that this applied to no one else. Amiss was one of those permanently battling with the backlog of drinks arrayed in front of them. The musicians—two fiddlers, an accordian-player and a man with a bodhrán [A hand-held, goatskin drum]—had arrived by now and having had a couple of pints, were getting ready for action. The bodhrán player uttered a few words of welcome and the music began.

Within a few minutes the pub was alive with people dancing what had been announced as 'The Walls of Limerick'.

'Let's join in,' said the baroness.

'Why?' asked Amiss. 'I thought all Irish dancing was anathema unless it consisted of a drunken old man . . .'

'Céilí dancing is different. Like country dancing in general, it is for letting off steam

198

and encouraging sexual intercourse. I'm all in favour of it. I hope you'll prove a worthy partner.'

'Are you out of your mind?'

'You're no fun. Pascal?'

'Never could dance,' O'Shea answered hastily. 'Never, never, never, never.'

The dance seemed so fast, demanding and complicated that even Taylor could not be bullied into acceding to the baroness's impassioned demand for a partner. She surveyed them with contempt. 'So much for you,' she said. 'I'll have to find a beau among the natives.' And carrying her pint she crossed the floor to a table of mountainy men and sat down with them.

'The Siege of Ennis' called the drummer. 'Take your partners for The Siege of Ennis.' Watched with fascination by her discarded comrades, the baroness leaped up and held out her hand to a tall man in wellingtons. Pausing only to drain his pint and wave at the barman, he took her hand and they joined the nearest group assembling themselves for a set.

Okinawa was mainly lost to them from then on, for although he returned for more whiskey rations from time to time, he was intent on filming the entire céilí. The dancers responded by cavorting ever more energetically in the hope of impressing him and posterity.

As the evening went on, Amiss struggled desperately to stay sober, but every time he refused a round he was ignored and when he drank slowly O'Shea or one of the other urgent drinkers would accuse him of being a party-pooper.

'When is closing time?' he asked, as the eighth round arrived.

'About an hour ago,' laughed O'Shea.

'What?' cried Taylor. 'You mean we're breaking the law?'

'In this country licensing laws are more honoured in the breach than in the observance, I think you'll find,' said O'Shea. 'Jaysus, you couldn't finish a céilí at 10.30 and all those people having driven miles for it.'

'Dinna fash yourself,' said Wallace thickly. 'You Anglo-Saxons are slaves to yourselves.'

'But what about the taxis? Surely they were booked for closing time?'

'Not at all. Pascal told them not to have a bother on them till midnight at the earliest.'

A look of sheer misery crossed Taylor's face. 'I haven't got the kind of stamina necessary for this kind of life. I'm already exhausted from two late nights.'

'Me too,' said Gibson and Pooley, as the baroness arrived red-faced but triumphant to order a round for her ex-friends before returning to her new.

'The Stack of Barley' bellowed the drummer, and the baroness took to the floor, this time in the company of a man in hobnailed boots.

'She's certainly approaching this *con brio*,' said Gibson.

'If a touch unorthodoxly,' said Pooley.

'I don't want to watch,' said Amiss. 'I might feel somehow responsible.'

'Another round,' said Wallace.

'Please, please no,' said Amiss. 'I've got three pints of lager lined up here and I simply can't drink them. My stomach doesn't have the capacity. I'm English, remember.'

'Why don't you move to the hard stuff then?' suggested O'Shea. 'There's a limit to how much you can drink of that ould lager. All that gas isn't good for you.'

'Well, just a small one,' said Amiss nervously, 'with plenty of water.'

'Sure, sure,' said O'Shea. 'That'll be grand.' And off he went to order a round of doubles.

*　　　*　　　*

Amiss was enjoying himself hugely when the taxis arrived. His group had been joined by several locals who seemed full of wit, spontaneity and merriment. The jokes and quips came even thicker and faster than the drinks. Amiss felt he had never been in better company in his life. When Gibson whispered to him that a taxi had arrived, he indignantly waved him away. His last memory of the evening was of O'Shea and the baroness on the dance floor performing what seemed to

201

resemble a wild mazurka. Amiss and his colleagues led the crowd in thunderous applause.

*   *   *

It took a few minutes for the shrilling of the phone to penetrate Amiss's consciousness. Fumblingly, he picked up the receiver and held it to his ear. 'Yes,' he croaked.

'Wake up, wake up.'

Amiss groaned. 'Oh, God, Ellis. What time is it?'

'Time to get up. And I want to talk to you. I'm on my way.'

Amiss looked at his watch, cursed, crept out of bed as quickly as seemed prudent and headed for the bathroom. By the time Pooley knocked he was out of the shower. 'What is it?' he asked, as he opened the door and resumed towelling himself.

'I'd better fill you in on last night.'

Amiss returned to the bathroom and began to apply toothpaste to toothbrush. 'But do I want to be filled in on last night? That is the question.'

'You need to be.'

As Amiss began to brush his teeth and tried to suppress the feeling of dread, Pooley perched on the bath. 'Well, that was certainly a memorable evening in the island of saints and scholars. Cheered me up, too, since up to now

I've been feeling utterly useless.'

Amiss brushed on.

'All I've been doing is sitting around saying nothing while all these tenth-raters fight amongst themselves and socially I've spent most of my time fending off questions about my mysterious millionaire from the sort of people whose only interest is trans-Atlantic freebies. Which of course is most of them.'

Amiss spat out the toothpaste and rinsed his mouth. 'True,' he said, dully.

'So it was good to be useful last night. Most of you wouldn't have got to bed without me.'

'Oh, God.' Amiss looked at him with that nervous expression that the drunkard gives the sober friend the morning after. 'How bad was it?'

'In what sense?'

'On a scale of one to ten, how embarrassed should I be?'

'Depends on how easily you're embarrassed.'

'For God's sake stop being playful, Ellis . . . that is Rollo. You know bloody well what I mean.'

'All right, all right, calm down and don't worry. Bearing in mind how some of the others were, I think you'd get away with five out of ten.'

Amiss looked at the razor and then at his right hand and, rather nervously, began to shave. 'Just tell me what happened. When did we leave the pub?'

'About two. Apart from Simon and Charles, who left not long after midnight.'

'Did we go voluntarily?'

'Well, no, not really. Most of you were keen to make a night of it and the remaining locals—not to speak of the publican—were enthusiastically concurring in the idea. You can't fault them on the hospitality front.'

'No trouble from the police?'

Pooley snorted. 'Well, let's just say that their notion of law-and-order isn't exactly mine. I mean there was a moment when the music stopped, we were all instructed to be quiet and the lights went out. That, it emerged, was because the local guard had rung to ask for this display of reverence for the law. We were told that since a local deputy became Minister for Justice he's become rather officious.

'Mind you, it was pretty difficult to keep Jack quiet. She kept demanding that we ask him in and get him to dance, but fortunately he wasn't trying to hear any disturbance so he didn't.'

'So what brought the evening to such an early end?'

'Me being a killjoy, really. I couldn't see any hope that left to yourselves you would stop before dawn or later, so I bribed the taxi drivers to say they were going home and threatened you all with a five-mile walk in the dark through the pouring rain.'

204

'Who was left?'

'Who do you think?' He ticked them off on his fingers. 'Hamish, Pascal O'Shea, you, Jack, oh yes, and Willie and Oki.'

'Did we come quietly?'

'If reluctantly. There were elaborate and affectionate farewells which went on for the best part of half-an-hour and extricating Jack from her friend with the wellies at one stage seemed an insuperable problem. They clung to each other like Romeo and Juliet.'

Surprised that he had so far managed to shave without incident, Amiss directed his attention to the right side of his face.

'The real problems began at the hotel. I should have thought to hire the taxi drivers to give me a hand in getting everyone to bed.'

'Oh God.'

'Oh, you weren't so bad. Indeed, with Oki—who admittedly, was red-faced, giggly and no longer able to point his camera—you made an effort to help me carry Hamish to bed. Jack helped too, which is why we dropped Hamish in the lift, but we got him to his bedroom eventually.

'But then Jack insisted on accompanying us downstairs to help with Pascal, who had passed out on the hall carpet. She felt that this was an appropriate moment to serenade him with a spirited rendition of "Thy tiny hand is frozen".'

Wiping the soap off his miraculously

uninjured face, Amiss began to cheer up. 'I've experienced her once or twice in Pavarotti mode. Not that she can carry a tune.'

'No. But she's got good lungs. And she *thinks* she can carry a tune.'

Amiss nodded. 'That's true. Sober or drunk.'

'Doesn't suffer from a lack of self-belief, our Jack,' said Pooley, as he followed Amiss into the bedroom and sat down on the bed, clearly looking forward to the next part of his story. 'You, Pascal and Willie were all on for another drink—as was Oki, insofar as he could get any words out through his giggles—but Jack suddenly decided it was time for bed and disappeared without another word. I suspect she felt miffed that we were insufficiently appreciative of her aria.

'Pascal was very hard to persuade to bed. He wanted desperately to share with you what characteristics of the English doomed Anglo-Irish relations to inevitable disaster, but I cheated him out of this by promising him we would all join him in his room for a drink within a few minutes and he was so fuddled that he didn't notice I was getting him on to his bed.'

'I'm very impressed, Ell . . . Rollo. I like that. El Rollo. We'll make an epic out of you yet. Anyway I'm impressed that to your normal resourcefulness you've added the necessary deviousness and prevarication to get things done in this environment. I'm glad you came. Otherwise I suspect I'd be feeling a lot worse than I am now.' He paused to consider that statement. 'No, perhaps not. If you think about it, I'd be more drunk and less hungover and therefore feeling not so awful.'

'Have some breakfast and you'll feel better.'

'That's a rash statement, but I'll try. Are you coming?'

'Not yet. I want to phone Mary-Lou.'

'Give her my love and tell her she missed something.'

'I don't think the natives would have stood the excitement,' said Pooley.

*   *   *

By the time he reached the dining room, Amiss's brief euphoria had evaporated and his health had taken a marked turn for the worse. He sat beside the baroness. 'Morning,' she said. 'What's wrong with you?'

He looked blearily at her. 'I wish you didn't look so well, Jack. I haven't had a head like this in a very very long time. And I don't want to have one like it ever again.'

'Stop moaning. Didn't you enjoy yourself?'

'In a way. But not like you.'

'Serve you right for not dancing. You wouldn't have had as much time to drink and would have got some of it out of your system through honest sweat.'

'I had never realized that you had aspirations to be an Irish dancer.'

'Just being cross-cultural. Applying to the Irish scene techniques I learned as a girl doing Scottish country reels.'

'I don't remember the end of the evening— though I've been filled in on it by Ellis—but I do seem to remember a few tumbles during it.'

'There were times when they were all going the wrong way except me. But, with due encouragement, that chap in wellies who partnered me most of the evening was able to direct the tide our way. On balance, I'd say we won.'

She smiled broadly. 'Ah, here's Philomena. Good morning, my dear. And what should I eat this morning?'

'The kippers. I made them get some specially. But have you heard the news?'

'What news?'

'There's been another accident.'

'What?' cried Amiss. 'Christ! Who? And is it bad?'

'That funny priest. Now, don't panic. It's not too bad.'

Amiss jumped up. 'I'd better do something about this. Talk to McNulty.'

'The Inspector's probably still at the hospital. Best thing you can do is sit down and have a decent breakfast. Father Cormac's been taken off to casualty and Pat says at worst he's got a broken leg.'

'But how did it happen? And when?'

'Seems to have slipped on the stairs coming down from his bedroom.'

'It couldn't happen to a greater pain in the arse,' said the baroness. 'Now about those kippers, Philomena, are they . . .'

The Sailor's Hornpipe drove Amiss out of the dining room.

'Have you heard about Father O'Flynn?' asked McNulty.

'Just.'

'It's worse than we thought. A lot worse. There's a possibility that he might die.'

'What? Philomena said he'd only broken his leg.'

'Looked like that at first. Along with mild concussion. But by the time he got to hospital he'd lapsed into a coma and the doctors think he's got a blood clot—and a dangerous one at that. They're operating as we speak.'

*　　　*　　　*

'My, my, we weren't exactly thick on the ground to begin with, but this really is becoming a most exclusive event,' said the baroness, as she sniffed at the kipper Philomena had put in front of her. 'This is excellent, Robert. You should have some.'

'Don't be so callous, Jack. What the hell are we going to do about the press?'

'I wouldn't do anything at the moment.

We'd better wait and see if he croaks. What does Simon think?'

'The same really. I rang him and he's going straight to the hospital to make sure he's been properly looked after.'

'Considering the way he feels about him, that's noble,' she said, removing the bones with great care. 'I'd be more inclined to bludgeon him to death with his guitar. Now, I suppose we'd better break the news to the survivors before we get stuck into a truly exciting session on negotiating our differences or marginalizing our attributes or whatever this latest member of the intellectual caravanserai wants to urge upon us.'

*   *   *

Pascal O'Shea crept into the dining room looking very grey. 'I wouldn't be up,' he quavered, 'only that they were on to me at the crack of dawn this morning about reactions to Billy's death. Apparently it's being claimed that it could be more than an accident. Anyway I explained that we had a wake for him last night—as cross-cultural a one as we could. Thank God I had the sense to toast him early on or there might have been criticism. Did you see the news this morning?'

'Yes,' said the baroness. 'I gather they burned bonfires in his honour last night on the Shankill Road. He'll be starring in a mural of heroic Protestant heroes defending the symbols of the state before we know where we are.'

Amiss gazed about him distractedly. 'Why?'

'Because his death is being seen as martyrdom since he died demanding parity of esteem for a symbol of British Ulster,' whispered O'Shea.

'Have some breakfast and calm down,' said the baroness. 'I recommend the kippers.'

O'Shea looked at her plate and his colour changed to white. Muttering a broken apology, he ran from the room.

CHAPTER FOURTEEN

McNulty's car came up the drive as Amiss finished telling Pooley about O'Flynn. They ran out to meet him.

He looked at them and shrugged helplessly.

'He's dead.'

'Cormac?'

'Yep. The hospital just rang. Died fifteen minutes ago apparently.'

'That's going to look great, isn't it?' said Amiss, with a note of self-pity in his voice.

'You're sure it was an accident?' asked Pooley.

'I don't know. Any more than I did with Billy Pratt.'

'You mean there's nothing to explain why he

211

slipped?'

'He seems to have slipped on some empty Guinness bottles.'

Amiss clutched his head.

'Come inside the caravan,' said McNulty. 'It'll be warmer there.'

When they were settled, Pooley asked, 'Where were the bottles?'

'Presumably on the staircase. That is to say, there were five of them around his body, one of which was broken.'

'Why would there have been bottles on his staircase, for God's sake?' Amiss was almost shouting.

'Maybe he was carrying them?'

'Why would he be carrying them? Couldn't he have disposed of them in his wastepaper basket?'

'Maybe he was a secret tippler and didn't want the chambermaid to know.'

Through the woolly miasma that was gripping Amiss's brain came a memory. 'Simon said he was keen on drink.'

'So he's covering it up. He takes the bottles out, drops them and manages to stand on them on the way down.'

'But why didn't he see them?'

'That's the most suspicious aspect,' said McNulty. 'It was dark. The bulb at the corner had failed.'

'An unlucky coincidence?' asked Amiss hopefully.

'Unless somebody planted the bottles and changed the light bulb,' contributed Pooley.

'Which would suggest they were prepared to put in danger anyone who came down that staircase—ranging from the maid to other guests. Seems very unlikely.'

'Not really, Robert. He was the only guest using that staircase. It's very narrow and leads up to just one turret bedroom. No one else would have been using it until the chambermaid arrived.'

'It still makes no sense,' said Amiss doggedly. 'If he'd dropped the bottles, he'd have advanced very gingerly, wouldn't he?'

'We'll call it an accident for the moment,' said McNulty. 'That's what Dublin will want. Rollo, I'd like to talk a few things over with you. And Robert, you'd better be getting back to whatever you're supposed to be up to. Something that'll take your mind off things, I hope.'

'You must be joking,' said Amiss. 'This morning's torture is "Hegemonic historicity or archipelagian marginalization?".'

'There are moments,' said McNulty thoughtfully, 'when walking around in wet grass in the middle of driving rain can seem almost attractive. Now look, all you can say about the poor Father is that you've heard the sad news that he died from an accident. Don't go into detail. It's enough to say he fell down the stairs. And then you can put out another of

213

those statements about how much you'll miss him.'

'And what'll you be saying?'

'That it looks like an accident, but we have to examine the remote possibility that the death might be suspicious.'

'If the ministry lets you go so far.'

'Indeed. They may try to make me say it must have been an accident. But I won't.' He looked at his watch. 'Nine o'clock. You'd better be on your way. I hope you don't have an outbreak of panic.'

'Shouldn't we simply cancel the rest of the conference as a gesture of respect to the two deceased?'

'That's the last thing I want you to do,' said McNulty. 'Think about it. I don't want these lads going out of this jurisdiction. If we've a murderer here, here is where he should stay or it'll all turn into tussles over extradition and God knows what. If anyone starts asking to go home, refer him to me. In fact you can tell them I'll be needing to speak to them all and will be along at coffee time to tell them what's going on.'

*   *   *

'Be solemn, for Christ's sake, Jack.'

'You do it, Robert. I mightn't get the tone right.'

She marched into the seminar room, which,

214

being minus O'Flynn, O'Shea, Pooley and Hughes, looked rather empty. Wyn and Taylor, who were talking to a stranger, looked up.

'Ah, Jack,' said Taylor. 'I don't think you've met Dr Schwartz, who's just arrived, and who, as you know, has this utterly fascinating theory about us all being of the same stock and there being no difference between Anglo-Saxons and Celts after all.'

'It'd take a lot to make me believe that,' she grunted, but she shook hands with Schwartz civilly and bade him sit beside her. 'Now,' she said, 'Robert's got something to tell you.'

Amiss, who had been wrongly optimistic that an adrenaline-rush would deal firmly with his throbbing head, stood in front of the group. 'I don't know how to tell you this,' he said. 'But we have experienced another bereavement.'

Laochraí leaped to her feet. 'It's Cormac, isn't it?'

'Well, er . . .'

'Isn't it?' she screamed.

'I'm afraid so. He's had an accident.'

'Accident?' she shouted. 'Accident? Don't lie. They've murdered him.'

*   *   *

Pooley and McNulty sat side by side in the caravan, brooding.

'What time did he fall?' asked Pooley.

215

'No idea.'

'What was he wearing?'

'A jumper and jeans. Though now you mention it, he certainly wasn't dressed for the daytime. He had no socks or underpants.'

'So why would he have left his bedroom dressed like that?'

McNulty frowned. 'He had a perfectly good bathroom of his own, so it wasn't that.'

'Would he have been looking for a book?'

'Where?'

'They've got some on those shelves in the fake-library corner of the bar.'

'He had books in his room.'

'Maybe they were all unreadable treatises on liberation theology.'

'Well, they weren't my idea of light reading,' said McNulty. 'But presumably people take with them whatever it is they want to read. Anyway he had a couple of political magazines: *Republican News* and some things about Marxism.'

'Maybe he was hungry or thirsty.'

'I can't really see him raiding the kitchen or the bar, can you?'

'Unless he was liberating capitalist property. But, no, I suspect not. Insomnia? Wanted to go for a walk?'

'With all the security people around and him being paranoid? And it lashing with rain? And with everyone having been warned it would be dangerous to go outside without first letting us know? Which he didn't.'

'A sexual tryst?'

'Now you mention it, it's a possibility. Unless he was up to no good where some other inmate was concerned. Which again, seems unlikely. The Father mightn't have been everybody's favourite priest but nobody ever suggested he was a terrorist.'

'There isn't much choice, is there?'

'Miss de Búrca, Miss O'Hara or Lady Troutbeck.' A slight smile crossed McNulty's harassed features. 'God, there's a choice. Now left to meself, I'd probably settle for her ladyship, but I wouldn't say a MOPEer would.'

'You are of course assuming his tastes were heterosexual.'

'Fair point. But I have a feeling it's one thing for a priest to take the risk of being found in bed with a woman at a conference full of his enemies. But he'd have to be a right eejit to take the risk of being found in bed with a man.'

'In these enlightened times?'

'I don't think the Jesuits are that enlightened.'

The William Tell Overture sounded and McNulty answered his phone. 'Right . . . right . . . That's timely. Thanks, Robert.'

'I think we have the lady. Robert says Laochraí is in a right state. Positively hysterical.' He thought for a moment. 'Look, Rollo, I'd like you to listen to the interview,

217

but you can't be seen. I'm taking over a small sitting room in the hotel that has a curtained recess. Would you mind sitting in there?'

'Delighted.'

'Right. Now I can trust my Sergeant Bradley, but no one else will know. Second floor, east wing, beside the lift. It's called "The Little People". Off you go and hide. We'll be along shortly with Miss de Búrca.'

*   *   *

Laochraí was surprisingly easy to crack. Listening from behind his curtain, Pooley felt almost sorry for her. She had recovered from her bout of hysteria, which she attributed to being a close friend and admirer of Father Cormac's, but she finally cracked up when McNulty said he agreed there was a chance he might have been murdered. She suddenly burst into tears.

'Who could have murdered such a great man? He was a leader. He would have saved the church from the reactionaries and the paedophiles and those that had always been too cowardly to help us in our struggles. Cormac knew that ours was a just cause and a holy war, whatever the Pope might say.' She stopped sniffling and went into aggressive mode. 'If he's been murdered, you don't have far to look. The securocrats. The opponents of peace. The RUC. MI5. MI6 . . .'

'Miss de Búrca,' said McNulty patiently, 'first we have to decide if he was murdered. That's stage one. Wild allegations like this are absolutely no use to me. And what I really need to know is what light you can cast on the fact that he was out of his bedroom in nothing except a T-shirt and jeans and with no reason for it except that he was visiting someone.'

'I'm not an informer.'

'What's an informer got to do with it?'

'Informing on someone's movements to the police is informing.'

McNulty surveyed her incredulously. 'Listen, Miss de Búrca. You say you admired this man. He is now dead. If he was in fact murdered do you want his murderer caught?'

There was a pause. Then a muttered, 'I suppose so.'

'So, will you please tell me if you know of any reason why he would have left his bedroom during the night? If there is no good reason, then no one could have been expecting him to do so. If there was a predictable reason, then murder is more likely.'

'I suppose I might as well tell you. Otherwise there will be nothing but harassment.'

'And anyway you know perfectly well I will find out somewhere else.'

'Probably. There are no depths to which you would not stoop.'

There was a pause. 'Come on, Miss de

219

Búrca. Spit it out. He was coming to see you, wasn't he?'

'Yes.'

'And it wasn't to discuss liberation theology.'

'There's no need to be crude. We were friends.'

'You were more than friends.'

'Yes. More than friends.'

'When did he arrive?'

'About two.'

'And he left?'

'About six.'

'Thank you. That is very helpful. Now I'd like to know how long your affair had been going on?'

'None of your business.'

'Miss de Búrca, I'm sorry for your trouble, but please stop being ridiculous. Of course it's my business. I need to know how many people are likely to have known of this in order to see who might have been able to predict his movements.'

There was a further pause. 'It started last summer at the festival.'

'What festival?'

'What festival? The only festival that matters in this country. Our Belfast festival of culture and protest.'

'You were attending?'

'We were co-organizers.'

'Of what?' McNulty sounded increasingly irritated. 'Just tell the story, Miss de Búrca.

220

It'll avoid me having to harass you.'

'I was one of those running the international side when Father O'Flynn came to me to suggest an event about international suffering and its relevance to our struggle. He thought it should be called the Rainbow Revolt.'

'Rainbow?'

'People of different colours. Like in South Africa.'

'Right. I think I see. He was going to provide you with a few blacks, was he?'

'He's very well connected in the anti-imperialist religious network. And very well respected. It was because of his drive and energy and contacts that we were able to devise an event with members of the ANC, the PLO, several South American resistance groups, veterans of the American Civil Rights Movement and, of course, the Basques.'

'Why do you say "of course the Basques"?' asked McNulty, almost idly.

'They're our closest allies in struggle. They and we are brothers.'

'Don't the Basques want to separate themselves from Spain whereas you want to become part of United Ireland? Aren't you the opposite of each other?'

'That's a simplistic interpretation.'

'Oh, never mind,' said McNulty, tugging his moustache hard, 'I'll never understand any of this. So the two of you got together this . . . what did you call it?'

'It was a performance in song, poetry and prose of the literature of the various struggles in which we shared our mutual suffering, praised the courage of our communities and communally pledged to overthrow the tyrannies we'd groaned under all our lives.'

'I know this is slightly off the point,' said McNulty, 'but isn't the ANC in power and haven't several of the other groups already got most of what they want?'

'As Father Cormac always pointed out, no struggle is ever over . . .'

'Till the fat priest sings . . . Oh, I beg your pardon, Miss de Búrca. I didn't mean that. It just slipped out.'

'I'm going to write a letter of complaint about your crudeness and cruelty.'

'I wouldn't bother your arse, Miss de Búrca. Those complaints always go in the bin. Save the stamp and get on and tell me about yourself and the priest.'

'We fell in love and then became lovers.'

'No problem about him being a priest?'

'Of course there was a problem,' she snapped. 'For as long as the church is dominated by outmoded, anti-feminism as well as anti-liberation prejudices there will be a problem. And he didn't want to be thrown out of the priesthood where he could do so much good for so many people.'

'If you say so, Miss de Búrca. If you say so. So you kept it quiet?'

'As quiet as we could, but inevitably, there were some people who guessed.' She burst into tears. 'When you're united in a search for justice and freedom, love sparkles with a passion that no bourgeois person could understand. People could see the aura around us and though we denied it we were not always believed. There were even some anonymous letters.'

'To whom?'

'To his superiors. To my husband.'

'Ah, your husband? And were these letters believed?'

'No. We denounced them as tittle-tattle, but it meant we had to be careful.'

'So who do you think sent them?'

'Securocrats, of course.'

'Why would the security forces care about a priest and a cultural activist having an affair?'

'They wish to destabilize our movement. They will use any means however foul. That's why they murdered him. They think it'll frighten me and my brothers and sisters in struggle. But it won't. While there is breath in my body I will fight for an Ireland united, Gaelic and free. And making a martyr of him will only make me more determined.'

She burst into loud sobs and then, after a couple of minutes, pushed her chair back and jumped up. 'The fools, the fools, the fools. They have left us our Fenian dead,' she thundered, before she walked out of the room and banged the door.

'The dead, the dead, the dead,' muttered McNulty to Sergeant Bradley. 'They have left us our Fenian Fools.'

He walked up and down the room for a moment or two. 'Mind you, Joe, what would you expect? I hear her people are from Cavan.' There was a moment's silence. 'And as we all know, Cavan people would tip a cat going through a skylight and come back for the kittens.'

CHAPTER FIFTEEN

'Well now, Rollo, from what you told me earlier about the shenanigans last night, 'tis yourself's in a position to tell us who could have done mischief to the priest.'

'More likely who couldn't, Inspector. Incidentally, are you sure she's telling the truth?'

'About the relationship with O'Flynn, yes.'

'And the times?'

'Can't see any reason why she wouldn't. Let's work on that basis anyway.'

'So the key time is between two, when he went down his staircase unharmed, and just after six when he went back to his room and presumably encountered the dark and the bottles.'

McNulty looked hopefully at Pooley. 'Can anyone be ruled out?'

'I'm not an expert on drunken behaviour but I'd be astounded if Wallace or O'Shea could have stirred after they reached their beds.'

'They couldn't have been faking?'

'I don't believe any of my flock could have been faking. I saw how much they drank and none of it was lemonade.'

'And that applies to all of them?'

'I suppose it's conceivable in certain circumstances that Robert Amiss, Lady Troutbeck, Willie Hughes or Tomiichi Okinawa might have been capable of engaging in a practical joke, though I'd expect most of them—even though befuddled—to steer clear of something with potentially lethal consequences. But even if any or all of them had tried something like that, they'd have broken the bottles, smashed the light bulb and woken up everyone within shouting distance.

'Apart from anything else, my room isn't far from O'Flynn's staircase, and though I didn't get to sleep before three, I heard nothing.'

McNulty gazed dispiritedly at his list. 'So, assuming the bottles were planted during the night, and leaving the couple of live-in staff out of it for now, the suspects are limited to you, Steeples, who was back here by eleven o'clock, Taylor, Kapur, Gibson, MacPhrait and the fat American. And of course, that academic who arrived after you'd all gone out and stayed in the bar reading alone until about ten thirty.' He pulled his moustache despairingly. 'There's as likely a line-up as I've ever seen, especially if we might be thinking of ye in relation to the flag-pole mullarky.'

'Inspector.'

'Yes?'

'Are you more inclined now to think Billy Pratt was murdered?'

'Are you?'

'Yes.'

'Me too. There was some funny business with the rope that I'll tell you about again. But they won't like that in Dublin.' He looked at his watch. 'I'd better go over and speak to them. And then I'll have a brief chat with everyone individually. Now do you want to hide there for the duration?'

'I'd like to. But how will I explain my absence?'

'Tell them . . . tell them . . .'

'. . . I've an urgent report to compose for my millionaire.'

'There you are. You're an inventive fella for an Englishman.'

Pooley looked at him demurely. 'I'm not wholly English, Inspector. I had an Irish grandmother.'

'Where was she from?'

'Cork.'

McNulty stopped dead. 'A grandmother

from Cork. Are ye serious? And ye never told me? What part of Cork?'

'Near Mallow.'

'That's even better.' He looked at his watch again. 'Can't stop now to talk. You can tell me more later.'

As the hitherto silent Bradley rose to follow McNulty, he paused beside Pooley. 'Do ye know the definition of a Corkman with an inferiority complex?'

'No.'

'Someone who just thinks he's as good as everyone else.' He left the room without looking back.

*   *   *

McNulty tugged his moustache. 'Look, ladies and gentlemen, I know this is distressing for all of you, but I have a job to do and I intend to do it. All I can suggest is that you do the job you came to do as well. If we can see all of ye today and ye're all cooperative, with a bit of luck we'll be able to let ye go tomorrow lunchtime, when the conference is due to end.

'Sergeant Bradley and I will have our headquarters upstairs. He'll be coming and going to tell you who we want to see and when. We'll try and disrupt things as little as possible. But please remember it's in all our interests to clear this up, and the more you cooperate, the quicker we'll all be out of here.

227

'Now I'll leave ye get back to your discussion.'

As he closed the door behind him, the conference participants sat in sullen silence. The baroness looked around the table. 'Look,' she said, 'there's nothing for it. Like it or not, we're stuck here. And we might as well be stuck here discussing whether we're separate races or just mongrels pretending to have pedigrees as well as anything else.'

She fixed Taylor with a steely eye. 'You've got off lightly this morning. Give us your opinion.'

Taylor looked at her miserably and then jerked himself into life. 'While, of course, I admire Dr Schwartz's obvious scholarship, I feel he takes too little cognizance of the clear proof of a singular Celtic genius which has given to Western Europe a profound spirituality, infused . . .'

Amiss sat in a reverie, envying Pooley.

*　　　*　　　*

McNulty was struggling to keep his temper with the maintenance man. 'Look, Peadar, for the hundredth time, I'm not accusing you of anything. It's not your fault that you were at your cousin's when we needed you yesterday. And no one's blaming you for what happened with the flagpole. Just tell me all I need to know about flagpoles.'

'What do you need to know?'

'Why it would collapse.'

'Sure you know that already, don't ye?'

'I want a full explanation of how this accident could have happened.'

'How would I know, and me not even here?'

'Peadar,' snapped McNulty, 'stop playing games. I know you're a Kerryman, but even so you'll answer my questions if I have to lock you up until you do.'

'And how would you be able to do that? Don't I have a brother a guard and doesn't he tell me ye . . .'

'Peadar,' roared McNulty. 'Why did the flagpole collapse?'

'Didn't someone undo the bolt that fastened the hinge?'

'How do you know?'

'Didn't I take down that flagpole only two weeks ago to paint it?'

'Yes. And?'

'And when I put it up again, didn't I put the bolt on?'

'Maybe ye didn't.'

'How could the pole have stayed up if I didn't?'

'Maybe ye didn't close it properly?'

'Why wouldn't I, and I closing it at all?'

'If that's the case, how could Billy Pratt have been killed?'

'How would I know?'

McNulty raised his voice to a level Pooley

229

thought would be audible in the dining room. 'Peadar Kennealy, you're so cute you'll disappear up your own arse if you're not careful. Now if you don't stop this oul shite this instant, I'm arresting you for obstructing the gardaí in the course of their enquiries.'

McNulty's eloquence had its effect. Though for his own self-respect Kennealy maintained his grudging tone, he changed tactics. 'You've no call to get so worked up. I'm the one has to put up them feckin' flags. Do you think I'd leave the feckin' bolts undone?'

'We all make mistakes.'

'Listen, guard, it'd be one thing to forget to close the bolt at all. But it'd be another to close it only a little bit so someone could be kilt. How could ye make that mistake?'

'You tell me.'

'If ye ask me,' said Kennealy, 'someone set that fella up. All he'd have had to do was slip the bolt nearly but not quite open.'

'How could he be sure it would hold long enough for someone to climb the ladder?'

'He probably couldn't. Maybe he was just lucky.'

'I want you to go up to the roof with a couple of guards and have a look.'

'At what?'

'Kennealy!'

'Oh, I'll go so.'

As Kennealy left the room with Bradley, McNulty tore back Pooley's curtain. 'Jaysus,' he shouted, 'them Kerry hoors wouldn't give Marilyn Monroe a straight answer if she offered them a ride.'

An obvious joke about necrophilia surfaced in Pooley's mind, but he repressed it firmly.

McNulty breathed heavily for a minute or so and then recovered his equilibrium. 'Right, Rollo. Now what with all Father Cormac business, I had divil the chance of telling you what came out yesterday about Billy Pratt.'

Pooley looked at McNulty eagerly.

'Willie Hughes and Simon Gibson thought Pratt was intending this as an election stunt. He was running for a council seat and the omens weren't looking good. Hughes had been expecting to win.'

'Seems a peculiar election stunt.'

'Of course it was peculiar. This is bloody Northern Ireland we're talking about. They're all peculiar.' McNulty handed Pooley a piece of paper. 'This was in Pratt's back pocket. He was obviously going to fax it through to the media as soon as he'd run the flag up.'

Pooley read it quickly. ' "Billy Pratt today raised the Union flag on Moycoole Castle in a symbolic demand for parity of esteem. 'The Irish tricolour flies in Northern Ireland as a gesture of respect to those who consider themselves Irish,' he said. 'Where is the reciprocation in the Republic for those who consider themselves British? If parity of esteem means anything, it must mean that our

Britishness is recognized throughout the island.

'"'I have raised this flag on Moycoole Castle as a protest on behalf of myself, my community and all British people living in Ireland'"'.'

'Now,' said McNulty, 'Hughes says and Gibson confirmed that Pratt knew he was getting too much of a reputation among his own people as a compromiser, so he had to find a way of showing he was a hard man. Indeed Hughes said he wasn't surprised at Billy's duplicity. Said he could be a treacherous wee bastard since he'd learned from republicans that the way to impress people was by words not actions.'

'So this exploit would have run well back home?'

'Very well, apparently. Especially if he was heavily criticized by nationalists. Indeed Hughes said he wouldn't have been surprised if Pratt had done some advance deal with a MOPEer or two to make sure they attacked him in terms that would win him votes.'

'What did our MOPEers say about that?'

'That they knew nothing about his plans. Anyway Pratt would have been more likely to tell his MOPE pals in Belfast. He didn't know our MOPEs well, apparently.'

He launched a new assault on his moustache. 'I can't think of any reason why he might have confided about the flag to anyone here. Especially to Willie Hughes, seeing he was his main rival for the seat.'

'So who killed him, then?'

McNulty uttered a sound close to a groan. 'Maybe it was an accident. Maybe Peadar's less efficient than he lets on. But he'll never admit to it. He doesn't want the blame and the management won't want to be sued for vast sums of money.'

'Surely Pratt's relatives wouldn't have a case. Even in the wilder shores of American compensation culture somebody who climbs a flagpole illicitly to put up an illicit flag wouldn't seem to me to have the strongest possible case.'

McNulty laughed. 'You're very new to this country, me boy. North and south, we've got a compo culture that's the tenth wonder of the world. The MOPEs have the hang of it, but the DUPEs are learning fast.

'However, let's forget about Pratt for now and get back to trying to make some sense of the priest.'

CHAPTER SIXTEEN

'It was a pretty boring afternoon for the most part,' reported Pooley to Amiss over a pot of tea. 'Almost made me briefly nostalgic for the fraud files. At least when I was working on them I could get up and walk around, make myself a cup of coffee and grumble to the others.'

'Huh,' said Amiss. 'Don't you talk to me about boring. You missed a paper by an EU enthusiast on how the challenge for the new millennium is to replace cultural nationalism by a Europe-wide renaissance if Brussels gets its directives right. Or something like that. I wasn't listening, and I doubt if anyone else was. The main excitement was each of us being fetched and returned by Garda Bradley.

'Laochraí and Willie weren't there, being on the phone most of the time I expect; Pascal slept soundly until Bradley came for him and Jack dozed several times and got cross with me every time I woke her up. Wyn made a bit of an effort and talked *ad nauseam* and irrelevantly about the state of the Welsh language and Charlie Taylor produced his usual bland guff, after which Jack said enough was enough and gave us the rest of the afternoon off, thank God.

'Now, what did you find out?'

'Not much, except that Peadar, the handyman, insists there was foul play. Apparently the halliard was tangled . . .'

'The what?'

'I suppose you were never a boy scout. The halliard is the rope that you attach to flags for raising and lowering. Peadar and the gardaí agree that the only reason Billy could have had

234

to use the ladder would have been because he had to disentangle the rope, which Peadar insists he always left in good order. Add that to the fact that the bolt had to have been almost undone, and it looks like murder. Unless you think Peadar is careless and lazy and a liar to boot.'

'Is he?'

'Haven't a clue.'

'Let me get this clear. Billy turns up with the flag, thinking he just has to run it up the pole.'

'Right. And then finds the tackle needs sorting out.'

'There happens to be a handy ladder.'

'Yes. In the little shed on the roof where Peadar keeps a few tools, flags and so on.'

'Billy climbs up the ladder.'

'Tugs at the rope.'

'And his weight detaches the bolt and sends the flagpole over the edge of the battlements.'

'That's it.'

'Why didn't he hang on to the rope?'

Pooley shrugged. 'Lost his grip, I expect.'

'You mean someone could have killed him simply by tangling up the rope and slipping the bolt.'

'That's right. They couldn't have been sure it would work, of course. But there were no risks involved.'

'And no one admits knowing he was planning this.'

'No one.'

Amiss sighed. 'What else emerged this afternoon?'

'Nothing, really. McNulty asked everybody the same questions and got virtually identical answers.'

'The questions were?'

'The same as he asked you. "Did you know or had you heard of Billy and/or Cormac before you came here? If so, how well and what did you think of them? And was there any possibility that they were murdered because they were friendly with paramilitaries?"'

'And the results?'

'No one thought the paramilitary connections were relevant. Hamish, Jack, Kelly-Mae, Oki, Chandra and Wyn had never heard of either of them before they came here. You had heard of Billy because he was down on your list, Gardiner thought he was "a wee scutter" that he wouldn't trust with sixpence, Pascal said everyone in Dublin believed him to be a fine man and Charlie had never met him but knew him as a man of peace who showed how enmity can yield to friendship.'

Amiss made a face.

'Apart from Simon,' Pooley went on, 'only the MOPEs and Willie Hughes had heard of O'Flynn before coming here, though Gardiner said he knew the Jesuits were up to no good. Jack added a bit of light relief by adding that she couldn't stand either of them, and that

Billy was a hypocrite and O'Flynn a lunatic. Simon intimated rather more elegantly that he took the same view, but added that he felt that in the context of Northern Ireland, where law-abiding citizens were instructed by international opinion to chum up and govern with mass murderers, it would be a strange person who would single out those two as particularly deserving assassination. Oh yes, and he thought O'Flynn was a fool rather than a knave.'

'Did McNulty find out if anyone knew about the relationship between Laochraí and the priest?'

'The only ones who admitted to it were Liam MacPhrait and—to a lesser extent—Simon.'

'How do you mean "to a lesser extent"?'

'He had heard rumours. But he said there's no lack of rumours about anyone at all prominent in Northern Ireland. Small place. Lots of scores to settle.'

'How many people might be denying knowing about it but actually did?'

'McNulty doesn't know. He thinks the loyalists might have known since they're all so thick with each other. But he doesn't have enough evidence to convince even himself that this is a murder enquiry. It just makes it slightly more likely since anyone who knew they were involved would have guessed they'd be getting together at night.'

'Why could it be predicted that he would go to her room? Why not the other way around?'

'It couldn't, which, of course, McNulty and I agreed, raises the possibility that somebody left the bottle there in the hope of getting Laochraí on her way up to him.'

'Somebody acting for a jealous husband?'

'Possibly somebody who just hated MOPEs.'

'I can understand that motivation all too well,' said Amiss with feeling.

'More tea?'

'Thanks, vicar. Now what happens next?'

'I'm not sure. There are the autopsy reports to come, but what will they tell us that we don't know? McNulty is stymied. And he's under relentless pressure from Dublin to treat both these events as tragic accidents.'

'I certainly hope they're right. Though I'm not so sure they were tragic.'

'You're getting as cynical as Simon, Robert,' said Pooley reprovingly.

'Would you blame me? The conference is a complete nightmare, quite apart from the corpses. Jack and I were tempted to cancel the rest of the proceedings but we decided to stagger on to the bitter end. The plenary session, where we all talk of what we've learned, is tomorrow morning. Then we can all get the hell out of here.'

The baroness stuck her head through the door. 'Ah, there you are.' She looked behind her and waved. 'Got them. Come on, Simon.'

Pooley jumped up and pushed two chairs towards the table. 'Tea, Jack? Simon?'

'No thanks. Just had some. Sorry you couldn't be with us this afternoon, Rollo. It was a cracker.'

'I'm sorry too. My master is very demanding. But Robert's filled me in on what I missed.'

'That's why you two've been AWOL for so long,' she said with a chuckle. 'Well that Eurocreep's gone now and we've had a call to say this evening's tame academic is on her way. I'd like to cancel her, but Simon's persuaded me we can't refuse to listen to her since she's gone to the trouble to come to such a remote spot through driving rain.'

'I don't know anything about this woman,' said Amiss, 'except that she's a last-minute substitute for someone famous.'

Gibson turned to the baroness. 'She's someone after your own heart, Jack. A woman who in her intellectual rigour, her majestic disregard for sacred cows . . .'

'Talking about me, again?' She smirked.

'No, Jack. If cow you are, you would more properly be described as profane than sacred.'

'How about a profane bull-in-a-china-shop?' suggested Amiss.

'Contrived,' said the baroness. 'Get on, get on, Simon.'

'As I was saying . . . in her implacable opposition to woolliness of mind or

239

meaningless rhetoric is a natural ally of yours.'

'Oh, God. You mean she's ghastly.'

'Depends on how you feel about a feminist nun who peddles a Freudian analysis of Anglo-Irish relations. If I remember correctly, the Brits are the super-ego, Ulster Protestants are the subconscious id and the Irish are the struggling reality principle.' He yawned. 'Or is it the other way round? Anyway, I seem to remember reading that she believes Irish revolutionary movements have been directed at the male symbol of the crown because of the Fenian Oedipus complex about Britannia the mother.'

'Surely the crown is vaginal,' said the baroness, puzzled. 'Anyway, how does that square with all our queens?'

'I don't know, Jack. She neither talks sense nor, in my experience, does anyone ever bother to challenge her. Feminist crap is cool these days in Ireland and most men are too timid to challenge it, even when it is the kind of unadulterated balls in which Sister Q specializes—if you'll forgive the male imagery.'

'What do you mean "Sister Q"?'

'She used to be Sister Concepta Ligouri, but then she renamed herself. And no, I don't know the significance of "Q".'

'After Sir Arthur Quiller Couch?'

'Jack, I know you take pride in being triumphantly out-of-date,' said Amiss, 'but if I remember correctly, that particular "Q" was in his heyday nearly a century ago. I doubt if he is the inspiration for a radical nun at the beginning of the third millennium.'

'Shall I sort her out?'

'What's a Freudian nun in the middle of all our other troubles? Let's just let her talk and be grateful she's the last torment to be visited upon us.'

The door opened and Gibson rose. 'Ah, Sister Q. How very kind of you to come to help us at our time of trouble.'

*   *   *

'Jaysus, you're great crack,' said Pascal O'Shea. 'Will you have another?'

'Certainly,' said the baroness.

'No, thank you,' said Pooley.

O'Shea signalled a repeat order to the barman and then looked at the baroness and sniggered. 'Fair play to you. You're a fierce wicked woman and no mistake. That poor nun.'

The baroness looked defensive. 'I was only asking her in a spirit of honest enquiry. It's always seemed odd to me about Catholicism that rules about sex are laid down by men in frocks who've never had it.'

'That wasn't what upset her,' said Pooley. 'It was the next bit.'

'You mean my straightforward enquiry as to whether being a life-long celibate mitigated

241

against fully understanding Freud?'

'You know bloody well that wasn't all you said,' interrupted Amiss. 'You also asked if she, like Father O'Flynn, regarded celibacy as no more than an optional extra which progressive clerics could ignore. She'd only just heard of his death, so I'm not surprised she was outraged. You'd no right to invade her privacy like that. Or his, for that matter.'

'Privacy? What right to privacy does anyone have if they go round the place talking about the castration complexes of the British establishment?'

'I liked that question of Gardiner's about the Catholic view of artificial insemination of cows,' said Gibson. 'Got her progressiveness, feminism and religion all in conflict.'

'Where is Gardiner?' asked the baroness. 'I owe him a drink for that.'

'Eating in his room, I expect,' said Amiss. 'He told me his friend's wife had given him a wee box of buns and he looked crazed with lust as he left the room.'

'Here he is now,' said Pooley.

'You're right,' said the baroness. 'If I ever saw a fellow exuding the lineaments of satisfied desire, it's him. Gardiner, Gardiner, come here. Jamsie, Jamsie, add a large Bushmills.'

'I can't stop, Jack. I'm away to my friends again.'

He waved and departed. The barman

arrived with a groaning tray. Pooley began to protest when given another gin-and-tonic, but O'Shea waved at him dismissively. 'A bird never flew on one wing, Rollo.'

'Thanks, Jamsie,' said the baroness. 'You make an excellent Martini.' She looked around the table. 'Now what are we going to do tonight?'

'Not the same as last night,' said Amiss firmly.

'Really? I wouldn't mind going back to Nelligan's. My swain might propose tonight.'

'Which swain?'

'The welly-man. He's quite a man of the world you know. Told me he'd been to Dublin once. I concluded he was serious when he asked me if I'd ever thought of living in Ireland, had I any experience of living on a farm, bragged about his "quotas", whatever that meant, and ended by enquiring if I fancied a bit of a coort.'

'What's a "coort"?' asked Pooley.

'A court,' said O'Shea. 'It was an invitation to go outside and fumble in the hay. But I wouldn't get your hopes up, Jack. I'm afraid he'd be needing a substantial dowry, seeing that if you'll excuse me saying so, you're probably past child-bearing age.'

'Oh, I don't know about that. I could always go to that Italian doctor.' She looked at O'Shea sternly. 'Are you suggesting that he is not simply a romantic who was swept off his

243

feet by my girlish charms?'

'He was swept off his feet a couple of times by your beefy arms rather than your girlish charms,' grunted Amiss. 'If you ask me, he thinks you're rich. Your jewellery was not exactly understated for a Mayo pub on a Sunday night.'

'He probably reckons you could swap your ring for a prize bull.'

'Pascal, that amethyst is not to be included in any dowry. My friend Myles would be very very upset. He places great faith in its magical properties.'

'Which are?'

'Warding off the effects of alcohol.'

'Is that so?' enquired O'Shea. 'I'd say I'd have to wear a tiara.'

'Which effects does it ward off exactly?' asked Amiss.

'Ill-effects. You'll have noticed that alcohol does me no harm.'

'It does lots of other people harm if they're in your company and you've been consuming it.'

'That's not what bothers Myles,' she said complacently. 'Nor me. However, I dare say you're right. It might be unwise to visit the scene of past triumphs so soon. And I wouldn't want to raise the poor fellow's hopes, for I fear my other commitments mean I am unlikely to be able to find the time to be his bride.'

'So what will we do tonight?' asked O'Shea.

'Sit in the bar with Sister Id,' suggested Gibson gloomily.

'Sister Id isn't even staying for dinner,' said Amiss. 'She claimed rather unconvincingly that urgent business meant that she had, after all, to be driven straight back to Galway.'

'So she chickened out,' said the baroness. 'She certainly seemed decidedly nervous about the risk of further tragic accidents.' She took another sip of Martini and smacked her lips appreciatively. 'You know I'll never understand about clergy. If they really believe that happiness can be found only in the next world, why do they seem so confoundedly reluctant to get there? Dammit, it should be us atheists who are quaking in our boots at the prospect of oblivion.'

O'Shea concentrated fiercely. Then his face cleared. 'What was it the fella said? "*Le dernier acte est sanglant, quelque belle que soit la comédie en tout le reste.*" '

'I don't do French,' said the baroness. 'And who was the fella?'

' "The last act is bloody, however charming the rest of the play may be." And it was your man Pascal, of the *Pensées.*'

'In whom you presumably have a proprietorial interest?'

'Old party trick of mine finding occasions to quote the poor tormented oul fecker. What else could I do, stuck as I was with a name like that? Though mind you I wasn't called after him but after me Great-Uncle Pascal who ran a pub in Magherafelt. But what I'm getting at is that at the end believers do worry about hell or purgatory.'

'I doubt it in Sister Id's case,' said Gibson. 'Like Call-me-Cormac, she's far too radical to believe in such out-moded concepts.'

The baroness shook her head. 'Well, I'm disappointed. I'd have enjoyed roughing her up a bit.'

'Nothing for it, Jack, but you'll have to make do with us,' said O'Shea. 'Now whose round is it?'

*   *   *

There were very few at dinner. As well as Steeples, Laochraí, MacPhrait and Kelly-Mae had been whisked away by their friends of the previous night and Wyn Gruffudd had been so outraged by Sister Q's talk that she was opting for prayer and room service. At nine o'clock the remainder gathered in the television room to watch the news. The five minutes allotted to the happenings at Moycoole Castle caused the baroness to snort so loudly as almost to drown out the newsreader and the interviewees. Billy Pratt had almost disappeared as a subject of conversation, as the propaganda reason for his fatal climb was now beyond doubt and the Irish media preferred to ignore it. 'They'll be laughing their bollocks off,' said O'Shea, 'but sure we have to keep a straight face because Billy's dead and all. They'll be playing it down in the interests of peace and that. But Jaysus, you have to laugh.'

Father O'Flynn was a different matter and now centre stage. There were myriad tributes to his selflessness, his dedication and his unremitting work on behalf of the oppressed. One MOPE interviewee went so far as to compare him to Roger Casement, whose heroic work in the early part of the twentieth century exposing cruelty towards natives in the Congo had been followed by his espousal of the cause of Irish revolution.

'There's a similarity, all right,' conceded the baroness. 'But he got hanged and Call-me-Cormac got bottled. And besides, the priest wasn't a queer.'

'For God's sake, don't let any of the MOPEs hear you talk like that,' said Gibson. 'They're so hot on gay and lesbian rights these days that the prevailing orthodoxy is that homophobia is a disease exported to Ireland by the Brits.'

'Don't tempt me,' she said, scowling at a clip of O'Flynn in full clerical rig blessing a group of anti-Orange protestors and another of him screaming as a policeman tried to remove a youthful protester from the middle of a road. 'Did I hear aright,' she asked, 'or was he shouting "Resist the forces of Satan"?'

'Sounded like it,' said Pooley.

'Whatever happened to turning the other

cheek?'

'You're so old-fashioned, Jack,' said O'Shea.

'Ghandhi-ji has been out of fashion for many a long day,' said Kapur. 'It is dacoits that we admire these days.'

'Dacoits?' asked Okinawa.

'Desperadoes. Miscreants.'

'Ruffians,' proffered Wallace.

Okinawa looked even more puzzled.

'And Che Guevara's more popular these days than ever, right-wing pope or no right-wing pope,' said O'Shea. 'Sure, the junior clergy in Ireland would make him archbishop and no questions asked if they'd half a chance.'

*   *   *

Conversation had come virtually to a halt by ten o'clock.

'It's like a bloody morgue in here,' said the baroness.

'Thanks, Jack,' said Amiss. 'Always the *mot juste*.'

'What about another round?' asked O'Shea.

'I'm going to bed,' said Taylor. 'Now.'

'And me,' said Gibson.

Within three minutes, there were only four of them left. 'Do you know,' said the baroness, 'I think this might be my last. I admit to feeling a trifle weary.'

Kelly-Mae's arrival at that moment did not lift their spirits. 'May I get you a drink?' asked

O'Shea.

'Water, please.'

'Sparkling or still?'

'Still.'

O'Shea called the order to the barman.

'Why don't you get it from a tap?' asked the baroness.

'I'm not going to put my health in jeopardy here,' said Kelly-Mae. 'You have to drink bottled water abroad.'

'We're not abroad,' said O'Shea, with a rare flash of irritation.

'No, but Kelly-Mae is,' said the baroness maliciously. 'To her, this is a Third World country, and it behoves her to take every precaution. Taking your malaria tablets, are you, Kelly-Mae?'

'Let it go, Jack, let it go,' hissed Amiss.

With a flounce, Kelly-Mae marched over to the bar, collected her water and left. Silence reigned. Even O'Shea joined in the general gloom, so it was only twenty minutes after Kelly-Mae's departure that the gathering broke up.

It was an hour later when the night porter rang McNulty to report that he had heard an explosion.

CHAPTER SEVENTEEN

When McNulty spoke to Pooley, half an hour or so later, he was ashen. 'God, Rollo, I've seen some grizzly sights in my time with traffic pile-ups and that, but when you know someone it's worse.'

'Laochraí's dead, is she?'

'Very.'

'What was it?'

'I don't know. Some kind of bomb. She's wasn't blown up, exactly. But bits of metal and wood have done awful things to her. We're hoping we can get the explosives experts up here by helicopter in the next few hours. But for the moment we'll have to say it's an explosion and we don't know the cause.'

'So you're allowing them the possibility that it might have been another accident?'

'Well they're not all complete eejits, so I'll have to tell them we think this time it was definitely done on purpose. Will you go and get Lady Troutbeck and Robert so we decide how to play it?'

*   *   *

'If I had time,' said the baroness darkly, 'I would go and lie down in a darkened room. As it is, I suppose I'd better get cracking on a statement about how much we're all going to miss Lucrezia.'

McNulty gazed distractedly at her silk blue-and-white-polka-dot robe.

'I'm flattered that you can admire my dressing-gown at a time like this, Inspector. It's my Noel Coward look.'

He buried his face in both his hands. 'Sorry, mam. I'm in that much of a state I don't know where I am.'

'Alive,' she said waspishly, 'which will probably soon put you in a minority.' She pulled out her pipe and began to stuff it with tobacco. 'You know, Inspector, I wouldn't say that I'm a nervous woman, but this is beginning to resemble Agatha Christie's *Ten Little Niggers*. You know, the one in which they all sit around in an isolated house from which there is no escape waiting to be murdered one by one for no reason that any of them can grasp. Just assuming that this isn't some lunatic coincidence, somebody has knocked off a house-trained loyalist, and two MOPEs, a priest and a cultural activist. Who's to say who might next tickle his fancy? A mustachioed Corkman? An aristocratic detective-sergeant? A humble baroness?'

'A deranged conference organizer,' added Amiss. 'I'm with Jack. Who could rationally have it in for that threesome?'

'Really only people who can't stand those who justify terrorism,' said Pooley.

'Oh great. That's very logical,' said the baroness. 'So the only likely murderer in these circumstances is somebody who's against murder.'

McNulty looked up and a faint smile crossed his face. 'This is Ireland, after all. Maybe it's an Irish solution to an Irish problem.'

The baroness lit her pipe and sucked vigorously. 'Enough of the merry badinage, Inspector. Are you going to break the news to everyone or what?'

Suddenly energetic, he jumped up. 'Yes, yes. I'll send Bradley to wake them all. I'll meet ye all in The Crock of Gold in about fifteen minutes.'

'Have I any little words of comfort to give them in the meantime? Or should they all be locking themselves in their rooms armed with defensive weapons?'

'You can assure them that security will be stepped up.'

'And perhaps warn them to stay away from flagpoles, Guinness bottles and whatever you in due course tell us did for Lucrezia.'

*   *   *

'I don't think anyone is likely to call this an accident,' said McNulty to the assembled gathering, who were sitting in their night-clothes in a frightened half-circle round the table in the seminar room. 'She was murdered and that's the long and the short of it. Which makes it more likely that Mr Pratt and Father O'Flynn were murdered too.

'I know ye'll be anxious . . .'

'Whadyemean "anxious"?' cried Kelly-Mae. 'Get me the American consul. I'm in danger of my life here.'

MacPhrait put his arm around her and patted her shoulder. 'You'll be all right, Kelly-Mae. It'll all be all right.'

'How can you say that when Laochraí's dead? And Cormac . . .'

'There, there. Let the garda speak. Don't worry. I'll look after you.'

'Promise. Oh, Gawd, I'm so frightened. I might be blown up.'

'Now you know what it feels like to be afraid of bombs, Kelly-Mae,' said the baroness. 'You can tell your IRA-loving friends back in the Bronx about it. That is, if you ever make it home.'

'For the love of Mike, will ye stop that, the pair of ye,' shouted McNulty.

'The thing to do is we all keep a steady head,' said Steeples. 'And say our prayers.'

'That's right,' said Wyn. 'We'll ask Jesus . . .'

'Miss Gruffudd. Please. I must get on. Now, as I was saying, I know you'll all be worried, but there's a bit of comfort for most of ye and that is that even if the three deaths are all murder, there's a paramilitary tinge to all the victims.'

MacPhrait and Kelly-Mae leaped up as one in protest. 'How dare you . . .'

'Don't give me that crap,' said McNulty. 'Sure wasn't Pratt as thick as thieves with the UVF and the other two with the IRA, whatever they said. So for all I know it's score-settling.'

'That's not much consolation to me,' said Willie Hughes.

'No, nor to Mr MacPhrait. But forewarned's forearmed and all that.'

'What about Gardiner Steeples?' shouted Kelly-Mae. 'The Orange Order is paramilitary.'

'It is not, so it isn't,' said Steeples. 'Any Orangeman having anything to do with paramilitaries dishonours his collarette, so he does.'

'That's right,' said Wallace. 'It's the same in Scotland.'

'You can't be sure this particular assassin is that politically sophisticated,' said the baroness. 'The trouble with people who . . .'

'Excuse me, mam. Now there's people scouring your rooms for relevant evidence, so I'm sorry to say I'll have to keep ye up for the moment. But the hotel staff are trying to fix up other accommodation so ye can get a night's sleep. It'll be a bit rough and ready, but it's the best that can be done.

'If I might make a suggestion, while you're

waiting, you might be well advised to have a drink to settle your nerves. I'll send in the porter.'

'There's an idea,' said O'Shea. 'It would never have occurred to me.'

'The trouble with this country,' observed the baroness as McNulty left, 'is that everything's an excuse for a drink. You use it to celebrate, to mourn, to help you think, to help you talk, to get you through a hangover and, now, it emerges, to keep up your courage when you're trapped in a remote castle with Bluebeard. Mind you, it's a philosophy that suits me. Mine's a large brandy.'

'Me, too,' said Steeples.

*   *   *

At two o'clock the explosives expert arrived.

'Now you'll be finger-printed and tested for contact with explosives,' McNulty warned, 'and then you can go to bed. But you won't be allowed back in your own rooms or given access to any of your possessions until all our tests are complete. You'll just have to make do tomorrow until we can organize someone to get ye some necessities in the nearest town.'

The baroness stood up. 'I'm sure we are all sticklers for duty and I'm sure we all have high concepts of *noblesse oblige,* but I'm inclined to think that to convene . . .' she looked at her watch, 'in five hours' time to discuss what we have learned from this conference would be high-mindedness to a fault. Does anyone have any objection if we abandon this conference finally? Now?'

There was complete silence for a moment and then Taylor gave a rare smile. 'We've reached agreement on something at last.'

'Very well. Henceforward you are in the care of Inspector McNulty. I wish you all a good night and hope you survive until the morning.'

She and Amiss followed McNulty out. 'Inspector,' she said, 'unless in the next hour or so you can prove without a shadow of doubt that Lucrezia and her priest committed suicide—and probably even if you can—I shudder to think what MOPE are going to do in terms of creating two new martyrs.'

'I know what they'll do all too well, mam,' said McNulty wearily. 'They'll blame the RUC, the gardaí, the securocrats, the British government and probably the World Monetary Fund. But what I've got to get on with is trying to find out as best I can what actually happened. So if you'll excuse me . . .'

He turned towards the front door and then looked back at them. 'If I were ye, I'd be careful, though we'll do the best we can. My lads are checking the whole hotel for weapons.'

'Considering one person's been killed with a flagpole and another with a Guinness bottle,' said the baroness icily, 'I don't see that checking for weapons is going to make much difference. The way things are going, I'm expecting imminently to be bludgeoned to death with a lavatory brush.'

'Oh, well,' she said to Amiss, as they went back towards the seminar room; 'at least we're out of that session tomorrow. Every cloud has a silver lining.'

'You didn't murder the three of them just to achieve that, Jack, did you?'

'No,' she said. 'I'd have chosen Kelly-Mae or Charles Taylor before Lucrezia. She was better-looking.'

*   *   *

Although by three, when he finally got to bed, Amiss feared he might die of exhaustion, he set his watch alarm to wake him for the eight o'clock news. It rapidly became clear that the British and Irish media knew they had what was potentially a wonderful story, but that they were so short of facts that they could do little but speculate wildly and interview people who knew either more or less than they let on. Dublin had the advantage of having been able to get hold of Sister Id, who spoke of Laochraí as a beacon of feminism whose eternal flame would never be snuffed out.

The baroness rang as the newscast finished. 'Good old Id. Never pass up an opportunity for a phallic reference. I don't know about you, but I'm getting up. There's something about being trapped in the den of the secret nine that makes sleep elusive.'

*　　　*　　　*

The Sailor's Hornpipe sounded. 'What am I to make of this, Robert?' asked Milton.

'Haven't you asked Ellis?'

'Couldn't reach him. I'm going to have to tell someone he's there, don't you think?'

'Can't you stick to the fiction for now?'

'No. I'll talk direct to McNulty. Stay safe.'

*　　　*　　　*

'It's all very well for Jim Milton to urge me to stay safe,' said Amiss to the baroness when they met in the dining room. 'But we don't even know what we're staying safe from.'

'Jesus and his Holy Mother,' said Philomena. 'If I were ye I'd get out of here as fast as my legs would carry me.'

'They won't let us go yet, Philomena.'

'And here have I been praying to St Jude to help you with the conference.'

'I fear he may have got his instructions wrong, Philomena. Maybe he thought you just wanted him to put us out of our misery,' offered Amiss.

'In case he doesn't know where to stop,' said

258

the baroness, 'look upon us as condemned men and give us a hearty breakfast.'

*   *   *

Pooley and the inspector were on their third cup of coffee. 'We're going to have to seal this place tight as a drum,' said McNulty. 'I thought it already was, but it obviously wasn't,' he added testily. 'Otherwise no one could have smuggled in a feckin' grenade, which is what the fella says it was. And it's got to be one of the conference attendees. Since Saturday, no one else, staff or tradesmen, got in or out without being searched and having a metal detector run over them.'

'And why weren't we searched?' asked Pooley.

'Because bloody MOPE protested to Dublin, Belfast and London about the indignity they suffered. Garda harassment, they called it. And of course authority caved in as usual. It was your woman de Búrca in the lead on all that. She's certainly paid a heavy price for being a pain in the arse.'

'Were the police and the army searched?' asked Pooley.

'No,' said McNulty heavily. 'And I appreciate you being ingenious and all, but if ye don't mind, I'll concentrate for now on slightly more likely suspects.

'Now we can be pretty sure, because of the

dogs, that the hotel was clean before everyone arrived. No one left the place on Saturday night, but everyone did on Sunday and there isn't one of ye, in theory, couldn't have taken delivery of a grenade on Sunday night.' He chuckled. 'Though from your evidence, Rollo, several of them would have blown themselves up before they ever got inside the door.'

'Look,' said Pooley hesitantly, 'I'm sure you've thought about this, but don't we need to know more about what these people were really up to behind the scenes?'

'You mean when they weren't spouting peace and culture were they up to any funny business?'

'Involved in internecine warfare, for instance?'

'Sure, even as we speak isn't there a fella from the RUC Special Branch on his way here to give us a confidential briefing on the corpses and any of the suspects they know about. It'd be a help, for instance, to know if de Búrca was the Virgin Mary or . . .' He paused. 'Well, no, she wasn't the Virgin Mary, obviously. But it'd be a help to know if she was a Jezebel.'

'Come again?'

'If she was involved.'

'Involved?'

'Actively involved in the IRA. A Volunteer, as they dignify themselves. But while I'd like to have you along when I meet him, to tell you

260

the truth, I daren't take the risk. As I said to your boss this morning, I don't want you known about yet. I'm uneasy about those gobshites in Dublin and I don't want to give any hostages to fortune. The boyo from the RUC's here on the sly as well.'

Pooley paused, cocked an ear, ran over to the window and opened it.

'What in the name of God is that racket?' said McNulty.

'Sounds like "Rent-a-mob" have arrived to protest about something.'

They ran out of the room, down the stairs, across the drawbridge and down the drive. There, at the gates, was a line of police and soldiers holding the gate against a dozen or so shouting protesters, who bore banners saying 'DISBAND THE GARDAÍ', 'GARDAÍ COLLUDE IN MURDER OF NATIONALISTS' and 'IS THIS PEACE? IT LOOKS LIKE WAR'.

McNulty pushed his way through, opened the gate wide enough to get out and closed it behind him. 'SS Gardaí, SS Gardaí,' chanted the crowd.

McNulty stood there patiently until they ran out of steam. 'Now look it, ye're upset and that's only natural. But we're doing everything we can and this doesn't help anyone. All you're doing is wasting police time which would be better spent trying to find out who murdered your friends—if they were murdered. Would you ever be sensible people

261

and go back home?'

Shouts of 'Shame, shame', 'Gardaí colluders' and 'SS Gardaí' echoed through the twilight. The accompanying media surrounded the demonstrators gratefully, clicking their cameras, pointing their microphones and shouting their questions. Then, as if in answer to a prayer, the heavens opened yet again and the rain came down in a deluge. As McNulty and Pooley ran for shelter the protesters and the media could be seen doing likewise. Only the police and the army were left to endure the force of the downpour.

'Jaysus,' said McNulty, as they shook themselves down, 'and here's me having to sneak out the back and go on foot to where I'm meeting this fella.' He reached into a corner and pulled out a pair of rubber boots and a vast waterproof cape. 'At least I'm prepared. I hope that shower get soaked.

'You'd better get back to the hotel when I'm gone. Have a rest and a bite to eat. I'll give you a ring the minute I'm back.'

Pooley stayed on for a few minutes, waiting until the downpour slackened. As he was about to leave, Sergeant Bradley came in and grinned at him. 'Tell me, Rollo,' he said, 'did ye ever hear the one about the IRA man who was killed in a bomb blast?'

'I don't think so.'

'He meets St Peter at the pearly gates. "I'm Kelly of the Belfast brigade," he says.

' "Well, you can't come in here so," says St Peter. "We don't want trouble in heaven."

' "I don't want to come in," says Kelly. "Ye've got ten minutes to clear the place." '

Pooley managed a titter. Bradley laughed uproariously, picked up the kettle and filled it at the sink.

*   *   *

'It's just been on the news, Ellis,' said Amiss. 'It was a loyalist grenade, apparently. Some outfit called the Protestant Defenders, who allege they're a splinter group of Orange Volunteers, who're a splinter group of the Loyal Volunteer Force who're a splinter group of the . . . Or am I getting confused?

'Anyway, whoever they are, they say they executed Laochraí in revenge for Billy.'

'But how in heaven's name could they get access to the castle, let alone to her room?'

'You're the cop. Not me.'

*   *   *

'Christ, this is a right snake-pit,' said McNulty to Pooley. 'First, there's all that codology about them loyalists, which I don't believe for a minute.'

'You don't think that maybe Willie Hughes or Gardiner Steeples . . . ?'

'Hughes is shaking like a kitten. He was

263

frightened enough when Billy Pratt was knocked off. He's terrified now. And it'd be pretty daft for a fellow with an explosives record to blow up someone he'd be suspected of blowing up even if he hadn't the faintest reason to want to do it. Which he had, being as how he couldn't stand yer woman, for all that she was so pally with Billy.

'Anyway the RUC are convinced Willie's clean. And as for Steeples, he hasn't had as much as a parking fine in his life. But what I've got to tell you is that that Laochraí de Búrca, her with that pious mouth on her, is only a double killer—part of a team who shot two off-duty policemen. And that only a few years ago.

'They know she did it, they had a witness, but she produced ten people to claim she was somewhere else and then didn't the witness have a mysterious and fatal accident?

'That's why she goes on about police harassment so much. It's a ploy. Lots of them do it to stop the cops following them. Any time they're pulled up by us or the RUC or questioned about anything they plead police harassment, get in some of those gullible human rights groups to take up their case and bingo, they're martyrs instead of unrepentant murdering villains like she was. Jaysus, but it's an Alice-in-Wonderland world all right when you get within spitting distance of the feckin' North.'

Pooley felt quite shocked. 'Would Father O'Flynn have known about this?'

McNulty shrugged. 'Who knows? If he had, no doubt he'd have excused her and her a freedom fighter and all. The fella was an eejit anyway. Would have believed anything she told him. I'd say on balance she wouldn't have. Most of these types keep their mouths tight shut.'

'Liam?'

'More complicated. From what you'd call an aristocratic republican family. That means that every generation some of them end up in jail and murder people, leaving the next generation feeling guilty if they don't do the same. It's one of the curses of this bloody country. Normal people want to leave their kids enough money to pay off their mortgages. Our fanatics want to leave their kids a licence to kill anyone who stands in the way of a United feckin' Ireland even if they die in the attempt. Liam's family was like that.'

He attacked his moustache. 'MacPhrait's been pretty lucky, all things considered. All right he was remanded in custody a few times, but though he was certainly active and almost certainly led two bombing campaigns in England, he always got off on some technicality or other. They've great lawyers, these lads.' He pulled the moustache so hard that he emitted a yelp. 'There's been a family split though, since this peace process stuff started, with a major falling-out a year ago. Him and his mammy took the Sinn Féin line and were in favour of doing a deal. Two of the brothers and the daddy were die-hards. Nothing short of a United socialist Ireland for them. One of the brothers is in jail now. The two of them were caught doing an armed robbery and one of them was killed when being arrested. Some say that a garda informer was responsible, others think one of the peace crowd sold them out.'

'Could that have turned him against Laochraí and the mainstream?'

'Anything's possible. But the word is there's no sign of it. He hasn't been to see the brother and he still doesn't see the daddy.'

'Anything on Kelly-Mae?'

'I've got lines out to the FBI. Nothing back yet. Now I'll have to leave you to your own devices. I've forensic reports and all sorts to deal with. Tell you what, though, you can expect to be back behind the arras first thing tomorrow morning. If I were you, I'd have a quiet evening with your friends and get to bed early.'

As Pooley was leaving the caravan, feeling anti-climactic, McNulty called behind him. 'Don't forget to lock your door.'

CHAPTER EIGHTEEN

'So how are you this morning, Rollo?'

'Much, much better, Inspector,' said Pooley. 'As are most people, I think. Well, more rested anyway. I saw a few of them at breakfast and they seemed calmer.'

'Well, I suppose it was a plus that the night passed without another corpse, but that's about all we've got to be pleased about. Have you seen any newspapers or heard the news?'

'I've heard the news, but I haven't seen a paper.'

'I can stand most of it. I expected all these MOPE demands for a public enquiry. I can stand all the accusations of collusion. But the hypocrisy gets to ye sometimes.' He threw a newspaper across to Pooley, who scanned the three pages devoted to the story.

There was a huge interview with Laochraí's husband, with a large photograph of their wedding. O'Flynn's ordination was pictured too, along with an encomium from one of his Jesuit contemporaries. A Belfast nun recalled his inspiring music-making in their 'Healing the Hurt' group. There was a 'why-oh-why?' cry of pain from an Irish columnist who wanted to know how any people could be so evil as to have murdered the best and the bravest of those in the forefront of the struggle for peace.

'Nothing's said about their affair, I see. Isn't that odd?'

'Not in Ireland, it isn't. It's not just that we like to speak well of the dead—publicly that is—but you wouldn't believe the libel laws.'

'But they're dead.'

'Mightn't stop the husband suing on the grounds his good name was being impugned and a jury giving him hundreds of thousands. Mind you, I hear some English journalist asked a question about the relationship at a press conference yesterday and was bundled out of the place by MOPE heavies.'

Pooley was shocked. 'But what about freedom of speech?'

'Let's not get into that. The RUC are sure the husband knew all about the affair. But he can hardly be a suspect. How could he have got through that security blanket to murder them over two nights?

'No. Our murderer is here, so we'd better get down to the interviews. But first, they're working on it still, but it's definite yer woman's wardrobe was booby-trapped with a grenade.'

'How?'

'Well, I'm no expert, but what our fella thinks is that someone stuck the grenade to the pole inside the wardrobe, screwed in a cup hook at the back of the door and attached a wire from the pin to the hook. Fiddly, but not that difficult.'

'Still, you'd need to know what you were about.'

'You would that. And plenty of nerve.'

'Right. Now to sources of supply. We've checked out Nelligan's and the owner and his wife knew everyone in the pub on Sunday night—apart from yourselves—and there weren't any suspect characters at all.

'Of course that doesn't rule out someone passing a grenade to one of your contingent, but it makes it less likely.'

'Gardiner's friends?'

'Possible. If you believe that a Presbyterian elder who has lived peaceably in the same Irish village for his whole sixty years running a grocery store and who is almost notorious amongst his neighbours for his respectability, honesty and belief in the supremacy of the law is a likely recruit to loyalist violence, then yes. But there's the slight problem that he's also known for driving miles to attend funerals of victims of loyalist violence on both sides of the border in order to show his contempt for murderers of his own religion.'

'MOPE's pals?'

'More promising in one sense. No one in the house they visited has a record, but there are serious suspicions of the older son and the local guard believes some IRA guys on the run have used it as a safe house. What does that prove? After all they were friends of Laochraí's, which make them an unlikely

269

source for the weapon that killed her. On the other hand there were several visitors that night—a couple of whom were definitely on the most benign interpretation ex-IRA—and who's to say one of them didn't provide Liam or Kelly-Mae or Laochraí herself with the means to blow her up.'

'Because we can't ignore the possibility that she had the grenade and someone else used it on her?'

'Far-fetched but possible. The lads are questioning all the neighbours as well as everyone who set foot in that house on Sunday or Monday night but sure there's nothing to be got out of them. Either they're innocent and they've nothing to tell us or they're guilty and won't tell us. Of course we'll rough them up a bit over the next few days if we have to, but as it stands no one saw anything suspicious and all deny being part of any splinter groups. What more is there to say?'

'Nothing.'

'In that case, Bradley, go and get Pascal O'Shea, and Rollo, go and hide yourself.'

*   *   *

It was not surprising that O'Shea was charm itself for, as Pooley had been able to report to McNulty, his hairs of the dog had already run to at least four large gins-and-tonic.

'Ah, is it yourself, Inspector?' he enquired

270

genially. 'God, this is terrible. Those poor people. And their poor families. Dreadful. Dreadful.'

'Could we just run through your movements at the relevant times, Mr O'Shea?'

'Of course you could. Not a bother in the world. Now what would you like to know about?'

'What were you doing on Sunday morning?'

O'Shea concentrated hard. 'Whenabouts?'

'If you remember, the morning began with a session on what you think of other cultures.'

His face cleared. 'Oh, yes. Jaysus that was good crack. I was glad I was up for that one. It was great being able to have a go at these people. I wouldn't want to say these things out loud, but you can be too nice. And you can let off a bit of steam when it's anonymous.'

'So you were on time for that?'

'I was indeed. Didn't I have breakfast with yer man Hamish about eight thirty and went straight into the room with him and stayed the whole time? And then there was coffee and that was an end to what we had to do that morning. So I went to the bar with a newspaper.'

'And you went to the ecumenical service.'

'I did indeed. Though given a choice I wouldn't have gone within an ass's roar of it. Are you a religious man yourself, Inspector?'

'Since you ask, I go to mass usually, Mr O'Shea.'

271

'Well to tell the truth, religion bores the behind off me, Inspector. Sure I have a bellyful of weddings and funerals that the wife drags me to without going ruining a peaceful Sunday morning listening to Protestant and Catholic clergy going on about love. But I went to it until I couldn't stand any more and ran for the bar. Then after lunch we heard about poor Billy Pratt.'

'And the night when Father O'Flynn had his accident?'

'Sure I was a walking Guinness bottle meself, that night. Or should I say, a rolling Guinness barrel? I couldn't tell you a thing that happened that night after about midnight till I woke up around eleven the following morning.'

'You've no evidence, no suggestions, no insights?'

'Arra, Inspector, look it, sure I'm an alcoholic and they don't make the best detectives. I only came to this conference because no one else would go. I've a decent pension since they eased me out of the civil service on medical grounds and they give me the odd bit of work like this, but I've as much interest in Northern Ireland as I have in your left toecap. And the same goes for the Scots, the Welsh, the English, the Indians and the Japs—in fact the whole heap. I like a night out, plenty to drink, a good sing-song, a bit of gas like we had on Sunday night and the rest of

272

them can all go hang.'

'I gathered from your questions about the flagpole that you're not very technically-minded, Mr O'Shea. Would I be right there?'

'I never looked properly at a feckin' flagpole in my entire life. I thought they were just things you tied flags on to. Ask my wife. She'd tell you I'd a better chance of being a ballet dancer than a handyman. I can't even drive a bloody car and I gave up the bike after I fell off it twice in the one week twenty years ago. Which pretty well looks after the explosives as well.

'God in heaven,' he said, as if the idea had just struck him. 'Sure I'd be terrified out of my wits just looking at a bomb.'

'It was a grenade.'

' 'Tis all the same to me. I was never cut out to be a man of action. Jaysus, we didn't even have toy soldiers when I was a kid. And me own kids can't even get me to go to James Bond films because they frighten me with all that violence.

'Now, I'll grant you that I might have managed the bottles escapade, but it'd be pushing it to think I could change a light bulb. In my house, that kind of thing is women's work.'

'What are your political views? Would you describe yourself as a nationalist?'

'Them fuckin' Northerners, they should be walled off behind that border. Let them in anywhere and there's nothing but trouble. The only thing that would drive me to violence is the threat that we might let any of these hoors into a United Ireland.'

'Have you any ideas or suggestions to offer?'

'The only idea I've got is that you should lock up them shagging Northerners—the ones that are left, that is—oh, yes, and that American pain-in-the-arse as well—and let the rest of us go home to our wives and families. And if you won't let me go, I'd like you to provide an entire detachment of the Irish army to accompany me day and night until this is sorted out.'

*   *   *

'What do you think, Mr Hughes?'

'I think this is a nest of vipers, that my life is in danger and no one seems to care and that Billy was murdered for his devotion to the crown and his loyalty to Ulster.'

'You knew Miss de Búrca and Father O'Flynn before this conference, didn't you?'

'I barely knew the priest. Taigs is one thing but Jesuits is another. There's limits. Laochraí and Liam, now, I wouldn't have had too much of a problem with. Well recently that is. Since we started to meet on committees and that. We have to acknowledge each other's differences, as they keep telling us. And find common ground. Well we'd found that OK. I mightn't have liked them much, but we agreed our main enemy was the old Protestant middle classes who'd ground us all down and we were united about the need for the British and American governments and the EU to give us the grants and the jobs.'

McNulty's eyes glazed. He changed tack. 'You definitely had no idea that Billy Pratt was going to raise that flag?'

'Inspector, I said it before and I'll say it again. I knew Billy when he hadn't an arse in his trousers, but he's learned a lot in recent years and one thing he learned good was how to get on. He wasn't putting up any flag for God or Ulster. He was putting up a flag for Billy in the hope of taking that seat off me. And if I'd known about it, I wouldn't have had to murder him. I'd only have had to tell that fat baroness and she'd have bawled him out and taken the flag off of him. But now he's dead, I'll probably lose the feckin' seat to one of his side-kicks anyway on a sympathy vote.

'As for that priest, I don't trust priests, let alone Jesuit priests, and I didn't like him one bit. He was full of himself, and I couldn't understand half of what he said—for all that Billy pretended he could—but if that was a reason to murder someone, I tell you there wouldn't be a lot of people left to go to conferences on Northern Ireland.

'And yes, I did serve five years for carrying

275

explosives, but if you were to look up what happened, you'll find that someone else made the bomb and gave it to me to plant. I put it in the boot of my car, I drove it fifty yards and it blew up. I was in hospital for three months, I still have the scars and quite apart from the five years I spent in jail, I can tell you it put me off the bloody things for life.'

*   *   *

'Mr Gibson, you're the only person at this conference who knew all the Northern participants at all well.'

'Guilty as charged, Inspector. And indeed I can see why I might be your favourite suspect. I didn't know that Billy Pratt intended that nonsense with the flag and had I known I would have done what I could to stop him. But I can't prove I didn't know. Indeed we'd had a confidential chat in the bar the previous evening about his election prospects.'

'Really, Mr Gibson. And why was that?'

'I'm supposed to know what's going on at the grassroots.' He sighed. 'And what's more, Billy was by way of being a popular pet with some of my political masters. I had been unofficially charged with passing on to him the information that someone would try to do something for his campaign in terms of giving him a political boost at an appropriate moment.'

276

'I get the impression that this was rather distasteful to you.'

'It was. Indeed Billy was rather distasteful to me. But not that much more distasteful than Mr Hughes or the majority of DUPEs. And certainly no less distasteful than virtually any of the MOPEs. I found it particularly distasteful that they received special treatment from people who seemed to have little grasp of morality or reality. It is no secret that I believe that far too many concessions have been made to people who don't deserve them.'

'What emerged from your meeting?'

'Nothing. Billy said he thought he'd probably win. I have here a note I made afterwards.' He passed it across to McNulty, who read it out loud, apparently for the benefit of Bradley.

'"Billy Pratt is confident that he can take the seat if HMG comes through with the community grant he's been demanding. He said he was suffering somewhat from a diminution in his street cred and was being accused of having sold his soul for a mess of government patronage and foreign junkets. It was therefore a relief to him that Willie Hughes had been persuaded to come to this conference too. He volunteered further allegations about Willie's involvement in the drug business and indicated that it would be extremely helpful if Willie were picked up on suspicion as long as he wasn't turned into a martyr.

' "I stressed to him that this was no concern of mine and that there was no collusion between politicians, officials and the RUC. He didn't believe me. But then they never do." '

McNulty gave him back his memorandum. 'And Father O'Flynn, Mr Gibson?'

'What is there to say? Ever since he arrived I wished him back in Peru. When you are trying to persuade people to take responsibility for themselves and stop crying "victim", the last person you want is someone as stupidly ideological as that useful idiot.' He shrugged. 'And yes, as I told you before, I knew about him and the wretched de Búrca. Or was pretty sure, anyway. And, yes, in theory I could have managed the bottles and the light bulb.' He yawned. 'Sorry, Inspector. I've found this weekend very, very tiring.

'But I really didn't need to resort to murder. I had reason to believe that certain words dropped in the ear of Call-me-Cormac . . . oh, sorry, force of habit . . . Father O'Flynn's religious superiors about unfortunate sexual entanglements would do the trick. They might leave him *in situ* to stir up merry hell and community conflict, but as a Catholic I know our clergy still get very worked up about sins of the flesh. Especially where priests are concerned. So I expected a rapid transfer for him.'

He yawned again. 'And as for her? Well,

Inspector, we officials have many failings, but on the whole we spend our time trying to stop people murdering each other rather than joining in to fill the void we've helped to create. Perforce I know a lot about explosives in theory, but that's as far as it goes. And frankly I'm at a bit of a loss to think of where I would have found a source of supply in County Mayo.'

*   *   *

'Mr Steeples. Can you help us?'

'I just want to go home, Mr McNulty.'

'So does everyone, Mr Steeples.'

'I must see my wife the night, for it's our wedding anniversary, my father's too old to be griping the silage, I'm to dedicate a banner the morrow and then be at the parent-teacher evening.'

'I'm sorry, Mr Steeples, but you'll have to hold your soul in patience and warn people that you may have to miss these events.'

'I've never missed my wedding anniversary in thirty-two years, or a parent-teacher meeting, or a commitment to the Orange.'

'I'm sure you're a very reliable fella, but it can't be helped. Your family and friends will understand. And anything you can do to help us find the murderer of Miss de Búrca will help you to get home all the sooner.'

'What do I know? What could I know? All

279

these things seem to happen very late at night when I've been in the bed many a long hour. There would be no cows milked or calves fed if people kept the kind of hours these ones do.'

'You have no loyalist connections, have you?'

'Not if you mean loyalist the way I think you do. I'm loyal to the crown and the bible, but I'll not touch any paramilitaries or anyone who supports them. I'm against violence. And that means I'm against anybody killing anybody. It's against the fifth commandment.' There was a pause and then he ended, in a voice that shook slightly, 'I know nothing and all I want is to go home to my family.'

CHAPTER NINETEEN

Pooley and McNulty were chatting when Garda Bradley returned after a long absence. 'Kapur's missing.'

'What do you mean "missing"?' asked McNulty.

'I mean I've looked for him everywhere and there isn't sight nor smell of him.'

'I thought he went to his room after breakfast,' said Pooley.

'I rang him several times and there's no answer.'

'Might he have gone out?'

McNulty looked at Pooley pityingly. 'In this? Sure what Christian would go out in this?' He caught Pooley's eye and laughed. 'Or heathen, for that matter. Whichever, I can't imagine him going out in the worst rainstorm even Mayo's seen this decade.'

'He'll be in a corner somewhere, meditating. I'll have a look.'

Having hunted around all the public rooms of the hotel and rung anyone he thought Kapur might conceivably have called on, Pooley was beginning to panic when a thought struck him. This time, instead of ringing Kapur's room, he knocked gently on the door.

'It is who?' called a faraway voice.

'Rollo, Chandra.'

'Please come in.'

Kapur turned out to be naked and standing on his head in the bathroom.

'I'm sorry to interrupt, Chandra.'

'Do not trouble yourself.'

'The police have been trying to get hold of you. They were getting worried.'

'Ah, so that is why the telephone has been ringing, ringing, ringing. I thought someone wanted something, but it is not good to interrupt a headstand abruptly. And usually, everything can wait without injury. Do they want anything in particular?'

'Just a chat. I'm glad I've found you. They're rather nervous.'

'In case I too should be another body? That

281

would be very amusing. It would give the whole affair a cosmopolitan flavour indeed. Perhaps the Indian embassy could arrange protestors to shout outside that I was a victim of racism.'

'What's wrong with sectarianism? Shouldn't we hold to the prevailing theme of the conference?'

'Ah, no. For that to be credible we would have to find a Muslim rascal and we would surely have to send to Dublin for one of those.'

In a single fluid moment he lowered his feet to the floor in front of his head and without using his hands, stood upright.

'I'm impressed.'

'Just showing off. What is the good of being an Indian sage if you can't show off the flexibility of your body occasionally? Maybe I should do a cabaret to provide amusement while we are all locked up together.

'Now, if you will excuse me, I will have a shower. Please be so kind as to reassure the inspector and tell him to expect me in ten minutes. Oh, but warn him that an Indian ten minutes is longer even than its Irish equivalent.'

*   *   *

'I am at a loss in all this, Inspector. I came here to oblige my old friend Lady Troutbeck.'

'You've known her a long time, Mr Kapur?'

'Since Cambridge. We shared a particular interest in nineteenth-century English literature and a common passion for the novels of Anthony Trollope and the poetry of Rudyard Kipling. Have you read Trollope, Inspector?'

'Can't say that I have, Mr Kapur.'

'Such few insights as I have had into the Irish until I came here have come from him, though I have to say that they are of limited use in these circumstances. Mr O'Shea, now, would be a recognizable Irish type from his pages—unreliable, irresponsible and essentially unscrupulous, but so charming as to be almost always forgiven. I refer you to the portrait of the Honourable Laurence Fitzgibbon in the Palliser novels.'

McNulty cleared his throat.

'Ah, yes, Inspector. Sorry. The problem with Trollope is that it was the southern gentry he understood mainly. He would be as puzzled by some of the people here as I am myself. The MOPEs and the DUPEs were not familiar Irish types as far as I was concerned. Which is not to say that I do not recognize aspects of them. They represent what one might call cloaked sectarianism. They have grown beyond the stage of parading it nakedly and have acquired rhetorical garments with which to cover it. It is, I suppose, evolution and therefore to be welcomed. Though there are moments when I would prefer the honesty of nakedness to the hypocrisy of clothes.'

'You're a man of the world, Mr Kapur.'

'It depends, Inspector, on which world you are talking about.' He looked at McNulty's blank expression. 'Forgive me. You have sufficient troubles that I should spare you the self-indulgence of mystical speculation. As I have explained to you, I have seen nothing that could be useful to you. Indeed while I have spent most of every day with these people, I have been with them little at night. I have never been able to adapt to a drinking culture. And devoted though I am to my friend Lady Troutbeck, I find her overwhelming when she is flown with wine.'

McNulty looked at him helplessly. 'I've been told you're intuitive. Is it your intuition that there have been three murders, two murders or just one?'

'Coincidence is part of life, Inspector. I believe in its long arm, but not an arm as long as this. I could be persuaded reluctantly to believe Billy Pratt was careless enough to bring about his own death. I do not believe the priest tripped over his own bottles.'

He threw his arms wide in a gesture of surrender. 'I'm sorry. I was brought here to act as an unofficial member of my friend Jack's praetorian guard. I understand words and ideas. But for most purposes, I live in my own head.' He smiled gently. 'Indeed, on it, as much as possible.'

'I observe little, Inspector. I lecord it. It is a besetting sin of Japanese culture that we are so enslaved by gadgets that we have turned ourselves into a nation of people who never enjoy the moment but instead lecord it in the hope that at some moment in the future they will enjoy it. We go to London, we watch a gleat celemony like Trooping the Coroul thlough the rens of our camcorder and sometime we hope we will sit down with our lelatives and actually enjoy the experience. I am not sure that we can do so plopally. You can see it and you can hear it but you can't feel the templature or the rain or the sun or the snow.' Okinawa looked sad for a few seconds, but then smiled. 'Still, I expect our technicians will lesolve this in time. And for me it is all light, for I can delude myself that I do this for a higher purpose, not because I am vulgarly obsessed with new equipment. I can say to myself that I do this for my students, to bling to them experiences they could not have had except through my filming. Yet more and more I find myself in the thlall of this object I take everywhere with me.'

He paused and giggled. 'That is one leason I enjoy getting dlunk. Japanese men like to get dlunk because it is an excuse to be irresponsible. Also, for me, it is an opportunity to become flee of my master. There is always the moment when I can no longer work it and I am thlown back on the enjoyment of the moment.'

'Is there any chance, Mr Okinawa, that you might have recorded anything that might be helpful to our investigation?'

'I have lecorded nothing that was not witnessed by other people. But you are of course welcome to see my films if they could help you.'

'How many hours of film would we be talking about, Mr Okinawa?'

There was a long pause while Okinawa calculated. McNulty noticed with interest that he counted on his fingers in a way he'd never seen before, resting his fingers one-by-one on the palm of his hand without assistance from the other. Eventually, having run through the fingers of both hands twice, he looked up. 'Maybe haughy-whore?'

'Come again.'

Okinawa held up four fingers on both hands. McNulty's face cleared. 'Oh, sorry. I've got you. But sweet effing Jesus, that's an awful lot. Let me think about it. I'll let you know.'

*   *   *

'I truly think you should,' said Pooley.

'Forty-four feckin' hours? And who's going to do the watching? It'd have to be someone who knew what they were looking for and who wasn't just going to fall asleep and miss any good bits.'

'I'd be prepared to do it.'

'For forty-four hours?'

'I'd be sampling it. Not going through the whole thing. I'd have a fair idea what to skip.'

McNulty chewed his moustache. 'Well, since you're offering, I'll have another word with him and find out about processing the film. I'll be back to ye. Go off and have some lunch.'

*   *   *

The baroness was cheerful. 'I never thought I'd be grateful for anything ersatz, but then I never thought I'd be marooned in a place like this. But by some miracle, that bogus bit of the bar that they call the library has actually yielded a few books worth reading. Someone bought a job lot from a country vicar, I'd say. I'm about to begin re-reading Maria Edgeworth. What are you doing with yourselves?'

'I'm still lurking behind the arras.'

'And I'm making myself available to anyone who wants me,' contributed Amiss. 'Smiling ingratiatingly. Hoping for useful confidences I can betray to the authorities. You know. The usual.'

'Seen anything?'

'Kelly-Mae and Liam seem very thick, I

thought.'

'Really,' said the baroness. 'I didn't think he was particularly thick. Rabid idealogue, yes. Thick, no. Though of course she is.'

'I didn't mean thick as in stupid, idiot. I meant thick as in cahoots.'

'It's hardly surprising,' said Pooley. 'She's on the verge of hysteria and there are very few people she's prepared to talk to. And vice-versa.'

'Well I suppose having your other two mates dead might depress anyone. What's everyone else doing?'

'Wyn's in her bedroom. Gardiner's wandering around the castle miserably and Pascal and Wallace are in the bar. I'm surprised you're not with them.'

'Robert, I may be a heavy drinker by English standards, but I know when I'm beaten. I have no aspirations to compete with a lush of such epic stature as Pascal O'Shea. Wallace, maybe, on a good day, but I've had enough good days for now. I'm off to my room with Maria and we will probably have tea.'

'Even Pascal's proposing an afternoon nap.'

'No one's proposing a walk?'

'In this? Are you kidding? McNulty says he's having real difficulties in keeping up his chaps' morale. I should think they'd probably fail to notice a convoy of armed terrorists if they were to brave the downpour.'

'That's comforting. See you later.'

'OK, Rollo,' said McNulty. 'I've talked to your boss again and he agreed I can keep you quiet for a while longer. There wouldn't be much more trouble if they found out later than if I told them now. Anyway I have you on the list of people completely ruled out, so the Special Branch shouldn't pay you any attention.

'Now, there's no need to process anything. Okinawa's going to give me all his tapes and you can watch them on the sly in your bedroom. We've got a video recorder for you.

'It'll be embarrassing if anyone finds out, but if you'll take the risk, I'll take the risk. And if you find anything out, I'll take the credit. Now let's get on with the rest of them.'

*   *   *

Pooley tracked Amiss down around six o'clock and gave him a run-down on the day's events. 'And then there was Liam, who was very mulish in the beginning, until McNulty brought home to him that to be uncooperative might imply he was complicit in her death. Like Laochraí two days ago, he eventually grudgingly admitted that he wanted the murderer caught and offered what assistance he could give, which turned out essentially to be virtually nothing.

289

'McNulty was very forthright with him and annoyed him by accusing him of being a dissident. Liam pointed out forcefully that he was so committed to the mainstream that he had been prepared to split his family on the issue. He made much of what we knew already—that he has nothing to do with his brother and that his father refuses to speak to him. There was no arguing his point that all this would have been avoided if he'd just dropped out of republican politics. "Violence is not just behind me," he said. "I'm making great personal sacrifices to try to make sure it's behind everyone." And he couldn't be faulted on his assertion that Laochraí and he had been friends and comrades for years and that her death was a grievous personal blow.'

'So that was that?'

'Not quite. He was quite emphatic about who had committed the murder.'

'Really? Do tell.'

'Guess.'

'Judging by your tone, I suppose he fingered me or you.'

'No. Jack.'

'Why should Jack give a stuff about Laochraí?'

'Oh you know. The usual. She's MI5 or MI6.'

Amiss groaned. 'One of the things that bewilders me these days is that on one level you hear everyone complaining about the government being hell-bent on appeasing terrorists, while the next minute you're supposed to believe that very same government, through its security agencies, is trying to rub out the very self-same terrorists.'

'It's a safe enough allegation. Rogue elements. All that sort of thing.'

'While I can see Jack as a rogue element in anything, I think Liam is overdoing it a bit this time.'

'McNulty saw him off pretty straightforwardly on that one by pointing out that since—fortunately mistakenly—they had decided that Jack was the prime target, she's been discreetly followed by a plain clothes garda at all times. Indeed she has one stationed outside her door all night. Ever since the IRA blew up Lord Mountbatten, they seem particularly frightened of losing another peer. So she would have had no opportunity to plant the grenade in Laochraí's wardrobe.'

'If I were Liam I would have suggested she had spotted the police and at some stage climbed out her window and across the ivy to Laochraí's room.'

'A highly likely scenario, especially in the driving rain. Anyway, it's fake ivy and wouldn't bear her weight.'

'What a pity. I cherish the image.'

'Did McNulty interview Kelly-Mae?'

'Indeed he did. She was hysterical and went on a lot about the securocrats, but mostly she claimed that the British government was secretly committed to the destruction of the peace process and the murders had been ordered directly by the prime minister. McNulty's attempts to extract information from her about her own links with republicans got nowhere. Was he asking her to be an informer? Never, never, never. There was nothing worse than being an informer: if it hadn't been for informers Ireland would have been free centuries ago. Anyway, she knew nobody. She had attended the Orange parade solely as a concerned American citizen. She knew nothing of the people involved. She followed Irish politics sufficiently to know about the evil oppression practised by the British occupying forces but she had nothing much else to contribute. As for evidence, there was nothing.'

'What's next?'

'You're to get everyone to the seminar room for seven to listen to McNulty.'

*　　　*　　　*

There was a full turn-out. 'I had hoped I might have some news for you about when you could go home,' said McNulty. 'But I'm sorry to tell you I haven't. However, there will be more news after dinner. Superintendent Maloney of Special Branch has arrived, he is reviewing the evidence as we speak and will bring you up to

292

date as best he can.'

*   *   *

Maloney was tall, silver-haired, pleasant-looking and in his early fifties. He shook hands with everyone first. 'Ladies and gentlemen,' he said, 'I'm sorry to meet you all in such tragic circumstances. Inspector McNulty has told me how forbearing you've all been and how helpful and courageous at this terrible time when I know you're grieving for your companions. And I know too that quite understandably some of you are feeling afraid that harm might come to you too.

'Now, I can reassure you that there is absolutely no reason for any of you to feel there is any danger. Only the guilty need feel any fear and I do not believe that any of you are guilty.

'I have spent several hours with Inspector McNulty sifting through all your statements and all the other evidence and I'm very clear in my own mind that what we're dealing with here is dreadful coincidence. We have had two accidents and one murder.

'Billy Pratt did a foolish thing and paid a very heavy price for it. Whatever way you look at it, accident is the only sensible interpretation of what happened to him. Let's go through it step by step.

'Mr Pratt wanted to put up a flag because he

293

thought it would help him in his election campaign. There was no one at this conference whom he would have told about this. The whole idea was the surprise element. He had his press statement in his pocket ready to release as soon as the flag was up.'

He smiled knowingly. 'For Mr Pratt to have been murdered, we would have to believe that he confided his plans to someone, and that he chose the very person who would take advantage of that confidence to sabotage the flagpole. We would also have to believe that this confidante knew enough about flagpoles to know they had bolts and guessed that Billy knew so little about them that he didn't.'

'I don't find either of those propositions difficult to believe,' said the baroness.

'If I may continue,' said Maloney, glaring at her and going back to his notes. 'Suicide, I think we can rule out. So we're left with accident.

'I know we're suggesting a failure on the part of the maintenance staff, but I don't think we need take that too seriously. If there was a failure, it's an oversight by whoever paints those flagpoles, but who cannot be thought to be culpable in any way, since normally anyone who was putting up a flag on the pole would check the bolts anyway.

'Now to Father O'Flynn and the bottles. In the name of God, how can this be murder? First of all, someone had to know that he'd get up in the middle of the night. Second this would-be murderer had to be equipped with a dodgy lightbulb.

'You may say "But how did the bottles get there innocently?" I'll tell you how they got there innocently. The poor priest himself. I don't believe in speaking ill of the dead and I'm not speaking ill of the dead when I say that the good Father liked a drink—and which of us doesn't?—and because rightly he didn't want to give scandal he brought the supplies with him in his own luggage.'

'Were his fingerprints on them?' asked the baroness.

'No, and nor were anyone else's. He'd obviously washed and dried them. But what with the police being around because of Billy's sad death and the possibility that his room might be searched, he didn't want to put the empties in his luggage. He didn't want to be the cause of talk. So he decided to get rid of them in the night and put them in some wastepaper basket away from his room. So, before he leaves his room to visit Miss de Búrca, he put them outside where he wouldn't forget them when he returned.'

The baroness exploded. 'What do you mean so he wouldn't forget them? Why didn't he leave them on his bed?'

'Now, your ladyship, it's easy from where you stand to make sweeping statements like that. And maybe in his position that's what

295

you'd do.'

Amiss savoured the expression produced as the baroness tried to imagine herself hiding empty bottles from puritans. 'But we all have our little ways of going about things. And what was more sensible for the Father than to put them outside his bedroom where he'd be sure to see them when he got back early in the morning and would be able to deal with them?'

'Why didn't he get rid of them on his way to her bedroom?' she asked.

Maloney winced. 'In case he ran into people. 'Twasn't that late. 'Twas only around two and there might have been people still up. This is Ireland. And indeed there were people still up, from all I hear. Including yourself, my lady. So, wasn't he right?

'Now, the Father leaves them there to make sure he doesn't forget them, but then he has the bad luck with the bulb. It's dark, he's tired and he's forgotten about the bottles and we know the rest of the sad story.'

'Surely if he fell over them, it meant he had left them lying on their sides,' said Amiss. 'Which would be strange.'

Maloney shot him an angry look. 'If you're going to be picky, you can find fault with everything. All this is the most natural thing in the world. Poor Father O'Flynn is blundering up there in the dark, he's half-asleep, he puts his foot over the step where the bottles are, kicks the top of one, they fall over like skittles, he steps on one, loses his footing entirely, and that's it. What can be plainer than that?

'And I'm sure Inspector McNulty would have seen that instantly if it hadn't been for the confusion over the unfortunate flagpole occurrence.'

The baroness opened her mouth. 'Not now, Jack,' hissed Amiss. 'It'll do no good. Wait till later.'

'So that should take away any fear ye might have of each other,' added Maloney.

'The business of poor Miss de Búrca is, of course, completely different. I have no hesitation whatsoever in pronouncing this to be murder.'

'You're sure it wasn't suicide?' blurted out the baroness. 'Maybe she decided on suttee, and thought blowing herself up was next best thing to climbing on the priest's funeral pyre.'

'I don't know what you're talking about, Lady Troutbeck, and I don't think this is an appropriate occasion for making jokes. In Ireland, we take death seriously.

'This was a very tragic murder of a fine woman who's been in the forefront of the struggle for peace and human rights for many a long day. And I know I speak for us all or at least for all right-thinking people when I say that the Irish nation is united in grief at this ultimate abuse of the human rights of Laochraí de Búrca. We cannot be certain yet

297

who's done it, but there's very little reason not to take the loyalist claim at its face value.

'Tragically, because of mischievous elements in the media, these people had believed that Billy Pratt had been murdered— which is a lesson to us all about the dangers of ill-informed speculation—and they used this as an excuse to exact vengeance.

'Now before anyone asks any hasty questions, there is no forensic evidence from anywhere that any one of you has been handling explosives. We know that a phone-call was made to the hotel to find out Miss de Búrca's room number—which is good clear evidence that there was no collusion with anybody present . . .'

'Or that someone was planting a red herring,' put in Amiss.

Maloney ignored him. 'I'm emphasizing that point in a very serious way in case anyone's speculating that Mr Hughes here might be involved in any way at all. Mr Hughes too, like Mr Pratt and Miss de Búrca, is a selfless worker for peace. And it does no good for peace and harmony on this island to be maligning people like this or questioning their motives or making wild accusations that can do only harm.'

He turned to his right, where McNulty was sitting gazing at the ceiling. 'It is no criticism of Inspector McNulty here to say that while the operation was as tight as anyone could make it, there were times when the cordon slackened and it had to slacken because of the demands on it made by the weather, journalists and so on.

'Now, we know that that bomb—or rather, as it turns out, that grenade—was in Miss de Búrca's wardrobe, so there seems no doubt that it was placed there the afternoon before she was murdered. Some fella bided his time and sadly got his chance.

'I know you all want to go home. And I'm very sympathetic. You'll be glad to hear you can all go in the morning.'

'I wanna get out of here right this minute,' shouted Kelly-Mae.

'Where would you go, mam, at this time of night?'

'Anywhere.' She turned to MacPhrait. 'Liam, couldn't I go stay with your friends? Just for tonight?'

'Better wait till the morning,' he said. 'You'll be safe here. We all will be. I'll take you to the airport in the morning.'

'Thank you, ladies and gentlemen. I hope you feel reassured now.' And before anyone had a chance to say anything more, Maloney had gone.

CHAPTER TWENTY

'What the hell is going on?' said the baroness.

Gibson shrugged. 'What do you expect? The politicians are taking charge. I've already been given a very clear message that no awkward questions are to be asked since it is politically helpful that this should be two accidents and a murder by persons unknown. Maloney is compliant. He wants promotion, and in the Irish Republic, that comes from politicians. It's that simple. Now, if you'll excuse me, I have to make a phone-call.'

*   *   *

'I don't believe a fucking word produced by Maloney's lying tongue,' said the baroness. 'But you have to admit, his line is convenient. For the governments, for us, the police . . .'

'And for the murderer,' said Pooley. 'It's outrageous. Absolutely outrageous and corrupt.'

'Of course it's corrupt. Politicians have become involved. Questions of principle are inevitably going to take a back seat to issues of pragmatism.'

'But what about truth?'

The baroness gazed at him pityingly. 'I do like you, Ellis. You're so endearingly naive.'

300

'But they're going to let someone get away with three murders.'

'I don't suppose for one minute,' asked Amiss hesitantly, 'that you think there's anything at all in the Maloney thesis.'

'No, and I don't believe in fairies either.'

'Who do you think did it?'

'No idea.'

'Ellis? Have you a candidate?'

'Yes.'

'And that is . . .'

'Don't want to say yet.'

'Why not?'

'If I told you why not, you'd know who it was.'

'Oh, God,' said the baroness. 'Cue for Ellis to be found with a knife in his back gurgling "It was . . . aaargh." After which no doubt Maloney would tell us he'd committed suicide while the balance of his mind was disturbed.'

'I'll be careful,' said Pooley. 'Anyway, I wouldn't expect that to happen if I'm right about who did this.'

'Or these?' asked Amiss.

'These.'

The baroness scratched her head. 'Is it someone who would kill only proles?'

'I don't think Jesuits can be classified as proles, however much Father Cormac would have liked it.'

'Irish people only?'

'Billy thought he was British,' pointed out

Amiss.

'Inhabitants of the island of Ireland only?'

'With paramilitary links,' added Amiss.

'I hope Liam and Willie are watching out,' said the baroness. 'Or maybe I don't. Are we warm, Ellis?'

Pooley smiled. 'It's much more straightforward than that. This person would never kill a red-head.'

'Ah, so you and the tinkers are safe, are you?'

She paused and smote her brow. 'Stap me. How come we've avoided having a representative of tinker culture?'

'We didn't,' said Amiss. 'It's just that she's dead.'

'Lucrezia was a tinker?'

'No, no. But she regarded herself *inter alia* as a spokesman. Of course you missed that row the other night when Pascal described some group as having as much culture as a coach-load of tinkers and Laochraí, backed up enthusiastically by Kelly-Mae, denounced him for racism. This heated up when Pascal asked if they'd ever had an encampment of tinkers move in beside them in Belfast or the Bronx, which of course they hadn't. "It's easy for ye to be sentimental," he concluded, "when ye don't have the tyres fecked off your car or the handbag off your wife." I had to do a great deal of soothing to get everyone to simmer down.'

'Wish I'd been there,' said the baroness. 'I'd have confused them all by waxing eloquent about my gipsy heritage. However, enough of this. Ellis, will you do something sensible like writing the name on a piece of paper, sending it to your bank and notifying everyone— particularly your putative murderer—that you've done this?'

'All the reassurance that I need is that neither of you tells anyone that I might be on to something.'

'How could we? We'd have to blow your cover.'

'I must go now,' said Pooley. 'I have tapes to view.'

'He loves being mysterious, doesn't he,' remarked the baroness, as he closed the door behind him.

'He certainly does. I can never decide if he is a living justification of, or a stern warning against, spending your youth reading detective fiction.'

'It beats that creep Maloney and indeed these governments he's serving so well, who obviously spent theirs reading Mills & Boon.'

'Any idea who Pooley's thinking of?'

'I could construct an argument for all sorts of people, but nothing sticks.'

'Me neither. But what difference does it make since we're off tomorrow?'

'Straight back to London? Should I book a flight?'

'We'll decide at breakfast. I might want to go to Dublin.'

'Why?'

'That'd be telling.'

Amiss glowered. 'All right. Play it like that if you want to. We'll talk at breakfast. Now, I suppose we'd better go and do our social duty in the bar.'

*   *   *

The baroness flung her arms around Steeples. 'Bye, bye, Gardiner. Well, you mightn't have learned much this weekend, but at least you survived it.'

'Oh, I learned a lot, surely. And it wasn't all bad, so it wasn't.' He gave her an enthusiastic kiss. 'You're a grand old doll, so you are. If you ever want some fresh air, come and stay on my farm.' He shook hands with Amiss, extended the invitation to him also and disappeared.

The baroness sat down again. 'I feel full of beans. I'm really looking forward to the drive to Dublin. But we must take care to avoid pothole country. I want to get there fast.'

'They may not be able to meet us.'

'Don't be so negative. God, this drisheen is delicious.'

Amiss looked suspiciously at her plate. 'What's drisheen?'

'A delicacy made of blood and oatmeal, encased in the narrow intestine of a sheep.'

She forked up a piece. 'Here, try it.'

Amiss waved it away. 'No, thank you. I don't even want to look at it. I'm sticking to my boiled eggs.' He picked up his spoon. 'As for the Dublin arrangements . . .'

Pooley slipped into the dining room and joined them. 'Just saw Gardiner on his way out. Anyone else left?'

'Wyn and Hamish are sharing his taxi,' said Amiss.

'The drisheen, Ellis. The drisheen. You mustn't miss it. It's one of the most . . .'

She was interrupted by the arrival of McNulty, who was followed by Steeples and his two travelling companions. McNulty looked around the room. 'Good morning, everyone.'

'Good morning,' they responded.

'I'm sorry to tell you this, but those of you of who have packed your bags had better unpack them now. Nobody's going anywhere. There's been another murder.' He stopped. 'I should correct myself on that. There's been another death, which may of course be a complete and utter accident.' The baroness dropped her fork.

'I wouldn't want to seem fussy,' continued McNulty, 'but I intend to find out the cause of it before letting anyone leave this place.'

'What's happened?' asked Amiss.

'Miss O'Hara is dead.'

MacPhrait jumped up. 'Oh my God. Not

305

Kelly-Mae. What happened? How? When?'

'I was notified when she failed to respond to her wake-up call. And after repeated attempts to raise her, the manager opened the door and found her dead.'

'Any sign of violence, Inspector?' asked Amiss.

'No.'

'So it could just have been a heart-attack or something,' suggested Pascal O'Shea.

'Anything is conceivable, Mr O'Shea, but we shall have to wait for the autopsy.'

'She wasn't well last night,' said MacPhrait. 'She left the bar early complaining of being very tired.'

'There you are,' said O'Shea. 'It'll be a heart-attack. You'll see. Inspector, surely there's no reason to keep us here.'

'I'm sorry,' said McNulty, 'but until the autopsy results come through I have to insist you all remain. And no, I can't tell you how long that will be, though I hope to have news by the afternoon.'

He quelled with a firm gesture the squawk of protest that arose from several of the audience. 'Superintendent Maloney went back to Dublin last night. I'm in charge again. This is the way it has to be.' He turned on his heel abruptly and walked out.

'Well, Ellis,' said Amiss in a low voice. 'Does this affect your theory?'

'Just don't know. Can't know until we hear

some details.'

'And all we can do is hang about.'

'I'll go on with Okinawa's films.'

'Nothing useful?'

'No. I stayed up half the night watching. Some of it is riveting, mind you, but for the wrong reasons.'

'Oh, good morning, Philomena,' said Amiss.

'God between us and all harm, but did ye ever hear the like of that? I don't think I'll be seeing any of ye again.'

'You think we're all going to be rubbed out?' asked the baroness, as she polished off the last piece of drisheen.

'No, but I've just rung my husband and he's lost his patience entirely. I've told him I'll be all right because I've put meself under the protection of Our Lady of Lourdes, but he says what with the botched job St Jude's made of it, he wouldn't be impressed if I got a guarantee of a safe passage from God the Father, God the Son and God the Holy Ghost.'

She took the baroness's hand and squeezed it. 'He's coming in the car for me now, so I'll say goodbye. And it's sorry I am to leave ye.'

The baroness got up and enveloped Philomena in an enthusiastic embrace. 'My dear Philomena, if it had not been for you, this place would have been unendurable.'

Amiss kissed Philomena on the cheek and Pooley shook her hand. She looked at them and a tear came into her eye. 'Now ye stay safe, won't ye. I'll say a whole rosary for ye when I get home.'

As she disappeared through the kitchen door, the baroness rushed after her.

'What were you doing?' asked Amiss when she returned a minute later. 'Kissing her again?'

'Just giving her something,' said the baroness gruffly.

'Oh, gosh,' said Pooley. 'We should all have tipped her.'

'It's OK. Gave her enough.'

'How much?' asked Amiss. 'And can I contribute?'

'Hundred quid. And no. I want it to be my present.'

'She'll probably spend it on rosary beads.'

'She said she'd spend it on having masses said for us, but I made her promise to buy herself a nice frock instead.'

'So what will we do now?' asked Amiss.

'I'm returning to my Victorian novels.'

'And after breakfast—if I get any now—I'm going back to the home movies.'

'Can I watch too?'

'Be my guest.'

*   *   *

Amiss spent his morning alternating between watching Okinawa's films and monitoring radio and television broadcasts. 'An extraordinary mixture of the fascinating and the unendurably tedious,' he commented, after watching the footage of the traveller row. 'Mind you, I can see how you could get to depend on it. You know that moment the day after a party when someone says "What did you think of the bit when . . .?" and you're kicking yourself for having missed it. Hey presto, and up it pops on your television screen.'

'There is a downside to this cinema *vérité*, Robert. Would you, for instance, want anyone—even yourself—to see your attempt in the pub the other night to rock-and-roll with the owner's wife?'

'You're having me on.'

'I'll show it to you if you like.'

Amiss whimpered. 'I'd have to be feeling much stronger. Perhaps we'll have an evening of selected clips when we get back to London. For now I'll go back to the radio.'

Superintendent Maloney's statement had been spun to the press in such a way that the consensus was that while the guilty loyalist murderer was still being vigorously sought, he had obviously gone back across the border and therefore the investigation was over as far as the gardaí were concerned. The news of Kelly-Mae's death was leaked early, and from the speed with which a republican source was called on to speak with deep suspicion of the circumstances of her death and talk about her contribution to peace in Ireland, it was clear, as McNulty put it when he rang Pooley to tell him about the autopsy, 'that that little shit Liam' had got in first.

'I'd cut off the phones and confiscate all mobiles only that Dublin would overrule me,' he grumbled.

'So what's the verdict?' asked Pooley, urgently.

'Smothered.   Drugged   first.   Then smothered.'

'With what? And how? And when?'

'Looks like she was smothered with her own pillow, sometime before eleven, at which time she had already swallowed a potentially lethal dose of sleeping pills. Commonly-available sleeping pills. But it was suffocation that killed her before the drugs had a chance to. The pathologist can't be certain they would have killed her, but thinks it highly likely.'

'But why would the murderer take the risk of going to her room and smothering her if he had already administered a lethal dose?'

'To be sure of killing her. Though it was very risky.'

'So when do you think the drugs were administered? Assuming she didn't take them herself.'

'Obviously before she went to bed pleading tiredness.'

'How long before they would have taken effect?'

'With that size of dose? Less than an hour,

310

apparently.'

'So we want someone who was in a position to administer them to her in her drink and then to gain access to her bedroom before eleven to finish her off.'

'That's what we're working on now,' said McNulty. 'Just the alibi-checking. Not worth your while attending for the moment. I'll let you know.'

Pooley put the phone down. 'That's it, Robert. Drugged in the bar and smothered in her bedroom before eleven. My theory's gone west.'

'What was it?'

'My candidate was Simon.'

'Simon! Blimey, Ellis, I know you go in for far-fetched ideas, but this one is completely preposterous. Did you think he was an agent for Laochraí's husband or something?'

'No, no. And I didn't really think he had anything to do with Billy Pratt's death. It was just that I knew he loathed Father O'Flynn . . .'

'Didn't we all?'

'Yes, but Simon's so fastidious, I thought it was really getting to him. I thought it wouldn't have been beyond him to put a few bottles on the stairs in the hope of giving the fellow a fall.'

'Well, I suppose that might be within the realms of possibility. But Laochraí?'

'He hated her.'

'Explosives, though?'

'Unlikely. Yet he was strong on motives for all of them, including Kelly-Mae, as it happens. He could have drugged her. But, as it happens, the whole edifice collapses over the smothering. He was with me in the bar until well after midnight railing against half the population of Northern Ireland and the whole of the Dublin and London governments. I couldn't get away, he was so angry.' He went back to his armchair. 'Back to the drawing-board.'

*   *   *

'Great, Robert,' said the baroness. 'So we can add pillows to the weapons to be decommissioned.'

'And sleeping pills, of course.'

She looked disapproving. 'Messy things, sleeping pills. Have different effects on different people. I prefer a Mickey Finn myself. More reliable.'

'You speak with the voice of experience?'

'I have in my time had occasion to use them. However, I didn't think to bring any to this conference. Any more than I thought to bring a suit of armour. Now what do we have to do next?'

'Wait to be interviewed about your alibi.'

'I've already been interviewed.'

There was a knock on the door and McNulty entered.

'Ah, Inspector. The very man. Is there any chance of getting out of this place for an hour or two? I'm going stir-crazy.'

'I'm sorry, mam, but there can be no question of anyone leaving today—and possibly not for some days to come. It entirely depends how our investigations go.'

'So we're left here with nothing to do except knock each other off. As opposed to up,' she added, laughing uproariously.

'Mam, our priority has to be to find the murderer.'

'Will we be allowed to leave the premises at all?'

'Only in the company of a couple of security guards, I'm afraid. But that's for your protection . . .'

'As well as our detention.'

'Precisely, mam. You've got it in one.'

'At least all this alibi-checking must get quicker the fewer of us there are,' she observed. 'Remind me of *Ten Little Niggers*, Rollo. Who did it?'

'Someone who was thought to have been murdered early on but had faked his own death.'

'Right. So if that precedent is followed, Billy—or possibly Call-me-Cormac—has crept nightly out of the morgue to do the business. I don't suppose Laochraí's been able sufficiently to put herself back together unless she was a practitioner in the dark arts.'

313

'Give over, Jack,' said Amiss.

'I shall return to my room.' She turned towards McNulty. 'You know, Inspector, I'm tempted to barricade the door, having of course first checked that the fearful fiend isn't hiding in the wardrobe.' She frowned. 'I wonder why Kelly-Mae didn't lock it from the inside. She was frightened enough.'

'It's something I wonder about too,' he said. 'Maybe the murderer was in there when she went to bed. Or perhaps someone got her to open the door.'

'Who would she open the door to?'

'Most of us probably,' said Amiss. 'Maybe not Willie. Maybe not you. But I don't think she was actually frightened by any of us.'

She rose. 'Right then. I'll leave you to it, Inspector, and retire to my bedroom with my improving book and a submachine gun.'

'Quite a character, Lady Troutbeck,' observed McNulty, as she left. 'Bit fiery at times. Would she have Irish blood in her at all?'

'Yes, if you count it as Irish. She has family in Galway.'

'What! A Galway woman. God, now you've really surprised me. I thought she was really intelligent.'

'And Galway people aren't?'

McNulty seemed very perturbed. 'It's not so much Galway, it's the West. Sure you know yourself, they're clannish, sly and pig-ignorant.

314

You could't trust anyone from the West.'

He walked over to the window, looked out and then turned round. 'What family is she from?'

'The FitzHughs of Knocknasheen.'

McNulty slapped his thigh. 'Ah for God's sake, why didn't you say she was a horse Protestant? I should have known. Right. I'm off. See you later.'

Amiss and Pooley looked at each other. 'What did all that mean?' asked Pooley. 'What's a horse Protestant?'

'A Protestant on a horse, one assumes. A member of the old Ascendancy. I suppose he was explaining that normal prejudices don't apply when talking about the Anglo-Irish gentry. Probably a whole separate set of prejudices apply to them.'

'The Irish are very strange people,' said Pooley. 'And you haven't even been exposed to Sergeant Bradley. I didn't tell you, but I ran into him after Maloney's speech the other night and he said, "He's a Dub, of course. Thinks we're all bogtrotters. And sure what can you expect from a pig but a grunt?"'

'All goes to show that Dr Johnson wasn't kidding when he said the Irish proved they were a fair people by never speaking well of each other.'

'Right. Once again, back to the movies.'

CHAPTER TWENTY-ONE

It was six o'clock, and Amiss had been dozing for more than an hour.

'My God,' shouted Pooley.

Amiss woke with a start. 'What?'

'Got him. Got him.'

Pooley rewound the tape a few feet and then pressed the play button. The scene was the bar. There was a buzz of unintelligible conversation. The camera seemed immobile and to be placed several yards away from what it was photographing—a table at which were seated Gibson, Hughes, O'Shea and Liam MacPhrait. What seemed like a desultory conversation ended when Hughes stood and appeared to bid them goodnight. As he moved towards the door, he turned back and seemed to ask a question. As Kelly-Mae, MacPhrait and O'Shea turned towards him, Gibson's hand snaked out and opened over Kelly-Mae's glass.

'I knew it, I knew it, I knew it,' said Pooley. 'I was right all along.'

'It doesn't prove anything. Doesn't show he'd anything in his hand.'

'I bet it will if we get the film magnified. There's no other rational explanation for his action.'

'Only you, Ellis, could still be looking for rational explanations after a long weekend in this environment.'

Pooley walked to the phone. 'Inspector, can you come and look at a film?'

*   *   *

'You're not seriously going to tell me you think that milk-and-water fella's committed four murders? Especially since you've proved yourself he couldn't have smothered her anyway.'

Pooley spread his hands out wide. 'Look at the evidence.'

'Fair enough, fair enough. I'm looking. And I'll grant you what I'm looking at looks like attempted murder. Yet he couldn't have done the smothering.'

'Assuming the pathologist's times are right.'

'Now, look here, Rollo, you're the one who gave him the alibi. And gave him one which leaves him nearly two hours to the good. That's got to be enough leeway. Now, if what you're saying to me is that there's two murderers applying themselves to Kelly-Mae, we have to consider how many were applying themselves to the others. Besides which, I find it frankly incredible that a fella whose life has been spent in the civil service should have been able to lay his hands on explosives let alone know what to do with them.

'I mean, we can show him this, but he's just going to deny it. And unless you're right about

317

magnifying it proving it, where does that get us?'

'Inspector, I don't mean to presume . . .'

'Now, Rollo, don't give me any of that ould shite. You've been a great help and it's much appreciated. Come on, what are you suggesting?'

'Gibson's doctor. Find out if he'd been prescribed sleeping pills.'

'How can we find out who his doctor is without tipping him off?'

'We need a pretext. Maybe we could ask everyone.'

'What pretext? And even so, that would still tip him off.'

There was a long silence. And then, with great reluctance, Amiss raised a miserable face. 'I can't believe this. Simon is a decent human being.' He paused. 'But . . .'

'But?' said Pooley eagerly.

'But I admit there's a *prima facie* case to answer.' He looked at them even more miserably.

'Yes?'

'I expect you'll find his doctor's name in his . . .'

'Of course. What was I thinking of? It'll be in his filofax.'

'No, no. Not a filofax. Nothing as vulgar as that for Simon. But he's got a little address book he carries round which is wonderfully comprehensive.'

318

'Where does he keep it?'

'Usually in his jacket pocket. But of course he's not wearing a jacket at the moment, so presumably it's in his bedroom.'

Pooley looked at his watch. 'Half past six. Ring him, Robert, and ask him to meet you for a drink.'

'I'll tell Bradley to come up here with the master key.'

'I don't want to do this, Ellis. I don't want to be Judas.'

'Simon isn't Jesus, Robert.'

'But he's a friend.'

Pooley looked at him straight and without another word, Amiss walked over to the phone.

*   *   *

McNulty chewed busily. 'That's it, then.'

'Looks like it.'

'Time to talk to him. I've been thinking. He might talk more freely to you, you know.'

'I'm not with you.'

'All I know is the fella's English and you're English so you probably speak his language better than I do. So would you oblige me?'

'It's a risk, isn't it?'

McNulty raised his eyes heavenwards. 'Listen. I don't think this is the time to be doing things by the book, do you? Even if we had a book. In any of our languages. Besides, from what I've seen of him, whether murderer or not, he's not the kind of fella's going to start complaining about you being an undercover cop. Are you with me?'

'I'm with you,' said Pooley.

McNulty turned to Bradley. 'Right, Joe, off with you and bring us Mr Gibson. He'll be in the bar.'

*   *   *

If Gibson was surprised to see Pooley, he showed no sign of it. He sat down, pulled up his trousers slightly to preserve his crease and smiled benignly. 'Is this official? I mean Rollo and you in partnership?'

'Yes and no. If you're wondering about Rollo here, well, to put it bluntly, he's an English policeman. I thought you might be more comfortable if he were to ask you the questions.'

'How ethnically sensitive of you, Inspector. Well, well, well, how interesting. I wonder how that happened without my knowing about it. It's always instructive to find one is trusted less than one thinks. But of course, in our world, it is even more interesting to find out who is the person not doing the trusting. I should have cottoned on, of course. I never could understand how this generous millionaire could have kept his identity secret.'

He looked at Pooley, who said nothing.

Gibson smiled. 'A conundrum for another day no doubt. Now, do tell me. What status of policeman are you? Inspector Pooley? Or are you too young to have risen to such heights?'

'I've passed my inspector's exams,' said Pooley blushing. 'But I'm still just a sergeant. But Inspector McNulty thought you wouldn't mind that.'

'Not in the least, my dear chap. I'm sure the reasons for this will all become clear shortly.'

Pooley looked at him steadily. 'We needn't delay getting to the nub of this, Simon. Okinawa unwittingly captured you on film dropping pills into Kelly-Mae's glass.'

'Really? How extraordinary.'

'And your doctor tells us you have a prescription for the very drug her body is full of.'

'Ah.'

He crossed his left leg over his right. 'And what doctor would this be, Rollo?'

'The doctor you've had for the last five years. Doctor Fraser.'

'I see. Would you be kind enough to play me the relevant piece of tape?

'Yes,' he said, when Pooley switched off the remote control. 'Not conclusive, but I suppose in conjunction with Dr Fraser's evidence, definitely tricky. Did he tell you anything else?'

'No. He was reluctant enough to tell us that.'

321

'I'm pleased to hear that. I always thought well of him.' He smiled pleasantly. 'What's next? Are you going to charge me?'

'First of all, Simon, it would be very helpful if you could explain things to us. Then we—or rather, Inspector McNulty—will think about charges. I have no authority in this jurisdiction, as you know.'

Gibson clasped his hands on his knees and gazed at the floor. After a minute or two he looked up and smiled again. 'This is a little unorthodox, is it not? But then it has undoubtedly been an unorthodox conference. The murders have been unorthodox and now it emerges that even the policing arrangements are unorthodox. Not that I'm complaining, you understand. However, this being the case, might I ask an unorthodox favour?'

Pooley looked at McNulty, who shrugged and said, 'Ask away.'

'For reasons which will emerge, I don't really feel like fighting my corner on this one. I'm happy to tell you the truth. In exchange, I'd be grateful if you'd extend my audience to include Robert Amiss and Jack Troutbeck. It seems to me that I owe them an apology for messing up their conference in such a dramatic fashion. Not, that is to say, that I don't owe apologies to others, but friendship rather comes into it with Robert, and Jack, I think, would enjoy the story.'

'If that's the way you want it, that's the way

you can have it,' said McNulty. 'Get them, Joe.'

'You know I feel more guilty about Gardiner Steeples than anyone,' said Gibson. 'No one ever wanted to come to a conference less than he did and no one ever less enjoyed the freebie and self-important aspect of it. And my activities have kept him away from opening the scout hut or whatever it was that is particularly plaguing him at the moment. Still into each life a little rain must fall.'

The door opened. 'Ah, Jack, Robert, do come in. I'm sure Inspector McNulty and Sergeant-soon-to-be-Inspector Pooley would wish you to make yourselves at home.'

He leaned back, stretched his arms wide, yawned and said, 'I often wonder that civil servants don't commit more murders. I do know from Robert that in his brief period as an official he was privileged to be intimately involved with such a rare phenomenon but it *is* rare and even in that case it was civil servants who were murdered while their natural prey— ministers—were left alone.'

He arranged himself more comfortably. 'Like most civil servants, I've had many fantasies of killing ministers, but since I was posted to Northern Ireland my homicidal fantasies have tended increasingly to focus on murderers. It's a matter of natural justice, really. Begins to get to you when you see people you know to be unpunished murderers and torturers being kissed by politicians, offered another canapé at a departmental Christmas party or topped up with champagne at an embassy dinner. Brings out the Jewishness in me. All that eye-for-an-eyery. Mind you, the Catholic side of me might have kept control had there been any sense that these murderers had repented and asked for forgiveness, but of course they hadn't. They don't. That's the rub.'

'Yes, but what about . . .?' began the baroness.

He looked at her and smiled seraphically. 'Jack, curb your impatience. It's not every day you hear a confession from a murderer. Surely I should be allowed to do this without interruption. I know you've a low boredom threshhold, but stretch a point.' He caught Amiss's eye and they both laughed. 'I'll give you the narrative and the explanation. The exegesis can wait for another time. But in deference to Jack, I'll skip my formative years, my Oxford days, my first years as a civil servant, disillusion, disappointment in love and all the rest of it and get down to what happened in the last week or two.

'The great liberation was what Dr Fraser confirmed after my tests a few weeks back. That I was going to die and die soon of liver

324

cancer. Incurable, unless you're going to go in for transplants, for which I have neither the inclination, nor, it emerged, the time. The condition was quite far advanced when spotted.'

He looked at Amiss's thunderstruck face. 'You're wondering why you didn't realize I was ill, Robert? Why should you? We only met face to face a few times before this weekend and it doesn't show yet. I never ate or drank much anyway and it hasn't yet started to be incapacitating.

'That I should hear this news at a time when I was being more than usually irritated by people I loathed and was about to be locked up with in a strange hotel was fortuitous—or not, depending on your point of view.

'I've often wondered how many reasonable people commit murder simply out of irritation. I've been intensely irritated, which is why what happened happened. I didn't come here intending to commit mass murder—or even any murder, though I did come here feeling anarchic and with a vague urge to do something. Otherwise I would have done the sensible thing, left the service instantly on perfectly justifiable medical grounds and gone off to put my affairs in order.

'I have a slight qualm about Billy. Infuriating little bastard, puffed up with his own importance and all that. But to the best of my knowledge, he's never actually killed anybody. As against that, he seems to me to have had absolutely no moral qualms about those of his pals who did. Even worse, he seems to have had no moral qualms any more about those on the other side who murdered his own pals. To see him chummy with Laochraí, whom he would have known had personally shot in the back of the head two exemplary young men whose crime was to be policemen, made me sick. And then he came and gave me the idea.

'Remember I mentioned that I had to tell him that his candidacy in the council elections was smiled upon by my masters. That's what we've come to, when a civil servant can be required to tell a jumped-up little paramilitary stooge that Whitehall smiles on him in a council election. Billy was delighted but not surprised. He knew he was popular with the establishment. But he had a problem which he explained frankly. It was easier for people who'd been known to do the business to do well in elections, so he was going to have to do something dramatic. Then he shared with me his masterplan. And because he wasn't exactly a man of action, he wanted my support, advice and if possible, practical help. Wondered if he'd need an assistant.

'I put it to him that it was unlikely that a middle-ranking civil servant could help to put a contentious flag up in a foreign country, but I promised to recce for him unofficially. Hence

I investigated the flagpoles and the means of getting to the flagpoles and discovered the bolts.

'It was ridiculously easy. I slipped up to the roof on Sunday morning when I knew I couldn't be putting the maintenance men at risk, undid the bolt almost completely, clapped Billy on the back as I went off to mass and he to his ecumenical service and told him I looked forward to seeing his emblem flying bravely when I got back to lunch.

'I have to say it was extremely difficult to contain my curiosity when I saw the flagpole was down, but it wouldn't have been wise to go and look for the body.

'Of course Call-me-Cormac wasn't a murderer either, I admit, but he was happily and hypocritically sleeping with one. And I didn't join the Roman Catholic church in order to see priests sleeping with murderers. Whiskey priests and Graham Greene-type sinners is one thing. Liberation theologians fomenting disorder is another. And he was even more irritating than Billy. What's more, you can argue that there is some excuse for people who were brought up in all this, but for outsiders to come in and espouse their cause is especially objectionable.

'And besides, it was another easy one. And it appealed to my puritan soul that he would be punished for his sexual as well as his other sins. I knew he'd go to her at night—or she'd go to him, which would have been even better. I spent some of those ludicrous sessions thinking of a suitable accident.

'I had a lot of luck. Late Saturday night I was able to pinch half-a-dozen empty bottles from a bin in the bar and early on Sunday evening my major problem was resolved when a bulb went in my bedroom. It felt like a divine omen.

'So when I got back from the pub on Sunday night I lurked, saw him leave his turret and go to hers and had it all set up before you returned. And magnificently successful it was too.

'Now, Kelly-Mae, as you know—oh, sorry, for those of you who don't, Okinawa's film spotted me dropping sleeping tablets into her Diet Coke. Kelly-Mae was straightforward too.'

McNulty interrupted. 'Hold on. What about Laochraí?'

'Sorry, Inspector. Laochraí? Nothing to do with me guv. Billy, yes. The egregious priest certainly. And I did my best to despatch Kelly-Mae, who was so typical of those dreadful Irish-Americans who are happy to encourage young idiots three thousand miles away to kill and die. And she was, as well, fearfully irritating.'

He shook his head disapprovingly. 'I'm afraid that when you begin to murder and it goes well and you don't care whether you're

328

caught or not, the grounds on which you do it become slimmer and slimmer. Had Kelly-Mae not been Irish-American I might still have been tempted to get rid of her because she was stupid, as well as really annoying about food. Corruption happens quickly.'

'But you didn't smother her?' asked McNulty.

'No.'

'Nor blow up Laochraí?'

'No.'

He chewed his moustache a bit more. 'Any idea who did?'

'Possibly, Inspector, possibly. As you might imagine, I've been giving this a rather considerable amount of thought. I can see it's a bit unorthodox to be discussing the identity of the second murderer with the first murderer, but . . .'

'Listen, Mr Gibson, I'd sup with the devil if he'd get me out of this feckin' mess and this feckin' place.'

'Very straightforward, I think. Unless there's another murderer who knocks people off for pretty arbitrary reasons, what you've got here is internecine warfare in the republican movement. I don't think this collection of fine intellects has to expend too much effort on identifying the likely perpetrator.'

'Liam MacPhrait.'

'Precisely, Inspector. My guess is that he's

329

actually a dissident, and that in addition to being a mole within the IRA he's taking revenge for what happened to his brothers. It may be that Laochraí had something to do with their betrayal. I'm absolutely sure she was still active in the IRA.'

'And Kelly-Mae?'

'Probably saw or heard something she shouldn't. Or maybe got involved disastrously in MOPE politics.'

'I'm expecting to hear from the FBI any time now,' said McNulty. 'In the meantime, Mr Gibson, I'm afraid I have to charge you with murder.'

'Be my guest, Inspector. At least this will give you the opportunity to rub the nose of Maloney in the dirt. And I won't even have to stand trial.'

The baroness stood up. 'Inspector, there's something I should explain. I've gathered that you believe that behaviour is frequently determined by the place of origin?'

McNulty nodded.

'There are a few lines that have come to my mind that might go some way to explain what happened with Simon. I admit the first two lines may not immediately strike you as reminiscent of him, but I think the verse as a whole will be helpful.'

'Go ahead, mam.'

'Kipling is speaking of the English. "Their psychology is bovine, their outlook crude and

330

raw. / They abandon vital matters to be tickled with a straw."' She paused and looked across at Gibson. '"But the straw that they were tickled with—the chaff that they were fed with—/ They convert into a weaver's beam to break their foeman's head with."'

Gibson bowed. 'I'll try to take that as a compliment, Jack.'

McNulty stood up. 'Isn't it a pity, mam, that there aren't more in that mould? Now can you all leave Mr Gibson with the sergeant and meself. We have business.'

EPILOGUE

THREE WEEKS LATER

'It's wonderful to be back in Ireland,' cried the baroness, as she drove out of the airport. 'We're on the road to Dublin,' she sang. 'We're Dublin bound.'

'We'll be off it soon, if you don't slow down.'

'More and more, Robert, you resemble a nagging wife.'

'Like most nagging wives, I've a lot to nag about.'

'No, there is much to celebrate.'

'How can you be so callous? Doesn't Simon's death bother you at all?'

'Could he have died at a better time? Elegant denunciation published widely. Two governments in a frenzy of self-justification. He went out on a high point. And here are we at last about to be reunited with the delectable Aisling and Siobhán.'

The Sailor's Hornpipe sounded. 'Hello . . . Inspector McNulty. Yes . . . Yes . . . Good God . . . Yes . . . No, really? . . . When? Are they sure? . . . Did she? . . . Him too? . . . It's hard to take it all in . . . What's the official line? . . . But of course . . . It would be . . . Yes . . . Thanks very much for letting me know. Good luck.'

The baroness was bouncing with impatience. 'What? Tell me. Tell me.'

'My hairdresser changing an appointment.'

'Do you want me to hit you?'

'I'll tell you if you stop the car. I'm not telling you anything interesting while you're driving like that. We'd go straight into the oncoming traffic.'

She bullied her way into the inside lane and drove on to the pavement in a squeal of brakes. 'Go on. Go on.'

'There is some justice. Even if McNulty couldn't make anything stick, Liam paid for what he did. Shot in the back of the head at home in Belfast. Republican sources say it was retaliation for Laochraí. And the FBI say he was in America last year and that Kelly-Mae may well have met him. She was definitely one of those conservative Catholic Irish-Americans who couldn't understand the new secular, political thrust of republicanism. And she definitely met Mickey Murphy there too.'

'Who?'

'The Slievenamná fellow. He hadn't moved on either.'

'So why was she killed?'

'McNulty thinks she was in Liam's confidence and probably knew or guessed he murdered Laochraí. Whether she shopped him or he feared she might we may never know.'

'That's it?'

'That's it.'

'Well, well.'

She switched on the engine. 'It reminds me of something. Did you ever talk to McNulty's side-kick, Sergeant whoever?'

'Not really.'

'He made an observation to me apropos what I can't quite remember.'

'Yes?'

' "If you lie down with dogs what will you get up with but fleas?" '

She switched on the engine, put the car into gear and slammed her foot down hard on the accelerator.